Bilingualism and Testing:
A Special Case of Bias

Second Language Learning

A Series Dedicated to Studies in Acquisition and Principled Language Instruction

Robert J. Di Pietro, Series Editor

Bilingualism and Testing: A Special Case of Bias

Guadalupe Valdés
Stanford University

Richard A. Figueroa
University of California, Davis

ABLEX PUBLISHING CORPORATION
Norwood, New Jersey

Library of Congress Cataloging-in-Publication Data

Valdés, Guadalupe.
   Bilingualism and testing : a special case of bias / Guadalupe
Valdés, Richard Figueroa.
      p. cm. – (Second language learning)
   Prepared for the National Commission on Testing and Public Policy.
   Includes bibliographical references and index.
   ISBN 0-89391-774-5 (cl). – ISBN 0-89391-775-3 (ppb)
    1. Bilingualism in children–Ability testing. I. Figueroa,
Richard A. II. National Commission on Testing and Public Policy
(U.S.) III. Title. IV. Series.
P115.2.V35 1994
371.2'6013–dc20   94-9902
                                                   CIP

Ablex Publishing Corporation
355 Chestnut Street
Norwood, New Jersey 07648

Contents

Acknowledgments

The idea for this book was first conceived during one of the five national hearings conducted by the National Commission on Testing and Public Policy on the impact of testing on minorities and women. The hearing, "The Impact on Testing on Hispanics," was held in San Antonio, TX, in February 1987, and included the testimony of many individuals who were particularly concerned about the testing and assessment of limited or non-English-speaking children.

In the years that this book has been in preparation, many individuals have lent their support and encouragement. We are, first of all, deeply indebted to the Commission itself for its financial support and especially to Dr. Bernard R. Gifford, Commission Chair, for inviting us to prepare a paper on the subject of bilingualism and testing for the Commission report. His enthusiasm for the project was an inspiration, and his support when the magnitude of the work became apparent to us was invaluable.

We are particularly appreciative of the time and effort taken by Richard Duran in carefully reading the entire volume and for offering detailed comments and suggestions. We also wish to thank Reynaldo Macias for using a preliminary version of this book as a class text and for requiring his students to prepare detailed reviews of its contents. We found these reviews to be most helpful in preparing the final version of this book.

We owe many intellectual debts to colleagues and students with whom we have had many conversations about the issues discussed here. We especially appreciate the work of Mark Lovaco who spent hours typing and proofing the manuscript during the summer of 1990.

We also wish to acknowledge the help given to us by Robert Di Pietro, editor of the Second Language Learning Series. We are grateful to him for his thoughtful response to our material, for his wise counsel, and for his friendship.

Finally, we wish to thank our families. We thank our children for their patience and our spouses for their encouragement, their gentle prodding, and especially for their willingness to read multiple versions of many of these chapters. Their deep commitment to educational equity helped us to believe in the importance of bringing this project to completion especially during those times when so many other activities competed with our writing. In particular, we wish to thank them for engaging us in discussions about the merit of our ideas, for contradicting us, and, in the end, for helping us to present our arguments more effectively.

Introduction by Series Editor

Second Language Learning is a series intended for the publication of new research on all aspects of second language acquisition and related programs of instruction and assessment. This series is distinguished from others that address similar topics in two major ways. First of all, the volumes in the series are focused in their orientation. They may be authored by one or more persons, but in all cases their findings and claims arise from theoretically coherent research projects. Secondly, they are motivated by the drive to uncover principles associated with the acquisition and use of languages and the application of such principles in designing effective instructional programs.

The present study of the testing of bilinguals by Valdés and Figueroa brings to mind a report completed over 80 years ago by a certain Leonard P. Ayres. Entitled *Laggards in Our Schools* (Russell Sage Foundation, 1909), this report portrayed children of Italian extraction as having the highest rate of retardation of any group in the schools of New York City. The tests administered to these children were the forerunners of those used nowadays to assess the capacities of bilingual school children. How much more objective have these tests become over the years? Valdés and Figueroa point to a 1978 study by the United States Office for Civil Rights attesting to an overrepresentation of Hispanic children in classes for the mentally retarded. Eighty years ago, "objective" tests were used to keep children out of special, prestigious educational programs. Somehow many of those children were able to overcome such handicaps, and their descendants have joined the ranks of the most productive and successful of Americans. Today's Hispanics are facing similar educational obstacles.

Their difficulties may be even more imposing with the deep entrenchment of testing within American education.

The authors of this book address the many problems in the testing of bilingual children with clarity and incisiveness. These problems begin with the very definition of bilingualism. What is a bilingual? How many different ways are there to be bilingual? What relationship, if any, obtains between bilingualism and the cognitive processes? The reader is bound to come away from this book overwhelmed with how seriously test makers and test givers have neglected and perhaps even maligned bilingual school children. In a country such as the United States, with its constantly shifting populations and its long history of linguistic diversity, the educational establishment needs to pay more attention than it does at present to the bilingual. Valdés and Figueroa conclude with the recommendation that all assessment of bilingual students should be stopped until more is known about the nature of bilingualism. Such a recommendation should be considered seriously because so much is at stake in the education of our youth.

Robert J. Di Pietro
Series Editor

Introduction

Testing is a fact of life in American schools. It begins early. Much faith is placed in the capacity of tests to diagnose problems, to identify talent, to measure achievement, and to evaluate school or program effectiveness. Tests, especially standardized tests, are considered by many Americans to be objective measures of talent, ability, potential, learning, and/or hard work.

Other Americans, however, have much less faith in standardized testing. Because these tests were originally used in schools in this country in order to exclude newly arrived immigrants from southern and eastern Europe[1] from certain kinds of education, their "objectivity" is highly suspect. A large number of practitioners and researchers believe tests to be culturally biased and specifically developed to favor students whose backgrounds provide them with the appropriate cultural capital.[2]

Testing, then, is a controversial subject. Whether it involves teachers coaching students on achievement tests or "doctoring" answer sheets,[3] or

---

[1]For a discussion of the initial use of standardized testing in American education, the reader is referred to Fass (1989).

[2]According to Bourdieu (1977) and Bourdieu and Passeron (1977) families with access to certain cultural resources (e.g., language, art, music) provide their children with "cultural capital" which can then be invested to maintain or improve their social position. Empirical work using this concept has found that the possession of high status cultural resources is closely linked to educational success.

[3]News stories such as those appearing on *60 Minutes* (Spring 1990) often report on teachers whose concern for their students' performance led them to "teach" to the standardized test directly and even to provide students with exam questions and answers

whether it involves testing companies suing states that insist on the disclosure of current versions of examinations,[4] it is clear that testing is serious business. Schools are ranked according to test scores, programs are cancelled or continued on the basis of student test performance, and discussions of discrimination at the university level center around the weight given in admissions decisions to SAT scores. There are many disagreements about what tests measure, how they should be used and interpreted, and even about possible alternatives to standardized testing.

Bilingual individuals have not done well on standardized tests. The reasons for such poor performance are as yet imperfectly understood. Views concerning "genetic" limitations have been offered[5] as have been views concerning the English-language weaknesses of individuals considered to be "bilingual."

This book is directly concerned with the reasons underlying bilingual children's poor performance on standardized tests. It is our contention that without an understanding of the nature of bilingualism itself, the problems encountered by bilingual individuals on such tests will continue to be misunderstood. In this book we bring together two different areas of research and practice: (a) existing scholarship on bilingualism and bilingual individuals, and (b) existing knowledge about the field of standardized testing. It is our position that although much has been learned about bilingual individuals by the fields of socio-and psycholinguistics, persons involved in the areas of educational psychology and psychometrics and persons who are called on to make decisions about bilingual students (in the light of their scores on standardized tests) often have little knowledge about the nature of bilingualism itself. This limitation in knowledge is a serious one because there is much to suggest that monolingual tests, developed by monolingual individuals and standardized and normed on a monolingual population, are being asked to do something that they cannot do. The bilingual test taker cannot perform like a monolingual, and the monolingual test cannot "measure" in the other language.

We contend that the testing of bilingual individuals has developed from the practice of testing monolinguals without the necessary examination of the assumptions underlying the measurement of monolingual abilities and the applicability of these assumptions and theories to the measurement of the same abilities in persons who function in two language systems. We would argue further that the testing of bilingual individuals as it is currently conducted is entirely lacking in a coherent theoretical foundation.

---

[4]According to *Education Week*, April 25, 1990, the College Board, the Educational Testing Service, and other testing agencies filed suit in federal court asking to be allowed to offer examinations in the state of New York without disclosing questions and answers as the current state law requires.

[5]For a recent view of such genetic limitations, the reader is referred to Dunn (1987).

The primary purpose of this book is to contribute to the development of a research, knowledge, and theoretical base that can support the testing of bilingual individuals. By reviewing and discussing both the nature of bilingualism and the nature of standardized testing and by presenting a detailed agenda of the questions that must be answered before measures of bilingual individuals can be interpreted and understood, we hope to influence existing and future policies which govern the use of tests and test results. Very specifically, our position is that in the absence of a knowledge base that can support the use of monolingual tests with bilingual persons, all testing of bilinguals should be suspended or, at the very least, viewed as unreliable and uninterpretable.

We begin the discussion which led to this position with an examination of the definitions of bilingualism and a review of the classification of different kinds of bilinguals. We argue that U.S. bilingual minorities are "circumstantial" as opposed to "elective" bilinguals and offer justifications for the use of this terminology for describing immigrant populations. We conclude this chapter by offering evidence of the confusion that has characterized the study of bilingual individuals within the fields of second language acquisition, language assessment of minority children, and educational psychology.

Chapter 2 continues this discussion by examining the cause of the confusion surrounding bilingual individuals. In this chapter, we introduce readers to the difficulties associated with the measurement and description of bilingualism itself. We describe the doubts and questions that have been raised about the "native speaking abilities" of bilingual individuals in *both* of their languages, and we discuss the appropriateness of the concepts of verbal ability and language proficiency for measuring the languages of bilingual persons. We then review the tendencies and trends that have characterized the measurement of bilingualism and conclude by contrasting the measurement of bilingual proficiency with the measurement of bilingual dominance.

In Chapter 3, we focus directly on the research that has explored the relationship between bilingualism and cognitive complexity. We discuss the investigation of cognitive development in bilinguals and briefly summarize principal controversies and debates as well as current directions in research. We then proceed to an examination of the neuropsychological work on hemispheric involvement in the learning and processing of first and second language and finally to the work on information processing in bilinguals. This section concludes with a description of the limitations of existing research in each of the three areas examined.

The next two chapters examine the testing of bilinguals in some detail. Chapter 4 reviews the area of intelligence testing and the problems and questions raised by the use of such tests with bilingual individuals. It also includes a discussion of achievement, personality, and vocational testing.

The focus of this chapter is on the performance on tests by bilingual individuals and the assumptions made by this practice about the nature of bilingualism.

Chapter 5 is concerned with diagnostic testing and the impact of this testing on the placement of minority children in special education. Court cases deriving from questionable practices are discussed at some length and the results of a recent study of decision-making accuracy are presented as an illustration of existing difficulties in measuring the abilities of bilingual children. This study, conducted by Figueroa over a 10-year period, empirically demonstrates the hidden effects of decisions based primarily on "objective" predictive scores.

Because of the many problems surrounding the testing of bilingual individuals, in the final chapter of this book, we present three possible options to both the testing and the policy communities. These options are: (a) to attempt to minimize the potential harm of using existing tests with bilingual individuals, (b) to temporarily ban all testing of bilinguals until psychometrically valid tests can be developed for this population, and (c) to develop alternative approaches to testing and assessment. In Chapter 6, then, we examine and critique the options we believe are available to the educational and policy communities and argue that decisions about bilingual populations must be made under different paradigmatic, theoretical, and procedural conditions.

For both of us, the writing of this book represents an effort to call attention to an area that is of increasing importance to American education. Current efforts to assess student progress, to measure teacher competence, and to produce the nation's report card are all directly based on the assumption that the same tests (with few changes or adaptations) can be used with both monolingual and bilingual students. If, however, it is the case that these tests are incapable of measuring the actual abilities or achievements of bilingual children accurately, we will have little meaningful information about the strengths and weaknesses of this rapidly increasing group of Americans. At a time when this country's future may depend on our identifying and developing the abilities and potentials of all our citizens, this is a serious problem.

The policy implications here are evident. What is not evident is the direction that new policies should take. In this book, we argue that current practices are seriously flawed and beyond simple repair. We examine options for developing both new practices and new policies about such practices that go beyond minimizing potential harm. The bottom line is that there is much that we do not know about how bilinguals differ from monolinguals and, because of this, we do not know how these differences affect performance on standardized tests.

CHAPTER 1

The Nature of Bilingualism

INTRODUCTION

In 1978, Beatriz Lavandera, an Argentine, American-trained sociolinguist, advanced the following theory about the nature of bilingual competence:

> Since the "communicative competence" of speakers who make everyday usage of two or more codes includes drawing on each of these codes, plus the ability to mix them and switch among them, the structure of each code taken separately is usually reduced in some dimensions. Therefore if the speaker's verbal ability is evaluated in a situation where he or she is forced to stay within a single code, such as in all contacts with the monolingual community, this speaker's communicative competence will seem to be less rich than it actually is. On the other hand, the speaker's total repertoire is fully exploited in those bilingual settings where the speaker can call on the resources from each of the available codes and on the strategies of switching among them. (p. 391)

In her own study of *cocoliche* in Buenos Aires, Lavandera found evidence to support this view and conjectured that the same might be true of Chicano and Puerto Rican bilinguals in the United States. She suggested that for these speakers, or at least for some of them, neither their variety of English nor their variety of Spanish would offer all the stylistic and social variation available to monolingual speakers of these codes.

Stated simply, Lavandera's position is that persons who use two languages in the course of their everyday lives are not identical to those persons who use only one language to carry out all of their communicative needs. It is highly likely that for such bilingual individuals their two codes may form a unitary whole. The result of this is that should the "verbal ability" of these bilinguals be evaluated in a setting in which only one code is allowable, this ability would appear to be "less rich."

Although Lavandera focused only on communicative competence and on spoken interaction, recent research on the nature of language competence and language proficiency suggests that her findings are also applicable to other dimensions of language ability or language competence. If this is the case, what Lavandera's theory implies for those concerned about the use of standardized tests with bilingual minority students in this country is that, if these students are tested monolingually, the seeming "reduction" of each code and/or the effects of this "reduction" might be manifested in those contexts in which ability is evaluated either directly or indirectly by means of standardized instruments. The existence of such a single code (i.e., the possibility that for bilinguals their two codes may form a unitary whole), in turn, suggests that the condition of bilingualism itself may impact directly on the test performance of bilingual individuals. How this impact occurs, what it might involve, and how test performance might be affected by bilingualism per se during the testing process are questions that have not yet begun to be examined.

By making this statement, it is not our intention to imply that language and/or degree of bilingualism have not been considered by other researchers. It is certainly true that researchers who have investigated factors underlying differences in test scores between English monolingual individuals and individuals who were raised in homes in which a non-English language was spoken are aware of the possible impact of low or limited English language proficiency on test scores.[1] It is also evident that they are aware of the fact that language itself (e.g., level and type of English language used in test items) might directly affect performance.[2] However, there is no indication that the relationship between what we call here "bilingual verbal ability/proficiency" and the nature of standardized testing has begun to be examined.

As was stated in the introduction to this volume, the purpose of this work is to bring attention to the study of the relationship between the nature of bilingualism and the nature of testing as well as to the investi-

---

[1]For evidence of this awareness, the reader is directed to studies such as Duran Knight, and Rock (1985) and Pennock-Roman (1986) in which background information about first language acquired, language used in the home, English-speaking ability of parents, and the like are examined against the scores obtained by Hispanic students on standardized examinations.

[2]For an overview of this research trend, the reader is directed to O'Connor (1989).

gation of the questions implied by this relationship. It is our intention to put into perspective the limitations of existing research, policies and practices on the testing of bilinguals and to describe a number of directions in which the exploration of this area might be channeled.

BILINGUALISM: DEFINITIONS AND TYPOLOGIES

The Question of Definition

One of the most serious difficulties encountered when one attempts to discuss the relationship between bilingualism and standardized testing involves the definition of the phenomenon of bilingualism itself. Simply stated, it can be said that *bilingualism* is the condition of "knowing" *two* languages rather than one. The expression "knowing two languages," however, is far from straightforward. A strict interpretation of this expression would require that one view bilingualism as a condition in which there are two "native" language systems in one individual. From this perspective, only those individuals able to function as native speakers of each of their two languages would be classified as bilingual.

A broader interpretation of the same statement, however, would argue that the key element in the expression "knowing two languages" is the word *two*. From this standpoint, what is a matter of concern is not the degree of knowledge possessed in each of the two languages, but rather the fact that there is knowledge present (to whatever degree) in *more than one* language.

As might be expected, students of bilingualism (e.g., Baetens-Beardsmore, 1982; Fishman, 1965, 1968; Grosjean, 1982; Hakuta, 1986; Hamers & Blanc, 1989; Haugen, 1956; Mackey, 1967; Weinreich, 1974) have either presented their own definitions of bilingualism and/or have reflected the range of definitions proposed by others. From the perspective of the formal study of bilingualism, then, difficult as it might be to offer concrete and unambiguous definitions of bilingualism, it is clear that the condition of "language contact"[3] and its resulting effects on the communicative alternatives developed by persons who are part of such a contact situation is a complex and multifaceted area of inquiry. Indeed, current research on the nature of bilingualism suggests that, rather than

---

[3]Two languages are said by Weinreich (1974) to be "in contact" when they are used alternately by the same speakers. More recently, Appel and Muysken (1987) adjusted this definition and spoke of two languages being in contact when through force of circumstances speakers of one language must interact with speakers of another in the course of their everyday lives. Such contact, Appel and Muysken argued, inevitably leads to the condition of bilingualism.

applying strict or narrow definitions of bilingualism to the study of bilingual individuals and bilingual societies, it is important to view bilingualism as a continuum and bilingual individuals as falling along this continuum at different points relative to each other, depending on the varying strengths and cognitive characteristics of their two languages.

Within this framework, bilingualism can be defined in its broadest terms as a common human condition in which an individual possesses more than one language competence. Expanding further on this notion, it can be said that bilingualism is a condition that makes it possible for an individual to function, at some level, in more than one language. Again, the key to this very broad and inclusionary definition is the descriptor *more than one*.

From the perspective of this framework, one would admit into the company of bilingual individuals who could, to whatever degree, comprehend or produce written or spoken utterances in more than one language. Thus, persons able to read in a second language (e.g., French) but unable to function in the spoken language would be considered to be bilinguals of a certain type and placed at one end of the continuum. Such persons would be said to have receptive competence in a second language and to be "more bilingual" than monolinguals who have neither receptive nor productive abilities in a language other than their first. The judgment here is comparative: total monolingualism versus a minor degree of receptive competence in a second language.

According to this perspective, a bilingual individual is not necessarily an ambilingual (an individual with native competency in two languages) but a bilingual of a specific type who, along with other bilinguals of many different types, can be classified along a continuum. Different types of individuals (all bilingual in Language A and Language B) might be classified in relation to each other as illustrated in Figure 1.1. Some bilinguals would possess very high levels of proficiency in both languages in both the written and oral modes, whereas others would display varying proficiencies in receptive and/or productive skills depending on the immediate area of experience in which they are called on to use their two languages and such factors as topic, interlocutors, nature of the interaction, and so on.

Helpful as Figure 1.1 may be in visualizing the fact that bilingual individuals may be very different from one another, it is nevertheless a simplification of a very complex reality. A bilingual individual, for exam-

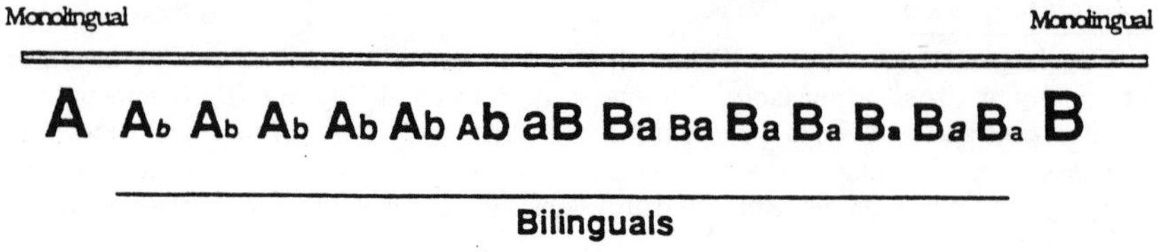

Monolingual   Monolingual

A A*b* A*b* A*b* A*b* A*b* A*b* a*B* B*a* B*a* B*a* B*a* B*a* B*a* B*a* B

Bilinguals

Figure 1.1. Types of bilinguals.

ple, represented in Figure 1.1 as aB, will actually fluctuate in her preference or perceived strengths in each language. Depending on the nature of
the interaction, the topic of discussion, the domain of activity, the for-
mality or the informality of the situation, and the like, she will display a
changing or fluctuating language profile as exemplified here:

Examples of Language Tasks, Contexts, and Conditions	Perceived Language of Greatest Comfort for Bilingual Individual	Language Profile for Bilingual Individual for Task in Question
1. To persuade school administrators in a public setting to increase student fees and to support minority activities.	Language B	aB
2. To argue with sister in a private setting about financial responsibilities toward mother.	Either Language A or B, with some preference felt for Language A	AB
3. To babble and coo to a newborn baby.	Language A	Ab

The true bilingual profile for this individual, then, could itself be con-
ceptualized as a continuum including perceived equivalent strengths in the
two languages for a number of limited tasks, interactions, and contexts,
but also reflecting the varying perceptions of limitation or strong preference for one or the other of the two languages for a larger range of topics,
domains, tasks, and contexts. A view of an immigrant bilingual's profile
limited exclusively to the home and work domains might be configured as
follows:

For most Topics Dealing with the Home Domain	For a set of very limited topics and tasks	For most topics dealing with the work domain.
Ab Ab Ab ab	AB or AB	Ba Ba Ba ba

Given this conceptualization, then, it will be appreciated that comparisons
between bilinguals are far more complex than what is depicted in Figure

1.1. In order to compare bilinguals, one would have to compare the total range of use for their two languages across a large number of different conditions. Such a comparison would need to take into account such factors as mode of use (written vs. oral modes), nature of participation (receptive vs. productive), purpose of participation (speech acts being carried out), setting, topic, domain, participants, audience, tone and style, plus a host of other variables. It should be evident, however, that because of the multidimensional nature of language use and the complexity of the factors involved, all characterizations of a bilingual individual's language profile involve simplification.

Types of Bilingual Individuals

Because of the fact that there are very different kinds of bilinguals, much effort in the study of bilingualism has gone into developing categories that might make the measurement and description of these differences possible. As might be expected, the categories used to describe different types of bilinguals reflect different researchers' interests in focusing on specific aspects of bilingual ability or experience. Researchers concerned about the age of acquisition of bilingualism, for example, classify bilingual individuals as either *early* or *late* bilinguals and further subdivide early bilinguals into *simultaneous bilinguals* (those who acquired two languages simultaneously as a first language) or *sequential bilinguals* (those who acquired the second language (L2) after the first language (L1) was acquired). Table 1.1 contains a summary of a number of different types of classifications of bilingual individuals and of the research perspectives from which classifications have been made.

As noted in Table 1.1, bilingual individuals can be categorized and labeled according to a number of different perspectives. The same individual, for example, can be said to be a circumstantial bilingual (whose parents' immigration forced him to acquire L2), a sequential bilingual who learned L2 at the age of 11, a productive bilingual who speaks both his L1 and his L2, a compound bilingual who learned his two languages in different contexts, and an ascendant bilingual whose abilities in L2 are still developing.

The usefulness of these labels and categories clearly depends on the specific interest one has in a bilingual individual. However, it should be obvious that meaningful comparisons of bilingual persons cannot generally be made unless attention is given to the differences and similarities between these individuals in terms of a number of these key dimensions. This is particularly important in the area of testing, because, as will be subsequently discussed, tests are hypo- and hypersensitive to some of these key dimensions.

TABLE 1.1
Different Types and Classifications of Bilinguals

Type of Bilingual	Definition(s)
1. Focus: Age of Acquisition	
Early Bilingual	Acquired L2 in infancy or early childhood
Simultaneous Bilingual	Acquired L1 and L2 simultaneously
Sequential Bilingual	Acquired L2 after L1 was acquired
Late Bilingual	Acquired L2 in adolescence or adulthood
2. Focus: Description of Functional Ability	
Incipient Bilingual	Beginning to acquire L2
Receptive Bilingual	Can comprehend spoken or written L2
Productive Bilingual	Can speak and/or write in L2
3. Focus: Description of the Relationship between the Bilingual's Two Languages	
Ambilingual	Is two native speakers in one individual
Equilingual	Has equivalent proficiency in L1 & L2
Balanced bilingual	Same as equilingual
4. Focus: Description of the Context of Acquisition and of its Effects on the Bilingual's Two Language Systems	
Coordinate bilingual	Definitions vary. Languages acquired in different cultural contexts. Language systems separate.
Compound bilingual	Definitions vary. Languages acquired in the same context. Language systems merged to some degree
5. Focus: Description of Stages in the Lives of Bilinguals	
Ascendant bilingual	Bilingual whose functional ability in L2 is growing
Recessive bilingual	Bilingual whose functional ability in L2 or L1 is decreasing
6. Focus: Description of Circumstances Leading to Bilingualism	
Circumstantial or natural bilingual	Is forced by circumstances to become bilingual. Is usually part of a group of individuals who become bilingual.
Elective, academic, or elite bilingual	Chooses to become bilingual. Elects to take courses in L2.

The Classification of Different Kinds of Bilinguals: Two Fundamental Categories

Although there is no universal agreement about what key categories or dimensions should be used in the description of bilingualism, most researchers have divided bilinguals into two fundamental categories: (a) the category of elective bilinguals, and (b) the category of circumstantial bilinguals.[4]

---

[4]The terms *circumstantial bilingualism* and *elective bilingualism* are used here instead of the terms *natural* and *elite/academic bilingualism* which have been used by others (e.g., Baetens-Beardsmore, 1982; Malmberg, 1977; Paulston, 1977; Skutnabb-Kangas, 1981).

Elective bilinguals are those individuals who choose to become bilingual and who seek out either formal classes or contexts in which they can acquire a foreign language (i.e., a language not spoken ordinarily in the communities in which they live and work) and who continue to spend the greater part of their time in a society in which their first language is the majority or societal language. The bilingualism of such elective bilinguals has also been referred to as "additive bilingualism" because these individuals are in a position of *adding* another language to their overall linguistic competence in a context in which their first language still remains the language of greater prestige and dominant usage.

Monolingual English-speaking Americans who learn French in foreign language classes, for example, are elective bilinguals. They remain bilingual by choice even when they travel to French-speaking countries in order to perfect their French. In contrast with circumstantial bilinguals, who will be described later, elective bilinguals put themselves in "foreign" settings for the principal purpose of expanding their language ability. They generally have no intention of living in the foreign country permanently and thus have no "real" need to use their new language in order to survive.

Circumstantial bilinguals, on the other hand, are individuals who, because of their circumstances, find that they must learn another language in order to survive. As Haugen (1972) put it, they are individuals whose first language does not suffice to carry out all of their communicative needs. Because of the movement of peoples and/or because of changes in political circumstances (e.g., immigration, conquest, shifting of borders, establishment of postcolonial states), these individuals find themselves in a context in which their ethnic language is not the majority, prestige, or national language. The result of this is that in order to participate economically and politically in the society of which they are a part, such persons must acquire some degree of proficiency in the societal language. Circumstantial bilingualism has been referred to as *subtractive* bilingualism because the condition of adding the societal language as a second language inevitably leads to a loss of the first language. Because of the strong pressures exerted by the majority society and the lack of prestige of the original language, for these individuals, the condition of bilingualism results in the gradual abandonment of L1.

Bilingual American minorities are, by definition, circumstantial bilinguals. They are forced by circumstances to acquire English, and they do so in a context in which their own first languages have little or no prestige. Whether they acquire English in formal settings (i.e., in voluntary ESL classes) or in natural interactions with English speakers, they are fundamentally different from elective bilinguals, that is, from persons who study foreign languages strictly by choice. Although immigrant bilinguals do have a choice of not acquiring English, the consequences of their not doing so are much more life impacting than are decisions made by elective bilinguals when they elect to learn or not to learn a second language.

The fundamental difference between elective and circumstantial bilinguals has to do, then, not just with conditions in which languages are acquired, but also with the relationship between groups of individuals. Elective bilinguals become bilingual as individuals. The group to which they belong has little to do with their decision to become speakers of another language. Circumstantial bilinguals, on the other hand, are generally members of a group of individuals who as a group must become bilingual in order to participate in the society that surrounds them.[5]

The principal characteristics of these two groups of bilinguals is summarized as follows:

Elective Bilingualism

1. Elective bilingualism is characteristic of individuals.

2. Individuals choose to learn a non-societal language and create conditions (e.g., enrolling in language classes) that help bring about such learning.

3. Communicative opportunities are artificially created in a classroom setting or sought specifically by learners. Some individuals may seek greater integration with the target

Circumstantial Bilingualism

1. Circumstantial bilingualism is generally characteristic of groups of people.

2. Group members respond to circumstances created by movement of peoples, conquest, colonization, immigration, and the like. A second language is learned because the first language does not suffice to meet all of the group's communicative needs.

3. Communicative needs may relate to either survival (minimal contact with the majority society) or success (ability to function totally in the majority society). Not everyone in the community will

---

[5]It is important to note that the categories used here (i.e., elective bilinguals vs. circumstantial bilinguals), although helpful, are not always mutually exclusive. For example, an individual whose circumstances demand that he or she acquire a second language may choose or elect to study this language in a formal setting. Similarly, an elective bilingual may decide to reside permanently in a setting wherein he or she is "forced" by circumstances to acquire levels of language not within his school-developed range. These distinctions, however, are useful for differentiating between two very different circumstances under which individuals first come into contact with a language other than their first.

language community. Such efforts are initiated by the language learner and may include marriage, residence abroad, etc.

have the same communicative needs.

4. In the U.S., elective bilinguals are generally middle class. Occasionally, working-class students are also successful in foreign language classes. Working-class bilinguals who acquire a second language in schools or neighborhoods because they frequently interact with recent immigrant populations are also encountered.

4. In the U.S., circumstantial bilinguals include both indigenous groups (American Indians) and immigrant groups. Among immigrant groups, there may be individuals of different class backgrounds depending on the characteristics and history of the original group. The Vietnamese group in the U.S., for example, includes persons from urban upper-class backgrounds as well as persons of peasant backgrounds.

5. In the U.S., foreign students who come here to study from overseas are elective bilinguals. Students who are products of immersion programs are also considered to be elective bilinguals. (Children raised in families in which two languages are spoken may be considered elective bilinguals if the circumstances requiring the use of two languages are created deliberately by the parents and are not present in the surrounding societal context.)

5. Circumstantial bilinguals include immigrants and original residents of territories conquered or colonized. (Children raised in families where two languages are spoken are considered circumstantial bilinguals if the circumstances requiring the use of two languages also exist outside of the home.)

6. For most elective bilinguals who study or use a second language for limited periods of time, their first language will remain their stronger language.

6. Circumstantial bilinguals will, over time, become stable bilinguals whose two languages play complimentary roles in their everyday lives. For most domains, topics, and styles, circumstantial bilinguals (even those whose two languages are very strong) will

have a momentarily stronger
language. This momentarily
stronger or preferred language
(Dodson, 1985) is one in which an
individual feels a greater facility
or capacity for efficient communication given the specific topic,
speakers, and function in question.

Types of Bilingual Individuals and Bilingual Communities

Individual circumstantial bilingualism develops within specific contexts
and in conjunction with specific experiences. It is the nature of these
experiences that results in a particular type of bilingualism and even in the
relative strengths of the two languages with regard to each other in
different contexts and domains.

In the United States, as was mentioned previously, circumstantial
bilingualism is generally the result of language contact that comes about as
a result of immigration. This type of bilingualism also developed when
territories (e.g., tribal lands inhabited by Native Americans, the states of
Texas, New Mexico, Arizona, and California) were taken over by English-
speaking populations. Most American circumstantial bilinguals, therefore,
acquire their two languages within the context of the immigrant community of which they are a part. What this means, in practice, is that the
nature and type of language proficiency individuals acquire and develop
depends on such factors as generational level, age, occupation, opportunity for contact with speakers of English, exposure to English media, and
so on. Although a number of generalizations can be made about immigrant
bilinguals at different stages of their residency in the United States (see
Table 1.2), it is also the case that there are many differences in language
proficiency between individuals of the same immigrant generation.

As Table 1.2 makes evident, differences in functional ability in both the
immigrant language and English can be found both between bilinguals of
different generations and between bilinguals of the same generation. The
acquisition of English by new immigrants depends both on the nature of
the community in which they settle and on the amount of exposure they
have to English in their everyday lives. It is possible for first generation
immigrants to become quite fluent in English after a brief period of
residence in this country. This is especially the case if they have had
previous exposure to the formal study of English before emigrating to the
United States. It is also possible, however, that depending on who they
marry, where they live, the number of bilinguals and monolinguals that

TABLE 1.2
A Sample of Some Different Possible Types of Immigrant Bilinguals

Type	Stage	Language Use
		First Generation—Foreign Born
A	Newly Arrived	Understands little English. Learns a few words and phrases.
	After several years of residence	
Ab	Type 1	Understands enough English to take care of essential everyday needs. Speaks enough English to make himself understood.
Ab	Type 2	Is able to function capably in the work domain where English is required. May still experience frustration in expressing himself fully in English. Uses immigrant language in all other contexts where English is not needed.
		Second Generation—U.S. Born
Ab	Preschool Age	Acquires immigrant language first. May be spoken to in English by relatives or friends. Will normally be exposed to English-language TV.
Ab	School Age	Acquires English. Uses it increasingly to talk to peers and siblings. Views English-language TV extensively. May be literate only in English if schooled exclusively in this language.
	Adulthood	
AB	Type 1	At work (in the community) uses language to suit proficiency of other speakers. Senses greater functional ease in his first language in spite of frequent use of second.
AB	Type 2	Uses English for most everyday activities. Uses immigrant language to interact with parents or others who do not speak English. Is aware of vocabulary gaps in his first language.
		Third Generation—U.S. Born
AB	Preschool Age	Acquires both English and immigrant language simultaneously. Hears both in the home although English tends to predominate.
a**B**	School Age	Uses English almost exclusively. Is aware of limitations in the immigrant language. Uses it only when forced to do so by circumstances. Is literate only in English.
a**B**	Adulthood	Uses English almost exclusively. Has few opportunities for speaking immigrant language. Retains good receptive competence in this language.
		Fourth Generation—U.S. Born
Ba	Preschool Age	Is spoken to only in English. May hear immigrant language spoken by grandparents and other relatives. Is not expected to understand immigrant language.
Ba	School Age	Uses English exclusively. May have picked up some of the immigrant language from peers. Has limited receptive competence in this language.
B	Adulthood	Is almost totally English monolingual. May retain some receptive competence in some domains.

16

they interact with, and so on, that they will fluctuate in their control and comfort in using the new language over the course of their lives. For most, first generation bilinguals who arrive in this country as adults, however, the immigrant language remains dominant.

This is not necessarily the case for second generation immigrants. Ordinarily, English exerts a strong pressure involving both prestige within the immigrant community and access to the wider community's rewards. it is frequently the case that by the end of their school years, second generation immigrants develop a greater function ease in English for dealing with most contexts and domains outside of the home and immediate community. Here again, there can be many differences between individuals of the same generation. Both the retention of the immigrant language and the acquisition of English depend on the opportunities available for use. In diglossic communities,[6] these individuals will have little access to a full repertoire of styles and levels of language. Because the immigrant language tends to become a language of intimacy and informality, their competence in this language may soon be outdistanced by their competence in English. Figure 1.2 illustrates the relationship of Language A (immigrant language) to Language B (English) for second generation bilinguals whose two languages develop in a community in which both diglossia and bilingualism obtain. As noted in Figure 1.2, although for informal styles both the immigrant language (A) and English (B) appear to be quite strong, the same is not the case for formal styles. Here, English has clearly outdistanced the immigrant language.

This same phenomenon (i.e., the outdistancing of the immigrant language by English) is also observed in the area of literacy. By the end of the school years (even when the first three may have been supported by mother-tongue teaching[7]), most immigrant bilinguals will have developed

---

[6]Diglossic communities are those in which one language or one variety of language is used for all formal (high) functions (e.g., interacting with official agencies, the presentation of formal speeches, the education of children, etc.) and the other language or variety is used for all informal (low) functions. In American immigrant communities, it is generally the case that English is used as a language appropriate to formal exchanges (political rallies, business meetings, announcements, sermons, lectures, etc.) and the immigrant language is used within the home and the community. The result of this is that U.S.-born persons of immigrant background will seldom have the opportunity to hear the immigrant language used for the high or formal functions. Thus, except for radio and television where available in immigrant languages, they will have no models for the use of this register of language and will not develop this level of language use.

[7]The term mother-tongue teaching is used here instead of the term bilingual education following the European tradition. In the United States, mother-tongue or bilingual teaching programs are designed to serve as a bridge to English. In public schools, attempts to produce biliterate individuals of immigrant background capable of functioning professionally in two languages are quite rare. For a discussion of this point the reader is referred to Valdés (1992).

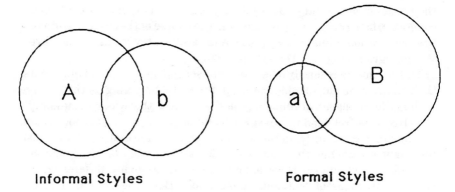

Informal Styles   Formal Styles

Figure 1.2. Functional Ability in Languages A and B

what skills they have in both reading and writing primarily in English. Again the impact of the wider society, the lack of opportunities for using the written immigrant language, the limited number of reading materials available in these languages, and the like, result in English language literacy, rather than in a bilingual and biliterate profile.

The same generalizations made about first and second generation bilinguals can be made for third and fourth generation bilinguals. Again, there is much variation within generations, and this variation depends on the access to both English and the immigrant language. Numerous factors can influence both immigrant language retention and immigrant language loss for different individuals. It is generally the case, however, as Fishman (1964) maintained, that by the fourth generation, immigrants become monolingual in English, the language of the majority society.

The Study of Bilingual U.S. Minorities

The study of bilingual U.S. minorities must take into account the fact that these individuals are circumstantial, and not elective, bilinguals. What this means is that, given the complexity of circumstantial bilingualism, one cannot easily group bilingual American minorities using one or two key variables, such as first language learned or language spoken in the home, as criteria. It must be remembered that individual circumstantial bilingualism can only be understood against the framework of societal bilingualism, that is, by taking into account the place and function of the two languages in question in the lives of particular groups of bilingual individuals who primarily share with each other the fact that they are not monolingual. The specific experiences of different individuals in using Language A or Language B will directly impact on the development of their functional ability in each language, as well as on the development of their linguistic competence in both languages. Factors such as the arrival and presence of new immigrants, the background of these persons (e.g., education, social class), the attitude toward these immigrants, and the opportunities for revitalizing the immigrant language play a large role in the retention or loss of this language by individual speakers. Elements such as the presence of other immigrant groups in the same community and the perceived need to use the societal language as *lingua franca* will also impact significantly on the degree to which community members use this language frequently. The language used for religious practice, carrying out business transactions, and entertainment (e.g., availability of movies and television in immigrant languages) will also affect the rate of acquisition of the societal language.

It is important to emphasize, however, that many of these same elements and factors and other similar elements and factors may be present repeatedly in the community at different times. Particular bilinguals will be affected by these factors to a greater or lesser degree depending on their individual circumstances. Thus, individuals might be affected by the presence of new immigrants in adolescence, be involved in activities which only require English during his 20s and marry (for the second time) a newly arrived immigrant from the home country. These different factors, then, will be reflected in the relative frequency with which they use each of the two languages over the course of their lives and the facility that they develop to discuss specific topics in each language.

More importantly, however, at any given moment, this same bilingual will reflect a sense of greater functional ease (not necessarily an awareness of such an ease) in one or the other of his languages, depending on his experience in similar contexts, with similar speakers, topics, or functions. Indeed, some researchers (Dodson, 1985)[8] have suggested that for any given interaction or function, all bilinguals have a momentarily stronger language. Whether or not it is possible for them to choose to function in that "stronger" language for that particular interaction depends on the circumstances in which they find themselves. Although systematic research has not been carried out on this question, It seems reasonable to conjecture that most bilinguals could be made aware about their momentary perceptions about which language might provide greater comfort or ease of expression at that moment.[9]

---

[8]Dodson uses the term preferred language for what has been termed here the language of greater functional ease. He defines preferred as follows: It is therefore proposed that the term preferred language be used to donate that language in which a bilingual, whether developing or developed, finds it easier to make individual utterances in discrete areas of experience at any given moment.

[9]This does not mean that most bilinguals would readily admit to such limitations. Indeed,

What this implies is that individual bilingualism that results from the real use of and experience with two languages is highly complex and variable. Although at the macrolevel one may be able to generalize about group tendencies or experiences, at the microlevel one cannot make assumptions about the relative strengths and proficiencies of a bilingual's two languages based on one or two factors about his background and experiences. Factors such as: (a) language spoken in the home, (b) age of arrival in the United States, (c) first language spoken, and even (d) language used most frequently can predict little about a bilingual's relative strengths in each language. Two bilinguals, for example, who share each of these characteristics may, nevertheless, have had experiences and contacts that resulted in very different strengths and weaknesses (e.g., strategic proficiency, linguistic proficiency, lexical range) in each of their languages.

THE STUDY OF CIRCUMSTANTIAL AND ELECTIVE BILINGUALS WITHIN THE FIELD OF EDUCATION: SOME FUNDAMENTAL PROBLEMS

The majority of the work carried out in the general area of the study of societal bilingualism and language contact has focused on the description of bilingual communities and of the circumstantial bilinguals who make up these communities. It is these individuals and the differences between these individuals in background factors such as age of acquisition, context(s) of acquisition, domains of use, degree of proficiency in each language, and so on, that have occupied the attention of those researchers and theorists. Specifically, these researchers have been concerned with describing and explaining the differences between different types of circumstantial bilinguals and with elaborating a set of theories that might account for both the similarities and the differences observed between groups of these bilingual individuals. They have also been concerned with describing different individuals who are members of such groups, the language production of these persons, the characteristics of their two languages, and the factors that lead to the choice of one language over the other.

Because of these concerns, very few descriptions of bilingual individuals have been presented in recent years without reference to the societal context in which this bilingualism developed. The tendency has been for

---

among certain groups of bilinguals, the pretense that both of their languages are equally strong is maintained even in the face of glaring evidence to the contrary. Awareness of a preferred language, however, would simply involve a momentary sense that the "other" language (the one not currently being spoken) provides one with greater ease or expressive range.

such descriptions to take into account the fact that circumstantial bilinguals are a product of a particular sociolinguistic environment which uniquely affects the type, level, and range of bilingual proficiencies described.[10]

These same trends, however, have not been operative in the study of bilingual individuals within the field of education. (Here, education is broadly defined to include the fields of second language acquisition, the language assessment of minority children, educational psychology, and psychometrics.) In these areas, the key distinction between elective and circumstantial bilingualism has seldom been taken into account. The tendency has been to view individual bilinguals as belonging to the same general type and to disregard the potential effects of context and use on language development and proficiency. This is particularly true in the area of psychometrics (Figueroa, 1990).

The Field of Second Language Acquisition

The study of incipient circumstantial bilingualism in school settings has been largely carried it out by scholars and researchers who see themselves as working within the general field of second language acquisition, rather than within the field of bilingualism broadly conceived. As will be made clear in the sections that follow, this is an important distinction.

Generally speaking, the field of second language acquisition itself is divided into two broad areas of focus. One of these areas sees second language acquisition as a domain of psycholinguistic inquiry that is independent of the concerns of the pedagogue and that, in Flynn and O'Neil's (1988) words, seeks "theoretically and empirically to establish the relevance of a theory of UG[11] for the adult L2 acquisition process" (p. 1). Researchers working within this framework are concerned with isolating and specifying "the properties of the underlying competence necessary for language learning." In studying second language acquistion, the principal objective of these researchers is to contribute to the development of a theory of UG in much the same way that researchers studying first

---

[10]For an excellent discussion of the trends and directions the study of bilingualism has taken, the reader is directed to Appel and Muysken (1987), Hamers and Blanc (1989), and Baetens-Beardsmore (1982). A view of the early work carried on in the field is provided in Haugen (1956, 1973).

[11]Universal Grammar (UG) in Chomsky's terms (1980) is "taken to be a set of properties, conditions, or whatever, that constitute the 'intitial' state of the language learner, hence the basis on which knowledge of language develops." Within this theoretical perspective, the human mind is considered to be endowed with an innate faculty for language, that is, with prewired linguistic knowledge. This innate knowledge or universal grammar makes possible, according to Flynn and O'Neil (1988), "the rapid and uniform development of language despite limited and often degenerate experience." It also explains "the richness and complexity of the system of grammar for human language" (Chomsky, 1981, p. 234).

language acquistion have been able to do so. The second area or branch of the field of second language acquisition, on the other hand, although also concerned with contributing to the development of theory, is primarily an applied science. As such, it is directly concerned with applying the results of its research to practical problems, particularly to the learning and teaching of languages within classroom settings. Within the general field of education, it is this second applied direction that has concerned itself with the investigation of how incipient bilingualism develops in classroom settings.

THE CLASSROOM AND BILINGUAL EDUCATION RESEARCH PERSPECTIVES IN THE STUDY OF SECOND LANGUAGE ACQUISITION

Although at first glance it might be expected that the classroom perspective on second language acquistion would focus primarily on incipient elective bilinguals and that the bilingual education perspective would focus on incipient circumstantial bilinguals, this distinction appears not to be an important one for either one of the two outlooks. The classroom perspective includes within it studies of elective bilinguals such as foreign students in U.S. universities enrolled in ESL classes and American students studying foreign languages in this country. This perspective also includes the study of circumstantial bilinguals such as newly arrived immigrant students who are placed in ESL programs in regular public schools. Similarly, the bilingual education perspective also encompasses the study of these two types of incipient bilinguals. Research carried out on second language acquisition in bilingual education programs[12] for non-English-speaking students in this country focuses on circumstantial bilinguals, whereas research carried out on Canadian immersion programs[13] for English-speaking students is concerned with elective bilinguals.

---

[12]Bilingual education programs in the U.S. involve the use of two languages in instruction. These two languages are the child's home language and English. Children eligible for bilingual education programs are normally children who come from homes in which English is not spoken. For a complete discussion of policies and practices in bilingual education, the reader is referred to Crawford (1989). It is important to note, however, that all children for whom bilingual education was originally intended would be considered here circumstantial bilinguals.

[13]Canadian immersion programs are designed for English-speaking children whose families choose this form of instruction for their children. In these programs, children are taught in the French language. They do not compete with French-native-speaking children and are instructed by bilingual teachers. It has been found that Canadian immersion students do not fall behind in their English language skills and at the same time learn French better than students enrolled in French as a foreign language classes. Children enrolled in such programs are considered to be elective bilinguals.

Within the bilingual education perspective, interest has largely centered on incipient bilinguals in formal classroom environments. Moreover, even though in the United States the children in question are members of bilingual communities (immigrant minorities or indigenous non-English-speaking minorities), most researchers have not taken the societal context into account in describing the process of acquisition or the factors leading to greater or lesser success in language learning.[14] The focus of many of these studies is the acquisition of the societal language (normally known as L2) and its use within the school context. What is examined are the factors impacting on L2 development in the classroom proper and the role of teachers, peers, and learners' individual characteristics on the acquisition process. Conclusions about growth and development in this language are often based on tests of academic achievement (i.e., reading, mathematics) or on specially constructed tests of language proficiency.

Within this tradition, little or no attention is given to the role in the acquisition process of normal, everyday, out-of-school events such as television, play with English-speaking neighborhood children, older siblings, and the like. From the point of view of many studies in this general tendency, studying the acquisition of English in the United States by minority children is not much different than studying the acquisition of French in foreign language classes in this country. In both cases, the process of learning or acquisition is viewed only in a formal setting. The key differences between the French-language student (the incipient elective bilingual) and the English-language student (the incipient circumstantial bilingual), which were summarized earlier in our discussion of elective and circumstantial bilinguals, are ignored altogether. The role of the surrounding English-speaking community is rarely taken into account for the English-language learner, and he/she is, in fact, studied from the same perspective as the foreign language learner. Indeed, if the circumstantial bilingual is of an interest to the second language acquisition researcher, he/she is interesting primarily as a learner of the societal language within a tutored context. Although this interest allows U.S. researchers interested in minority children who are incipient bilinguals to work closely within the same tradition as Canadian researchers working in immersion programs and with researchers who focus on foreign language learners, it tends to obscure the important differences between the elective or additive dimension of bilingualism and the circumstantial or subtractive dimension of the phenomenon.

---

[14]Although there are exceptions to this trend (e.g., Cancino & Hakuta, 1981; Fantini, 1985), most researchers working within this tradition have primarily focused on second language acquisition as it occurs in formal or instructed contexts. For a review of research trends in this field, the reader is directed to Beebe (1988) and Klein (1986).

THE CANADIAN IMMERSION AND BILINGUAL
EDUCATION PERSPECTIVES ON BILINGUALISM

Both the Canadian immersion and the bilingual education perspectives on second language acquisition have sought to understand the growth and development of second language abilities primarily in tutored, classroom environments. By carrying out research in such contexts, researchers have endeavored to contribute to both policy and practice. Very specifically, they have sought to provide for policymakers and practitioners a set of guiding principles that might inform the education of linguistic minority students both in this country and in other areas of the world.

Unfortunately, the view of developing bilingualism emerging from this research is somewhat narrow. As was noted earlier, most studies in this tradition have focused exclusively on classroom settings and have concerned themselves with examining either the linguistic characteristics of the children's two languages or the performance of these children on standardized tests. A large number of the researchers engaged in this type of study are either psychologists or psycholinguists who work very much within the traditions of these two fields.[15] Although apparently concerned with the same object of study as students of bilingualism, scholars who view themselves as second language acquisition researchers have views about the the development of circumstantial bilinguals' second language that are unlike those of students of societal and individual bilingualism. This difference will be apparent in the following summary.

Views of Students of Second Language Acquisition.

1. The primary focus of this research is the period of incipient bilingualism.
2. The assumption is made that an individual will arrive at a "full" or native-like stage in the target language. The learner is viewed as moving through a series of stages toward this goal. The *monolingual norm* of the target language is used, therefore, to judge the adequacy of the learner's progress at different stages.
3. When a native-like stage is not reached, this is viewed as a problem in need of explanation. Explanations offered include:
   • limited access to monolingual mainstream variety of target language,
   • exposure to flawed language data,
   • negative learner attitudes toward target language or speakers,

---

[15]For a discussion of the limitations of the fields of linguistics and psychology in the study of bilingualism, the reader is referred to Fishman (1968).

- fossilization of particular forms, and
- insufficient formal instruction.

Views of Students of Societal Bilingualism.

1. The primary focus of this research is "steady-state" bilingualism[16] and the various factors that affect the use of each language at various stages in a bilingual individual's lifetime.
2. The assumption is made that, for reasons not well understood, second languages are seldom acquired "perfectly" by most circumstantial bilinguals. Indeed the assumption is further made that circumstantial bilinguals rarely exhibit total monolingual-like competencies in either of their two languages simply because they are not monolinguals. Additionally, the use of monolingual norms for evaluating these speakers is thought to be inappropriate because it is considered that their language behavior and use is governed by *bilingual* and not *monolingual norms* of interaction.
3. When a native-like stage is not reached, this is viewed as normal. Because circumstantial bilinguals use both languages in accordance with varying home and community standards, such use may never include the total broad range of registers and styles and competencies found in a monolingual community. Language proficiency and communicative competence in each of the bilingual's two languages, therefore, is seen to depend on factors such as:
   - age of first exposure to the language,
   - amount of exposure to either or both the contact variety and monolingual variety of the language,
   - nature of the bilingual community's norms of usage,
   - function of the language within the community, and
   - frequency of use.

As might be conjectured, the contrast in perspective between the two fields has resulted in pronounced differences in their study of bilingual individuals. For example, although students of bilingualism consider ambilingualism to be an idealized condition that is seldom achived by most bilinguals, second language acquisition researchers often speak of "full" bilingualism, a concept that is poorly defined but that suggests the presence of "equivalent" or close to "equivalent" abilities in two languages. Similarly, although students of bilingualism believe that all bilingualism is limited to some degree for some functions and domains, students of second

---

[16]This term is used by Hyltenstam and Obler (1989) as a synonym for mature-stage bilingualism.

language acquisition use terms such as *limited* bilingual or *semilingual* to refer to individuals who do not attain the desired ideal state.[17]

The Fields of Educational Psychology and Psychology

Similarly, within the fields of psychometrics and educational psychology, there is seldom an interest in differentiating between elective and circumstantial bilinguals or even in determining the degree to which bilingual individuals differ in terms of language abilities and/or proficiencies. Research is conducted on bilingual subjects and on the effects of bilingualism on some other construct (e.g., memory, perception) and in most cases bilinguals are identified casually. For example, potentially "bilingual" subjects are asked to self-identify as bilinguals (with no definition of bilingualism provided), or they are assumed to be bilingual if a language other than English is spoken in the home.[18]

When there is a concern about degree of bilingualism, it is present only to the degree that there is a sense that the only "real" bilinguals are individuals whose proficiency in their two languages is equivalent. For this reason, the tendency has been to search for *balanced bilinguals* and to include in experiments or studies only subjects found to have "equivalent strengths" in both their languages. Equivalence is considered to be manifested by different researchers in different ways but includes such indicators as scores on sociolinguistic background questionnaires, self-ratings in receptive and productive modes for oral and written language, performance on "equivalent" reading tests in the bilingual's two languages, and so on.

Generally, no differentiation is made between elective and circumstantial bilinguals by most researchers.[19] In some studies, for example, a French native who learned English in France as a foreign language and subsequently came to the United States as a foreign student for a period of five years would be considered to be a *balanced bilingual* of the same type

---

[17]The debate surrounding these issues is a serious and complex one. For a view of questions involving the concept of semilingualism, the reader is referred to Edelsky, Flores, Barkin, Altwerger, and Jibert (1983) and Martin-Jones and Romaine (1987).

[18]Typical of these are studies on bilingual memory by Lopez, Hicks, and Young (1974) and Lopez and Young (1974).

[19]Typical of this tendency are studies such as that conducted by Lambert (1972) in which he describes his subjects as "college or university students with extensive experience in both English and French languages" (p. 53). In this particular study, subjects were classified as *separated* if they spent at least an entire year using the acquired language either exclusively or primarily and *fused* if they did not. This classification scheme allowed an elective French bilingual Canadian who had spent a year living in France at some point in his life to be classified as the same type of bilingual as an individual who grew up in France and then went to live in Canada.

as an American raised in a French-American bilingual community in Massachusetts and educated in English since the first grade. The basis for such classification would be that these two individuals both performed equally well on a test of their French reading ability and on an "equivalent" test of their English reading ability. It would not matter if one of the individuals obtained higher scores on both reading measures. In order to be considered similar types of bilinguals, that is, "balanced bilinguals," both individuals would simply show no advantage when tested in one language as opposed to the other. This "equivalent" performance in two languages (although in only one functional area) would be reason enough to place both of these individuals within the category of balanced bilinguals.

Needless to say, for the student of societal bilingualism, many problems arise if two individuals, such as those described earlier, are considered to be similar types of bilinguals. There can be no doubt that, because of each individual's life experiences, persons categorized in this manner as balanced bilinguals will have very different ranges of functional ability in each of their languages. They may indeed score "equivalently" on one measure of English and French reading, but this does not mean that they are ambilingual (equally able to function in L1 and L2 in all contexts) or even similar with regard to the majority of their language characteristics.

From the perspective of the study of both societal and individual bilingualism, the assumption that performance on narrow measures of linguistic ability can be used to categorize and group bilinguals is most suspect. Moreover, given what is known about the conditions in which bilingualism develops naturally, it is unlikely that many circumstantial bilinguals are actually able to develop balanced functional abilities in both their languages. When such balanced bilinguals are found, they are generally the products of familial or geographical accidents or of a carefully considered effort by an individual to develop "equivalent" strengths in her two languages.[20]

It can be concluded from this discussion, then, that even though the field of education has had an ongoing interest in the study of the performance of bilingual individuals, educational researchers have often not been concerned with trying to understand how various differences in bilingual background and experience affect this performance. Because of this limitation in perspective, research conducted on bilingual populations by a number of education-related fields may not accurately reflect the

---

[20]It is often the case that circumstantial bilinguals decide to go into fields such as interpreting or the teaching of languages. In those cases, these individuals will deliberately work to develop parallel strengths in their two languages in domains, topics, and areas they have normally only encountered in one of their languages.

actual competencies or lack of competencies of these individuals. In the sections that follow, we briefly explore a number of the reasons why this seeming disinterest exists among educational researchers, and we indicate how existing questions and controversies about bilingual speakers in general have impacted on what we currently know and do not know about bilingualism and testing.

CHAPTER 2

The Measurement of Bilingualism

THE SOURCE OF THE PROBLEM: MEASURING AND DESCRIBING BILINGUALISM

Although there are many reasons why fields outside of the general area of the study of societal and individual bilingualism might not take into account the natural variation that exists among bilinguals, one of the key reasons for this state of affairs has to do with the difficulties and problems encountered in trying to assess or describe individual bilingualism. The fact is that currently there is no agreement among researchers about how bilingualism should be measured or even about whether it can be measured meaningfully. The field has moved little beyond where it was in 1967 when, at the Moncton Seminar, scholars gathered to discuss key issues in the measurement and description of the phenomenon as a whole. At that time, foremost scholars in the field (MacNamara, Hasselmo, Fishman, Mackey, Lambert, Haugen, Leopold, Ervin-Tripp, Gumperz, Hasselmo, Kloss, Oksaar, Tabouret-Keller, etc.) carefully considered existing approaches and concluded that ascertaining just how bilingual an individual is can be most complex. It was evident to everyone there that researchers can, in fact, assess whether a particular person can function well enough in Language A or Language B to carry out particular tasks, but it is a far more complex matter to try to describe a person's bilingualism as a whole.

It is not surprising then that the questions that were focused on during the Moncton Seminar[1] are still unanswered. We do not know how to

---

[1]The proceedings of the seminar were published in Kelly (1969).

measure, for example, the extent to which one of the bilingual's languages influences the other, the roles which a bilingual's two languages play in his everyday behavior, and most especially the extent of a person's bilingual proficiency.

In the sections that follow, a number of the questions that contribute to making the measurement of bilingualism difficult will be reviewed. In the first section, we review the difficulties involved in establishing standards of language ability. In the second section, we examine a number of theoretical issues having to do with the bilingual individual himself; and finally, in the third section, we critique the different types of approaches and strategies that have been applied to the measurement of bilingual proficiencies and abilities.

What Does it Mean to Know a Language?

The language knowledge or competence of native speakers is generally taken for granted by most researchers. It is assumed that normal human beings are endowed with an innate capacity to acquire language, and that they do indeed develop their inborn capacity to become linguistically competent and communicatively able users of the language that surrounds them from birth.

Different researchers, however, have focused on separate aspects of this native-speaker ability. Some researchers, for example, have focused on linguistic competence, that is, on the largely implicit knowledge of language structure which includes such elements as: knowledge of the sound system of the language, knowledge of the meanings of words in the language, creativity (ability to create novel sentences), knowledge of sentences and nonsentences, the ability to recognize more and less grammatical sentences, the ability to recognize relations within sentences, the ability to recognize relations among sentences, and the ability to recognize ambiguous sentences.

Other researchers have argued that in addition to such implicit knowledge, native speakers also have the ability to use their language for actual communication. This ability, which has been termed *communicative competence* (Hymes, 1985, 1972), includes the capability to use the language appropriately, to carry out actions by means of speech, and to follow complex interactional rules for speaking with different interlocutors.

In spite of the research carried out on numerous aspects of both the linguistic and communicative competence of native speakers, it is not the case that this research has led to complete descriptions of native-speaker ability or to standards for comparing the relative facility in the language between different individuals. Except for speech pathologists who examine children thought to be language delayed, the assumption is generally made that native speakers of a language do not need to have their linguistic competence tested in order to prove that they are native speakers. Moreover, except for verbal IQ tests, the comparison of native speakers in terms of their different kinds of language competencies has not been pursued broadly. It appears to be simply taken for granted that individuals will vary in their ability to use language. This variability, however, whether it involves articulateness, inarticulateness, breadth of vocabulary, or quick verbal wit, is not seen as reflective of greater or lesser degree of native ability in the acquired first language.

The concerns are much different within the field of second language acquisition and particularly within the field of second language testing. For individuals involved in this area of endeavor, conceptualizing and describing the linguistic and/or the communicative competence of native speakers is fundamental. Without such a description and without standards against which language learners can be compared, assessing second language "proficiency" becomes an impossible task.

Within the second language acquisition field, then, much work has been carried out in attempting to define the various different components of native-speaker competence. Early efforts generally focused exclusively on linguistic knowledge and on particular sounds or structures. More recently, however, researchers have tried to develop a theory about what it means to know a language that encompasses both knowledge about its structure and the ability to use such knowledge appropriately. Bialystok and Sharwood-Smith (1985), for example, argued that knowing a language involves the "mental representation of systematic, organized information about the target language and the procedures for effectively and appropriately retrieving that knowledge in appropriate situations" (p. 106). Canale and Swain (1980), on the other hand, proposed a model of language competence that involves three types of related competences: (a) grammatical competence (knowledge of lexical items and of rules of morphology, syntax, sentence-grammar semantics, and phonology), (b) sociolinguistic competence (sociocultural rules of use and rules of discourse), and (c) strategic competence (verbal and nonverbal communication strategies).

More recently, Bachman (1990) proposed a model of communicative language ability (CLA) in order to provide "a broad basis for both the development and use of language tests and language testing research" (p. 81). In developing his model, Bachman took into account work carried out in the area of language proficiency assessment and in the area of communicative competence. Figures 2.1 and 2.2, which are taken from Bachman (1990, pp. 85, 87), offer some sense of the complexity of this model.

As is apparent from Figure 2.1, Bachman attempted to account for the various components of language ability when language is actually being

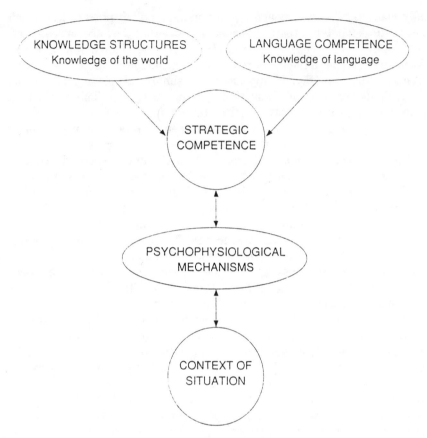

Figure 2.1. Components of Communicative Language Ability in Communicative Language Use. (Reprinted with permission from Oxford University Press.)

used. For Bachman, these components include not only knowledge about the world and knowledge of language but also a strategic competence, that is, a "mental capacity for implementing the components of language competence in contextualized communicative language use." Psychopysiological mechanisms, on the other hand, refer to the "neurological and psychological processes involved in the actual execution of language."

Additionally, Figure 2.2 is intended by Bachman to serve as a visual metaphor of the hierarchical relationships among the components of language competence. He emphasizes, however, that in spite of the static nature of the diagram, these components are not separate and distinct but rather interact with each other and with the situational context.

If this diagram and this presentation of the complexities of communicative language ability are important, it is because they help to emphasize the enormous complexity of the construct in question. A view of the

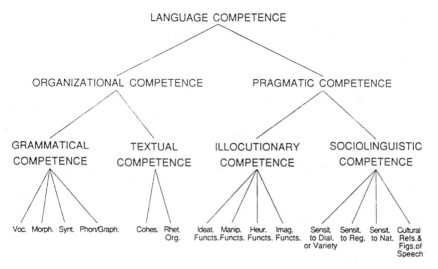

Figure 2.2. Components of Language Competence. (Reprinted with permission from Oxford University Press.)

components and subcomponents of each of these elements will underscore this perspective:

Organizational competence:
- consists of grammatical and textual competences,
- comprises those abilities involved in controlling the formal structure of language.

Pragmatic competence:
- is concerned with relationships between utterances and the acts or functions speakers intend to perform through those utterances,
- includes illocutionary competence that consists of the ability to carry out functions by means of language. Functions can include ideational functions, manipulative functions (regulatory, instrumental, interactional, phatic), heuristic functions, and imaginative functions.
- includes sociolinguistic competence that involves the understanding or control of the conventions of language. It entails sensitivity to differences in dialect and register as well as strategic competence, that is, the ability to compensate for breakdowns in communication.

For Bachman and for the researchers on whose work his proposed model is based, communicative language ability is a multifaceted, complex phenomenon that involves not only intuitions and innate knowledge about the structure of the language, but also the ability to select appropriately, from among an enormously large set of options, the linguistic form(s) that will most effectively enable the speaker to realize her momentarily changing goals.

From the perspective of second language testing researchers, then, what it means to know a language goes much beyond simplistic views of good pronunciation, "correct" grammar, and even mastery of rules of politeness. Knowing a language and knowing how to use a language involves a mastery and control of a large number of interdependent components and elements that interact with one another and that are affected by the nature of the situation in which the communication takes place.

What Is It That Needs to be Measured or Described: Native-Speaker Ability or Second Language Proficiency?

Given the previous discussion, it can be appreciated that the question of what needs to be measured or described if one intends to assess the language abilities of bilingual individuals is quite complex. To begin with, there is the question of whether one is attempting to measure the bilingual's innate grammatical knowledge of each of her two languages (in Bachman's terms, her organizational competence in L1 and in L2) or whether one is trying to measure her functional ability in each language (in Bachman's terms, the pragmatic competence in L1 and L2).

Secondly, there is the question of whether when assessing the competence or ability of a bilingual speaker one is assessing abilities or proficiencies in one of the languages as a native language and in the other language as a second language, or whether one is assessing both languages as native languages or both languages as second languages. This is a matter of fundamental concern. The issue is: Is a bilingual speaker a native speaker of at least one of his languages? Is the native language always the language acquired first? If so, does the bilingual remain a native speaker of this language in spite of his almost exclusive use of a second language during most of his life time? From what perspective, then, should each of a bilingual's two languages be assessed?

The Concept of the Native Speaker

The Concept of the Native Speaker in the Field of Linguistics. From the point of view of the field of linguistics, the concept of the native speaker is both important and complex. Coulmas (1981), for example, pointed out that linguists of every conceivable theoretical orientation agree that the concept of the native speaker is fundamental in the field of linguistics. For example, for some linguists, native speakers are the essential source of linguistic data. For other linguists, the principal goal of the linguist is to describe a language in a way that makes explicit the innate ability (competence) of such native speakers.

In spite of the centrality of native speakers in linguistic research, however, there has been much disagreement about the use of native speakers in both field work and theory building. The important point for this discussion is the fact that regardless of the position taken about the use and importance of native speakers for linguistic research, the sense that native speakers are fundamentally different from nonnative speakers underlies every discussion of the concept.

Not surprisingly, for many researchers, bilingual speakers do not qualify as native speakers. From some perspectives, for example, Coulmas (1981), only those speakers of a language qualify as potential informants "whose first language it is." According to this view, there is a qualitative difference between a first and second language. By insisting on "nativeness" the linguist guarantees that the data he acquires is not distorted by possible interference from another language.

Other students of the concept of native speaker take an even more extreme position. Ballmer (1981), for example, said this about the inappropriateness of considering bilingual individuals to be native speakers of one or the other of their languages:

> We may conjecture that every speaking human is a native speaker of a language. This is not true either, as results from bilingualism-studies show. The typical case is that bilinguals are not native speakers of either language. Moreover there are those people who have forgotten their native language for various reasons, e.g., because of living abroad in an environment linguistically different from the native one. Hence, the implication from *speaking human being* to *native speaker* does not hold. (pp. 54–55)

Although we might disagree with the contention that "bilingualism studies" actually have shown that bilinguals are native speakers of neither of their languages, the point here is that bilinguals are often seen by researchers as unusual human beings, as individuals whose language abilities and or intuitions may not be totally reliable, a quality considered essential if these intuitions are to form a basis for theories or descriptions of language.

Popular Views of the Concept of Native Speaker. In the popular mind, the concept of the native speaker is less complex than that encountered in the field of linguistics. For most individuals, a native speaker, or a near-native speaker,[2] is one who can function in all settings and domains in which other native speakers normally function. However, to be considered fully native, a speaker must be indistinguishable from other native speakers; that is, it should not be evident to most other native speakers that there is something particularly different or nonnative about him or her. Upon interacting with the speaker, they should assume that he or she acquired the language in question as a first language.

Circumstantial Bilinguals and the Concept of the Native Speaker.
As might be noted, the concept of the native speaker, even as a popular concept, is difficult to apply to most circumstantial bilinguals. As can be recalled from Table 1.2, many such bilinguals actually acquire two languages as a first language. Thus, the question of which language is a first language may not be answerable in simple terms. One might reasonably argue that such bilinguals would, in fact, qualify as native speakers of two languages.

On the other hand, as we also made clear in our earlier discussion, the language strengths and abilities of circumstantial bilinguals change over time. It is possible for bilingual individuals to "forget" their first language, that is, to use it less, to feel that it is less comfortable than the language they acquired as adults. The implications of this are clearly critical, for if it happens that these bilinguals do reach a stage in one of their languages in which they no longer are able to function capably and comfortably in all domains in which most normal native speakers function, they would not meet even the most basic elements of the popular definition of the native speaker.

The standard of indistinguishability is equally as problematic for circumstantial bilinguals. Because they acquire both of these languages among bilingual speakers of both languages, it is often the case, that they speak a *contact variety* of each of their languages.[3] What this means is that monolingual speakers of one or the other of their languages might view them as either learners of the language in question or as speakers of a

---

[2]The term *near-native speaker* is often used to refer to individuals whose proficiency in a second language is, except for a few features, nearly equivalent to that of a native speaker. In the foreign language teaching profession, for example, when an academic department advertises for a native or near-native speaker, it is assumed that the individual will have excellent pronunciation and nearly total "mastery" of a second language. Such mastery includes being able to interact in all intellectual and social domains with comfortable appropriateness with only an occasional slip-up (perhaps during moments of great stress) in areas such as verb usage or form.

[3]Contact varieties of Spanish spoken in Mexican-American bilingual communities, for example, have been found to exhibit traces of English vocabulary and syntax. Contact varieties of English in these same communities, on the other hand, have been found to exhibit traces of Spanish pronunciation.

nonstandard or nonprestige variety of this language. For monolingual speakers of prestige varieties of language who are prescriptive in their orientation to language and who believe in strict norms of correctness, contact features often suggest foreignness and lack of mastery of the language being spoken.

In terms of "passing" among native speakers, circumstantial bilinguals would be less detectable among speakers of less-than-standard regional or local varieties. Among such monolinguals, they might simply be thought to be native speakers from another region of the country.

Native Languages, Second Languages and Language Assessment

The question of whether bilinguals are or are not native speakers of one or the other or both of their languages is a difficult and complex one. It is so complex, in fact, that ordinarily one might want to view it as a matter of theoretical interest and yet not involve oneself with its resolution.

Unfortunately, for those of us concerned about assessing degrees of bilingualism, levels of proficiency, and the like, the question cannot be avoided. It is clear that both the procedures for assessing native languages (as opposed to second languages) and the theoretical assumptions underlying these procedures are quite different. In attempting to decide how to approach the assessment of the language competence of bilinguals, therefore, one must first decide whether one is assessing a native language or a second language. Specifically, one must decide whether it is appropriate to assess the *language proficiency* or the *verbal ability* of the bilingual speaker.

Although at first glance this might appear to be a trivial distinction, the notion of whether one is assessing proficiency or verbal ability is a most pivotal one. As Duran (1985) noted, the term verbal ability is used by cognitive psychologists and psychometricians to refer broadly to language skills, whereas the term language proficiency is used by researchers in the area of elective bilingualism and nonnative language assessment to denote familiarity with a language system.

As was argued previously, what this reflects is that monolingual native speakers are considered to have certain "natural," taken-for-granted verbal abilities in their only language. Even though it is evident that certain abilities might vary across monolinguals, language competence per se is assumed to be "normal" and is seldom assessed except in cases in which there is evidence of speech and language "disorders" (e.g., stuttering, delayed language acquisition). No normal monolingual speaker is ever assessed in a school setting and asked to prove his or her competence as a first language speaker.

The same is not the case for individuals who acquire a second or foreign language or even for individuals who are fluent circumstantial bilingual speakers. In these cases the assumption is made that there are limits to the individual's abilities or proficiencies. Assessment, then, involves identifying these limits by comparing the nonnative speaker's performance with a monolingual norm or standard or by testing for conscious knowledge about the language. In both cases, the individual is perceived as a "learner," as one who is in the process of acquiring a fully native system and who may in certain areas fall short of this standard.

Although this may indeed be appropriate for elective bilinguals and even for circumstantial bilinguals in the periods of incipient bilingualism, it is not clear that this is the case in assessing fully fluent bilinguals who can function as native speakers in everyday interactions with other native speakers in each of their languages. The question still remains: Is the bilingual individual a native speaker of both of his or her languages, or of neither of these languages? What criteria can be used to decide this? What instruments or measurement strategies should be used to make such a determination? How should the measurement of bilingual individuals be approached? Which group(s) should they be compared to?

There are clearly no simple answers. If one assumes that the bilingual is a native speaker of at least one of her languages, this would imply that, should one want to "assess" how competent a native speaker she is, one would have to use instruments or procedures currently used to make such assessments. What one would find, however, is that there are few models or precedents available. Again, except for the field of speech therapy that evaluates the language abilities of native speakers only when a pathology is suspected, it is normally not the case that the abilities of native speakers of the standard dialect are ever suspect.

If one assumes, however, that the circumstantial bilingual is a nonnative speaker of one or both of his languages, other questions arise. These questions are equally as perplexing as those surrounding the concept of the native speaker when applied to bilingual individuals.

The most fundamental question has to do with the entire notion of acquisition. The question is: To what degree is a circumstantial bilingual who is a fluent speaker of two languages still an *acquirer* or *learner* of his second language?

This question is a central one, because it is, in fact, this issue that may most clearly separate the elective bilingual from the circumstantial bilingual. The elective bilingual, almost by definition, is considered to be in the process of continuing to acquire his second language throughout most of his life. His proficiency, then, is considered to be "measurable" by comparing his performance to that of an idealized educated native speaker.[4] It is rarely the case, however, that most foreign language learners (elective bilinguals) reach this level of proficiency. Generally, therefore, failure to achieve this native-speaker norm is interpreted as being due to the fact that the individual is still in the process of acquiring the target language. Nonnative elements found in his or her production are considered to be either characteristic of the learner's developing system in L2 or to be the result of fossilization.[5]

Underlying the entire theory of fossilization and interlanguage is the assumption that all individuals who are native speakers of A can potentially learn or acquire Language B to the point that they will control the system totally and become indistinguishable from native speakers of B. Given this assumption, a native speaker of A who performs in Language B (his second language) in a manner that is not native-like (i.e., not identical to a monolingual speaker of the standard variety of Language B) must be seen as still being in the process of acquiring Language B.

As was noted previously, however, the circumstantial bilingual cannot be viewed as a language "learner" simply because her production in one or both of her languages is not identical to that of a monolingual speaker. Seemingly non-native-like features may not be the product of an approximative system or of "fossilized" forms, but rather part of the fully developed system of a speaker of a contact variety of Language A or Language B. What this means is that the circumstantial bilingual has acquired one or

---

[4]Procedures such as the *Foreign Service Institute Oral Interview* and other similar measures (e.g., *ACTFL Oral Proficiency Interview*) assess an elective bilingual's proficiency by comparing his performance in an oral interview with descriptions of different levels of "proficiency." These levels, in theory, cover a broad range of abilities beginning at the elementary level for an elective bilingual (e.g., can understand only memorized phrases) to the "educated-native" level (e.g., has the vocabulary normally expected of a native speaker in the same profession).

[5]Essentially, according to developmental variation theory, second language learners, in the course of acquiring a second language, develop learner's systems (approximate systems that are very different from those used by adult native speakers) or interlanguages (ILs). These learners' systems change over time and come to approach the native norm more closely as the learners become more fluent or proficient in the language. Often, however, for reasons not entirely understood, elective bilinguals appear to retain certain forms or features that are characteristic of early learners. When this occurs, the early form or feature is said to have "fossilized."

Some researchers believe that when a certain approximate form can be used to carry out a function without undue difficulty by the learner, the approximate form tends to "fossilize," that is, to remain in the speaker's developing or developed system. From this perspective, adjustment of form comes as a result of unsuccessful communication. Other researchers, however, believe that forms fossilize because learners have not been made conscious of their "infelicities" through direct grammar instruction. For a review of research in this area, the reader is directed to Beebe (1988) and Tarone (1988).

both of the languages in question among speakers who themselves speak an A-influenced variety of Language B or a B-influenced variety of Language A.[6] They are as legitimate varieties of fully developed native English as are other varieties of English whether stigmatized or not.

What this discussion implies is that in order to assess the language(s) of circumstantial bilinguals with instruments designed for use with elective bilinguals, one must first establish the fact that the circumstantial bilingual is indeed a "learner" of one or both of these two languages. As these arguments have intended to make clear, it is not evident that one can view the circumstantial bilingual as still being in the process of acquiring one or both of his or her languages.

Summary: Should We Measure Verbal Ability or Language Proficiency?

In deciding what needs to be measured or described when assessing the languages of a circumstantial bilingual, one has the following choices:

1. One can decide to view the bilingual speaker as a *native speaker* of *both* of her two languages.
2. One can decide to view the bilingual speaker as a *native speaker* of *one* of her languages and a *second language speaker* of the *other* of her languages.
3. One can decide to view the bilingual speaker as a *native speaker* of *neither* of her two languages.

From the point of view of Position 1, the bilingual individual would be assumed to have "verbal ability" in each of his languages. Unless one sought to compare the differences between his verbal abilities in Language A and Language B, one would generally not expect this individual to be asked to demonstrate his ability in either language beyond what is expected of other native speakers.

---

[6]Some researchers (e.g., Wong Fillmore, personal communication, 1988) are of the opinion that persons who reside in bilingual communities exhibit certain nonnative-like characteristics in their language because they have received "junky" data as input. We would maintain that whereas the language input provided by members of a bilingual community who speak Language A and Language B at varying degrees of proficiency will indeed include "junky" or approximative data from those acquiring either A or B, it will also include "good" (though not standard monolingual-like) data from individuals who have fully acquired A or B or are even monolingual speakers of the contact varieties of A or B. The language data provided by these speakers can only be considered "junky" data if one accepts monolingual native-speaker production as the only (i.e., "nonjunky") language data.

From the point of view of Position 2, however, the bilingual individual would be seen as having one native language and one second language. Problems might arise, however, in identifying the language that exhibits "native" strengths and the language that is either still in the process of being acquired or that has already been acquired and yet displays certain "nonnative" characteristics. Depending on the circumstantial bilingual's experiences, both the individual's "first" language and the language acquired subsequently might display certain "nonnative" features.

Position 2 would expect that the bilingual would be "proficient" to some degree in his second language and would attempt to discover the depth or level of this proficiency using instruments designed primarily for the study of elective bilinguals. In using such instruments, the assumption would be made that the circumstantial bilingual is a language "learner" of his second language and therefore similar to the elective bilingual.

Position 3, on the other hand, would speculate that both of the bilingual's two languages would fall short of native-speaker norms and would seek to measure the individual's level of proficiency in each language. In each case, procedures used for measuring this proficiency would be those developed for measuring the growth and development of elective bilinguals. Once again, the circumstantial bilingual would be viewed as a language learner.

Not surprisingly, given the issues raised here, the task of deciding whether to assess the *verbal ability* or the *language proficiency* of circumstantial bilinguals has caused difficulties for educators, educational researchers, and other individuals concerned about the study of bilingual individuals. As was stated previously, currently there is no agreement among students of bilingualism about how these matters should be resolved. In the absence of such agreement, however, individual researchers continue to use "bilingual" subjects and to arrive at far-reaching conclusions based on the use of methods of assessment which may be entirely inappropriate.

HOW HAS BILINGUALISM BEEN MEASURED: AN OVERVIEW OF TENDENCIES, TRENDS AND QUESTIONS

Attempts to measure bilingualism have generally sought to answer two fundamental questions: (a) What level of ability or proficiency does a bilingual individual have in each of his two languages, and (b) What is the status of his two languages relative to one another? In the first case, what is of interest is describing or assessing the bilingual's abilities in one or both of his two languages. In the second case, what is of interest is determining which one of a bilingual's two languages is "dominant."

In general, these two fundamental questions have been approached by researchers as though they were very separate issues. As a rule, researchers concerned about dominance have had little interest in presenting a full descriptive profile of a bilingual's dual-language abilities. They have been concerned, rather, with identifying the bilingual's weakest or strongest language in as efficient a manner as possible. Researchers, on the other hand, who have been concerned about describing the functional ability or proficiency of bilinguals have sought to present as full a picture as possible of what bilinguals are able to do in each of their two languages when speaking, listening, reading, and writing.

In this section, we briefly review the general trends and tendencies that have been followed in the measurement of bilingualism by each group of researchers. First we describe measures that have been used to assess overall ability and proficiency, and then we describe the strategies and procedures that have been used to measure bilingual "dominance."

Measuring Overall Competencies in One or Two Languages

Efforts directed at measuring bilingual proficiency or competence have had two principal purposes: (a) to determine to what degree bilingual individuals can speak, understand, read, and write each of their two languages', and (b) to determine whether a particular bilingual individual has enough mastery of one or both of his or her languages to carry out a given task or set of tasks. Although superficially similar, these two purposes are fundamentally different. Determining whether an individual can speak one of his or her languages well enough to work as an airline stewardess or a bilingual teacher, for example, is a far easier task than determining and describing the extent of a person's total speaking, reading, or writing ability in two different languages. Because of this, approaches to measuring or assessing proficiency have been used that are closely tied to these two distinct purposes. Investigators concerned about determining whether individual bilinguals can handle one or both of their languages at a level necessary to carry out a specific job or a set of activities can be described as involved in *assessing bilingual proficiency for specific purposes*. On the other hand, investigators concerned about describing or measuring to what degree bilinguals can function broadly in their two languages can be said to be involved in *assessing bilingual abilities in one or two languages*.

Trends in Assessing Language Proficiency for Specific Purposes. The development of assessment instruments or strategies for measuring bilingual proficiency for specific purposes has focused on analyzing the tasks or functions to be carried out for a particular job or purpose and determining the specific abilities needed in Language A and Language B in order to carry out those functions. As might be expected, assessment is carried out using direct measures, that is, by having the examinee actually use the language for a specific set of functions and judging whether he or she can use the language(s) being tested at the level required.[7] An example of such measures is the Federal Court Interpreters English–Spanish examination designed to certify federal court interpreters. On the oral part of this examination, examinees are required to demonstrate their ability to sight-read and translate from one language to the other, to interpret consecutively from Spanish to English and from English to Spanish, and to interpret simultaneously from English to Spanish. Examinees who are able to perform these tasks at the level determined to be essential in order for court procedures to be carried out are certified as federal court interpreters.

This same procedure of using real-life tasks in measuring language ability is generally used in the assessment of bilingual proficiency for specific purposes. From the perspective of the test designer working within this tradition, the question to be answered by the language assessment procedure is: Does this individual have the particular abilities in Language A that are required to carry out activity X? He or she is not concerned with overall ability or with the relationship between the bilingual's two languages.

In comparison to other approaches to language measurement, the assessment of language for specific purposes is both straightforward and limited in scope. Once the key tasks and functions associated with a specific purpose or domain of activity have been identified, a researcher can directly examine an individual's ability to carry out all or some of these tasks.

Trends in Assessing General Language Proficiency. Most of the activities relating to the measurement of language abilities have been directed at elective bilinguals, that is, at foreign or second language learners. Indeed the major language tests in existence today (for example, the Test of English as a Foreign Language (TOEFL), the Oral Interview of the Foreign Service Institute, the IEA Achievement Tests of Proficiency in English as a Foreign Language) are intended for persons who have studied language formally and who usually have conscious knowledge about a given language's structure, vocabulary, sound system, and the like.

According to Spolsky (1975), foreign/second language testing has passed

---

[7]For a description of the development of instruments designed to assess bilingual proficiency for specific purposes, the reader is directed to Valdés (1989b).

through three stages of development during this century: the prescientific stage, the psychometric-structuralist stage, and the psycholinguistic-sociolinguistic stage.

At the prescientific stage, tests were primarily of the translation, composition, and sentence completion type. They were intended exclusively for foreign and second language learners and closely followed existing beliefs about how language should be taught and what it meant to "know" a language. At that point in time, most language courses followed a grammar-translation approach, and students were said to "know" a language if they could translate in both directions using the target language and the native language. Oral skills (both productive and receptive) were not taught and consequently were not tested.

During the second stage in the development of language testing, attempts were made to achieve validity by relating tests to existing theories about language. Because it was assumed that problems experienced by learners in the language under study were due to the transfer of elements from the first language, the native language and the target language were normally subjected to contrastive analyses, and classroom activities, particularly pattern drills, concentrated students' attention on these elements. During this period, to "know" a language meant that students could recite previously practiced and memorized dialogues with good pronunciation, that they could respond orally to drills that asked them to transform sentences in order to change verb tense, subject pronouns, and so on, and that they could use traditional grammatical terminology to talk about the language. Few expected learners to actually speak the language itself.

As a result of these approaches to language teaching, tests were produced that sought to measure students' mastery of particular points of difficulty. This contrastivist/structuralist view of language resulted in the development of discrete point tests—tests that Oller (1979) defined as those that attempt to focus attention on one point of grammar at a time and in which each test item is aimed at one and only one element at a time. As Davies (1982) recalled, the structural testing school that gave rise to analytical, discrete point tests assumed that language is learned by successive progression through skills and that, in order to test those skills, language had to be broken down into its linguistic components (e.g., phonology, morphology, syntax, and vocabulary). Typical discrete point tests purported to measure one such component at a time and were subdivided into sections each of which focused on only one subskill. Individual items in a phonology section of an English as a foreign language test, for example, might ask that examinees distinguish between two similar words heard out of context (e.g., watch and wash, pill and peel). Interestingly enough, the majority of students who scored well on such discrete point tests were often not able to use the language on which they had been tested in real-life communication. On the other hand, individuals who had traveled abroad and had learned a foreign language in a context other than the classroom generally did poorly on such tests. They generally lacked the ability to analyze language in the manner in which such analysis is carried out in foreign language classes and experienced much difficulty in dealing with language elements out of context. As might be expected, circumstantial bilinguals, because they normally have no familiarity with terminology used to examine and analyze the structure of the language(s) they speak fluently, also performed poorly on such tests.

More recent approaches to language teaching have argued that the focus of language instruction should be actual functional competence, that is, the ability to communicate with real speakers in the target language. Although questions about methodology, classroom practices, and the like that result in such functional development or acquisition of proficiency are still in a state of flux; dissatisfaction with testing practices in general and new advances in theory have led to the third stage of the language testing tradition—the psycholinguistic/sociolinguistic stage. The emphasis during this stage, which is still ongoing, is on integrative or global tests, that is, on instruments or procedures that Davies (1982) described as attempting "to assess proficiency (both in production and comprehension) of the total communicative effect of a message" (p. 131). Basic to this approach to testing is the assumption that language elements are never actually processed independently of one another by real speakers, and that language involves actual communication of meanings.

Within this tradition of integrative or global testing, two principal types of approaches to test development have emerged. One approach (the purely integrative) is simply the direct opposite of discrete point testing in that it attempts to assess the learners' ability to use many linguistic elements simultaneously. This assessment is carried out by using test items that are not isolated elements, but rather "texts" of connected discourse that the learner must respond to or manipulate in some fashion. Test items are considered to be integrative if they require the examinee to process a segment of language as a whole. They need not be actual tests of oral production or comprehension.

The other approach (the integrative and pragmatic) attempts to measure learners' production directly by examining their performance on tasks that involve actual listening, speaking, writing, and reading. An example of one integrative and pragmatic measure of proficiency is the OPI (the Oral Proficiency Interview), which involves the use of oral interview examinations modeled after the Foreign Service Institute's (FSI) Oral Interview Process. According to Dandonoli (1987), the OPI "is a face-to-face test of foreign language speaking competence, lasting 10–30 minutes." Through a conversational interview the examiners rate the examinees' ability to function in the target language on a scale of 0–5 (from novice-low to superior) according to a set of proficiency definitions. The three areas of focus during each interview are: function, content/context, and accuracy. Each of these areas are further subdivided. For example, the accuracy dimension includes such elements as pronunciation, vocabulary, fluency, and grammar–each element contributing in different amounts to the overall production depending on the level of proficiency of the examinee. Although a great advance over previous types of language tests, the OPI and other similar procedures have provoked strong criticisms from many language-teaching professionals.

Summarizing briefly, in developing language tests, the language teaching and testing profession has primarily addressed the needs of persons involved in the process of learning language; and in all cases, theories about language testing have mirrored theories about language teaching and learning.

It will be seen, then, that the foreign/second language teaching and testing profession has little to offer to individuals concerned about measuring the abilities of circumstantial bilinguals. At its best, even the Foreign Service Institute's interview procedure (the FSI Examination), which is used to decide whether individuals speak a language well enough to serve in the foreign service, reveals little about the abilities of circumstantial bilinguals. Because the interview seeks to determine how close a prospective member of the foreign service comes to speaking the target language like an "educated native speaker," it is concerned with a particular style and range of language. As critics of the procedure have pointed out (Savignon, 1985; Valdés, 1989), the use of the educated native-speaker norm would result in most native speakers of a language being rated as "3s" on the 0 to 5 scale, but never as "5s." In the words of the *ILR Handbook on Language Testing* (1982):

> Finally, we return to the point of whether a "native" speaker non-5 would be accepted as a native in his homeland. The answer, of course, is "yes"–a native auto mechanic would be accepted as a native-speaking auto mechanic. He would not be accepted as a "native-speaking" journalist. In the last analysis, the government not only wants to know whether a person will be accepted as a "native" speaker, but at what level. Thus, it is perfectly possible to have "native" housewives who are "3s"; semi-educated "natives" who are "3 + s", etc. In any society, there is not a majority of "5's". (as cited in Savignon, 1985)

The range of abilities such an educated native speaker has and does not have is generally left undefined. To date the questions of what exactly a native speaker can and cannot do with language and how accurate he or she is in real life are the subject of much controversy. What is evident is that rating a monolingual native speaker who can function effectively in a native environment a "3" because he or she does not control the prestigious variety of the language, and rating a nonnative learner of the language also a "3" because he or she does not control some aspects of syntax, morphology, or vocabulary, is most suspect. Clearly both individuals do not have the same or even similar language abilities.

The fact of the matter is that because circumstantial bilinguals are not the products of academic programs, the foreign/second language testing profession has not directed much attention to measuring their linguistic abilities. On the other hand, individuals concerned with measuring the achievement of English native-speaking students in language-related areas, have paid little attention to the fact that these instruments may also be used with circumstantial bilinguals.

Problems in Measuring the Language Abilities of Circumstantial Bilinguals. The assessment of overall proficiency in one or the other of a bilingual's two languages, then, is complicated by the fact that procedures and instruments available for such measurement have not been developed for use with circumstantial bilinguals.[8] They have been designed either for native speakers or language learners. Because it is never entirely clear whether circumstantial bilinguals should be tested using instruments intended for native speakers of the language or for language learners, it is often the case that, when bilingual language abilities are measured, the entire question of instrument selection and instrument appropriateness is simply ignored. No mention is made, for example, and no explanation is given by researchers when a bilingual is measured in the same language using both a test of reading developed for native speakers and a test of listening designed for language learners. For example, the fact that in reading Language A the individual is considered a native speaker and is being compared with standards set for native speakers appears not to affect the decision to use an instrument intended for language learners for measuring another aspect of the same language, for example, his or her listening comprehension ability. The fact that the same

---

[8]As a result of legislation and litigation regulating the education of non-English-speaking and limited-English-speaking children in this country, much attention has been given by schools to assessing the language proficiency of children who are suspected of belonging to one of these categories. In general, the intent of such assessment is to determine whether children "know" enough English to profit from English-only instruction. Several instruments, therefore, have been developed (e.g., the Language Assessment Scales [LAS], the Basic Inventory of Natural Language [BINL], and the Bilingual Syntax Measure [BSM]) for identifying language "dominance" and for determining correct program placement for children who are, in theory, incipient circumstantial bilinguals.

TABLE 2.1
Instruments Available for Measuring Different Language Modalities

Types of Examinations	Developed for Native Speakers	Developed for Language Learners
ORAL LANGUAGE		
LISTENING	Normally not available	Listening comprehension examinations
SPEAKING	Normally not available	Oral proficiency examinations
WRITTEN LANGUAGE		
READING	Reading achievement examinations	Reading proficiency examinations
WRITING	Writing achievement examinations	Writing proficiency examinations

individual is being treated as both a native speaker and a learner of the same language appears to be of little importance to a number of researchers.

The problem is, in part, that the availability of tests designed to measure language across modalities is limited. This limitation results from the fact that tests of oral proficiency and listening comprehension, in particular, are not normally developed for use with native speakers in their native language. It is assumed that native speakers can both speak and understand their native language.[9] On the other hand, tests that seek to measure reading ability and writing ability or vocabulary in native speakers are considered to be tests of reading and writing achievement as such and not tests of language proficiency.

In terms of availability of instruments, Table 2.1 details the existing situation. As noted in the table, there is a basic difference between these achievement tests and tests of language proficiency. Reading, writing, and vocabulary achievement tests are designed to measure knowledge gains made in specific subject matter areas. They are, in theory, not tests of language per se, and they are normally expected to be administered to a population that is native speaking or has received instruction in the language of the examination. By comparison, language proficiency tests (whether or not they test reading, writing, or vocabulary) are designed for language learners and are first and foremost tests of language even though they correlate highly with ability tests (IQ, speech, and language). They are devised to measure how well individuals who are learning a language or who have learned the language as elective bilinguals know and use this

---

[9]This may not be the case when this variable becomes crucial for other uses such as IQ assessment. Under these circumstances, low verbal scores may be seen as a measure of low intelligence.

target language in the oral and written modes. Tests of language proficiency are not intended to reveal much about native speakers.[10] At the same time, reading, writing, and vocabulary achievement (or placement) tests designed for native speakers are considered to be problematic when used with language learners or even with fluent speakers who have learned the language as a foreign language.[11]

Unfortunately, the implications of this distinction and the possible confusion resulting from the use of both proficiency and achievement tests to measure each of a bilingual's two languages has been given scant attention. To our knowledge, no one has commented on the fact that simply by choosing a language assessment instrument, one makes an assumption about the type of bilingual individual being studied. If one chooses instruments for measuring Language A that are designed for language learners, one is taking the position that the bilingual is not a native speaker of A. If one chooses instruments designed for measuring reading or writing achievement in native speakers, one is taking the position that the bilingual is indeed a native speaker. Finally, if for measuring Language A, one chooses a combination of instruments (e.g., a reading instrument designed for native speakers and an oral proficiency measure designed for language learners), it is not clear whether one is avoiding taking a position on the issue or if one is unaware of the importance of the distinction between the assumptions underlying the development of each type of instrument.

Except for students of bilingualism (e.g., Mackey, 1962; Weinreich, 1974), who have discussed the enormous complexity of measuring the productive and receptive abilities of bilingual individuals in both of their

---

[10]Research, which has as its purpose comparing the performance of native and nonnative speakers on instruments intended to measure the proficiency of nonnatives or foreign learners, is infrequently undertaken. However, some studies have been conducted that reveal the types of problems that native speakers can encounter on tests produced for persons who have studied language formally as a foreign language. Angelis (1977), for example, summarizes results of several studies which demonstrated that native English speakers performed poorly on the TOEFL (Test of English as a Foreign Language). In one case (Angoff & Sharon, 1971) it was found that in the Structure and Written Expression and in the Reading Comprehension and Vocabulary sections, 80% of the native-speaking subjects answered one-fourth to one-fifth of the items incorrectly. It was conjectured that the lack of conscious awareness of grammatical structure in English as well as the nature of the vocabulary included resulted in unexpected difficulties for these native English speakers. Additional evidence of the fact that the TOEFL has been considered inappropriate for use with native speakers of English is found in Clark (1977).

[11]The reader is directed to Alderman (1982) for a discussion of problems encountered by foreign students with the SAT and for a discussion of problems encountered by foreign students when taking the GRE. Both the GRE and the SAT are considered to be placement examinations (i.e., academic achievement tests of native speakers of English as opposed to language proficiency tests for foreign students of English).

languages, most individuals engaged in research have tended to use available instruments. Such instruments, moreover, have often been used for purposes other than those for which they were intended.[12] Unfortunately, there has been no widespread objection to these practices.

Trends in the Use of Self-Report Data in Assessing Bilingual Abilities in One or Two Languages. Self-report data have been used by researchers of different backgrounds in an attempt to determine the relative language proficiency or ability of bilinguals. In general, two different kinds of self-report data have been used: (a) self-rating of language abilities in different modalities for each language, and (b) sociolinguistic background questionnaires.

Self-Rating of language abilities. Procedures designed for the self-rating of language abilities by bilinguals ordinarily present individuals with scales of some type and request that they indicate on such scales their degree of competence in each language. Depending on the researcher's interests, bilinguals may be asked to rate and compare their ability to speak, understand, read, and/or write each of their languages. As is the case with other kinds of self-rating, the use of this procedure assumes that, for the most part, ordinary speakers are aware and conscious of their language abilities and limitations. It specifically assumes that circumstantial bilingual individuals will be able to rate their abilities in both the societal and the minority language reliably.

Unfortunately, it is not always the case that bilinguals can rate their ability in both languages accurately. For example, they may over-or underrate their ability in one or the other of their two languages depending on the norm that they utilize for comparing their own perceived performance. Because it is rare for researchers to define precisely what an excellent versus a good or a fair command of the written or oral language will be, it is the bilingual him- or herself who must both define the levels of ability conveyed by a researcher in using, for example, the terms poor,

---

[12]An example of this is the use of achievement test for measuring the English language proficiency of children placed in bilingual education programs. In many instances, scores obtained on the CTBS below a certain cut-off point (e.g., the thirtieth percentile) are interpreted as evidence of limited English proficiency. For a discussion and critique of this practice, the reader is referred to Baker, (1986).

Another example of the use of tests for purposes for which they were not intended is seen in Hakuta and Diaz (1985). In this study, the researchers assessed children's ability in Spanish by means of an adaptation of the Peabody Picture Vocabulary Test. The authors commented that both the English and the Spanish versions of the Peabody were used, not as measures of intelligence, but as "a measure of relative abilities within each of the two languages" (p. 334) for their bilingual sample.

fair, good, and excellent, and rate his or her own competence according to this definition.[13]

The result of this, as Macnamara (1969) found, is that elective bilinguals tend to rate their skills depending on the grades obtained in school in the formal study of each language. On the other hand, circumstantial bilinguals are no more accurate than elective bilinguals in rating their own proficiency in two languages. Given the circumstantial bilinguals' limited exposure to the monolingual norm in the minority language and their everyday exposure to the monolingual norm in the societal language, it is often the case that very different criteria will be applied to the latter language as opposed to the former. An individual, because of his or her exposure to many educated speakers of standard English, may be aware of limitations in the use of certain registers in this language. At the same time, if this same individual has had little contact with the educated standard in the minority language, he or she may not be conscious of how his or her own language abilities would compare to those of an educated monolingual native. The individual may overrate such monolingual competencies and thus underrate his or her own abilities in comparison. On the other hand, he or she may have an incomplete awareness of a what full monolingual competence in the minority language might actually involve. For example, she may not be aware of the range of registers that monolinguals might ordinarily have. She might, therefore, expect monolingual speakers of the language to have the same range of abilities found in bilingual communities, a conclusion that would lead to an overestimation of her own abilities in this language vis-à-vis the imagined monolingual native.

The problem, then, in the use of self-rating procedures has to do both with the general validity and reliability of this kind of measure with an added confusion resulting from undefined standards of competence and from the bilingual's experience with bilingual speakers of both languages. It is generally agreed that in order for such measures to be useful, researchers must carefully describe the standards against which bilinguals should compare themselves. More importantly, it is generally recommended that researchers use such self-report data in conjunction with other more direct measures of language performance in order to control for possible misperceptions and or exaggerations of actual language abilities.

Although the use of self-report data has been defended by a number of researchers (e.g., Rose, 1980) because of its positive correlation with translation ability, it must be used with caution. Even though self-rating in

---

[13]An example of an attempt to define levels of proficiency more precisely is found in Vaid (1984).

situations in which no reward or punishment is expected is generally considered to have a high degree of face validity, there is little evidence, for example, to suggest that it can be used with children. Unfortunately, this limitation has not been obvious to a number of researchers.[14]

Sociolinguistic background questionnaires. Beginning with Hoffman's work (1934), students of bilingualism have used questionnaires in an attempt to obtain a detailed profile of the role played by each of two languages in a bilingual's everyday life. Ordinarily such questionnaires include queries that focus on the age of acquisition of each language, the domains in which each of the languages is used (e.g., home, neighborhood, school, work), the frequency of use of each language, the persons with whom each language is normally used (e.g., family members vs. outsiders, siblings vs. parents), and the topics and areas of experience that are handled most comfortably in one or the other of the two languages.

The best designed questionnaires (e.g., Fishman, Cooper, & Ma 1971; Institute of Education, 1983) include a large number of questions designed to elicit information about the respondent's actual use and ability in each language. The Linguistic Minority Project's Secondary Pupil's Survey,[15] for example, contained a total of 60 questions. Among them were such questions as:

When I'm talking to my father, I usually speak _____ .

When I'm spoken to, my father usually speaks to me in _____ .

(The above questions were asked for each member of the family.)

Before I went to school, I only used _____

    mostly used _____

    also used _____

Can you speak this language now?

    Yes, quite well.

    Only a little.

    No, not now.

    Never could.

---

[14]An example of the use of self-rating scales with children is found in Myers and Goldstein (1979).

[15]The Institute of Education (1983) was concerned with the minority languages widely used by large numbers of people in England. It was funded by the Department of Education and Science and was based at the University of London Institute of Education from September 1979 to April 1983. The Secondary Pupil's Survey was developed for examining the language use and perception of linguistic diversity among secondary school pupils.

When well constructed, sociolinguistic background questionnaires are both detailed and thorough.

Based on what is known about bilingual communities and circumstantial bilinguals, such questionnaires seek to paint as complete as possible a picture of a bilingual's life experiences in using two languages. Of necessity, because of the nature of societal and individual circumstantial bilingualism, the picture obtained from these instruments is often both inconsistent and complex. Simple expected relationships (e.g., the language first learned will be the language spoken ordinarily by the mother) may not be found. Moreover, the scaling properties of these questionnaires are undefined and suspect since these items may comprise nothing other than nominal properties though the scoring schema may assume interval characteristics.

Used in conjunction with other measures, especially with self-ratings of ability and with observations or with evaluations of actual performance, sociolinguistic background questionnaires have been found to be useful tools for obtaining baseline information about the role and function that two languages play and have played in a bilingual's life. They may not, however, validly assess individual proficiency, because this is mediated by many more uses than included in such questionnaires.

Unfortunately, not all questionnaires administered to bilinguals in an attempt to assess their relative proficiency in each language are of the type described above. Census questions about language, for example, limit themselves to asking one or two questions about language background which are thought to reflect the actual language use or proficiency of the interviewee. Questions such as: "Is there a language other than English spoken in the home" followed by self-rating or frequency-of-use questions seldom lead to answers which reveal the degree of proficiency in the non-English language of either the respondent or the other members of his family.

Other short questionnaires (for example, those supposedly limited to key questions thought to be most revealing about a bilingual's language abilities) are equally as problematic. As can be recalled from Table 1.2, circumstantial bilingualism is most complex, and it is difficult to predict the language abilities that will be found even within the same generation of immigrant bilinguals.

For the most part, in examining the relationship between language background and/or proficiency and standardized testing, researchers (e.g., Duran et al., 1985) have followed this latter trend and have tended to ask a limited number of questions that are expected to be most revealing of the examinees' English language ability and of his or her use of and/or ability in the non-English language. Such questions normally focus on language spoken in the home, language spoken by parents, language learned first, language perceived to be stronger for respondent, and so on. It is assumed that answers to such questions are valid indicators of the respondent's ability, especially in the minority language. Questions, however, that do not take into account factors such as setting of language use, topic, and relationships between speakers, may actually reveal very little about both a respondent's overall abilities and about his bilingualism in general. Such questions do not take into account the extraordinary complexity of societal bilingualism and its impact on bilingual individuals. For example, it may in fact be the case that a person whose mother only speaks a minority language is nevertheless an English-language preferrent college-age student who is only literate in this language. His younger sibling, however, (because of exclusive attention from his mother after older siblings had left home) may be far more comfortable in the minority language than in English. Conclusions reached about an individual's language ability strictly on the basis of generalizations about home language use, then, are simplistic. Contrary to what might usually be expected, there are few background factors that by themselves or combined with a small number of other factors can be used as measures of how well bilinguals function in both of their languages.

Measuring Bilingual Dominance

The problem of measuring "bilingual dominance" is one that has preoccupied most students of bilingualism who have sought to study bilingual individuals. The very concept of bilingual dominance, however, is problematic. As Weinreich (1974) argued: "The complex term dominant covers what is indiscriminately lumped together under mother tongue, . . . All criteria of dominance, of course, may be socioculturally determined" (p. 75).

As this statement argues, the very term *dominant* has suggested a number of different kinds of language strengths to different researchers. It appears to include the kinds of abilities that one would associate with a mother tongue; however, as Weinreich also pointed out, the entire notion of what a mother tongue is may be socioculturally determined. For Weinreich, the "formidable difficulty" to be resolved in measuring bilingual dominance has to do with the fact that the criteria by which a language may be characterized as dominant are numerous (e.g., proficiency, age of acquisition, range of levels, or varieties mastered.)

Few researchers interested in the area of bilingual dominance have approached it taking into account Weinreich's concerns. In essence, most researchers have assumed that the concept of dominance does not need to be defined precisely (i.e., dominant and stronger were considered to be synonymous). They have sought to answer questions such as: Is it a fact that bilinguals have a dominant or "stronger" language? Is it possible for bilinguals to be equally proficient in their two languages and thus not dominant in either? How can dominance, if it exists, be measured?

Much of the early work on bilingual dominance was carried out by researchers interested in various different questions. Some, for example, sought to describe the structure of memory, cognitive development, and the like, and wanted to find "true" or "balanced" bilinguals in order to do so. Others hoped to understand the relationship between language transfer and a bilingual's weak and strong languages.

More recently, the placement of children from non-English-speaking homes in school programs led to a new interest in measuring language dominance. Because in many states, instruction is or was mandated to take place in the child's most proficient or dominant language, identifying such dominance led to the development of numerous language assessment strategies, procedures, and instruments which were to be used especially with young children. This application and the problems resulting from this application is discussed at greater length next.

Trends in Determining Language Dominance. In comparison to the researcher interested in describing how proficient a bilingual might be in one or the other or both of his or her two languages, the researcher interested in bilingual language dominance is generally only interested in determining which of a bilingual individual's two languages has greater functional strengths. Once this determination is made, the researcher either considers his or her task done or embarks on the investigation of major areas of interest for which the measurement of bilingual dominance was a desirable or necessary preliminary.

In theory, in order to determine which of a bilingual's two languages is dominant, a researcher can use two principal approaches. One approach involves measuring the performance of bilingual individuals across a wide (or narrow) variety of tasks, contexts, settings, modalities, and functions in each of the two languages and then comparing the two total performance scores obtained for each language. In this approach, if scores obtained in one language are consistently higher than those obtained in the other language, the language in which the higher score was obtained can be designated the dominant language. The other approach involves comparing a bilingual's performance on a set of tasks in each of his languages with the performance of monolingual speakers of each language on the same set of tasks. In this case, the language in which a bilingual more closely approaches the monolingual performance norm is designated the dominant language.

Comparing scores obtained by the same bilingual on the same or similar measures. If a researcher elects to follow the first approach described, he or she can, for example, test bilingual individuals using parallel and equivalent instruments in their two languages (e.g., tests of reading comprehension, tests of vocabulary, tests of listening comprehension) and from the score obtained in each language determine which of the two languages is stronger. Although this strategy presents a number of difficulties—particularly the problem of developing "equivalent" instruments or measurement procedures across languages—it appears to have some legitimacy. However, as Weinreich (1974) predicted, the notion of what is acceptable as evidence of dominance varies widely and reflects researchers' socioculturally defined perceptions. Because it is clearly impossible to develop measurement strategies for assessing the bilingual's competence in all possible areas of experience and ability, a limited number of domains, functions, or levels of language must be chosen for study. The choice itself, that is, the selection of timed tests of vocabulary, for example, as opposed to tests of listening comprehension, is directly influenced by the researchers' assumptions about the nature of bilingual dominance. If the researcher believes that "truly competent bilinguals" are able to engage in joking behavior, for instance, he or she may choose to use "participation and response to joking" as an index of language strength or weakness. On the other hand, if the researcher believes that a bilingual's dominant language will be one in which he or she has the widest range of vocabulary, the researcher will test for differences in vocabulary strengths across languages.

What is important here is that because it is clearly a difficult undertaking to assess bilingual competence across the various levels of both languages, and because all possible skills and areas of performance cannot be sampled, a specific selection of measurable skills or features to be tested must be made. However, the mere selection of one skill or area of performance and the exclusion of another will result in an incomplete view of the bilingual's full competence in each of his languages and, therefore, of the total comparative strengths and weaknesses in each language.

In practical terms, what this means is that it is possible to test bilinguals on specific skills (e.g., reading comprehension) and find that they display no difference in performance. This result—if one is using the first approach to measuring dominance—can lead to the conclusion that both of the bilingual's languages are equally strong (or equally weak). For many researchers, such performance would result in the subject's being classified as a "balanced" bilingual. As is apparent from this discussion, however, it is not evident, from the measure used, that such a bilingual balance would exist in other areas of language ability. Strictly speaking, the researcher could talk about balance only in terms of performance in one modality (reading) as measured by one instrument with two equivalent versions. If, however, the instruments used were different and developed to be used, for example, to measure reading achievement in different countries, the significance of the "equivalent" scores obtained would be even more difficult to interpret.[16]

Comparing the performance of bilinguals using indirect measures in two languages. Another important trend in the measurement of bilingual dominance which is based on the comparison of the bilingual's performance in his two languages is the use of one or of a series of indirect measures often used with monolinguals for other purposes. According to Hamers and Blanc (1989), these measures are based on the assumption that whenever a task involves "a certain degree of verbal competence a balanced bilingual's performance should be the same whatever the language used in performing the task" (p. 17). Typical of these indirect measures are: (a) reaction or latency-time measures in which encoding or decoding or both are examined, (b) completion and word-detection tests, (c) verbal association tests, (d) interlingual flexibility measures, and (e) interlingual ambiguity measures. Examples of these include: measuring how rapidly bilinguals respond to oral instructions in each of their two languages (Lambert, 1955), measuring how many objects in each language subjects can name when such objects are presented pictorially (Ervin, 1961), determining how many words in each of his or her two languages a bilingual can recognize in a string of nonsense syllables (e.g., DANSONO-DENT) (Lambert, Havelka, & Gardner, 1959), measuring speed of reading aloud in both languages (Macnamara, 1969), measuring speed of translation (Lambert et al., 1959), and counting the number of responses made in each language when cross-language ambiguous words (e.g., French PIPE and English PIPE) are read aloud.

For the most part, these measures have been used by psychologists and psycholinguists for whom such measures are part of a research tradition. However, they have been criticized by sociolinguists and others (e.g., Baetens-Beardsmore, 1982; Fishman, 1968; Hamers & Blanc, 1989). For the most part, these criticisms focus on different aspects of the measures used, but include concerns about the validity of using speed as a measure of bilingual dominance[17], about the degree to which differences in lan-

---

[16]For a discussion of the limitations of the various approaches to research on bilingualism that have depended heavily on the notion of bilingual balance, the reader is directed to Fishman (1968).

[17]For a criticism of the use of the notion of speed in the psychological research on bilingualism, the reader is directed to Fishman (1968). Summarizing briefly, Fishman argued that such research has been carried out without an explicit theory as to the significance of

guages might make it impossible to find comparable tasks, and about the use of written stimuli (e.g., for the identification of cross-language ambiguous words presented in written form) with bilinguals who have had access to schooling and to reading instruction in only one of their languages.

For sociolinguists, in general, procedures which involve, for example, presenting single words to bilingual subjects by means of a tachistoscope are of questionable validity because of the uncertain relationship between such tasks and actual language use. Moreover, because, as Dodson (1985) has argued, a circumstantial bilingual's language of greater functional ease can shift from moment to moment depending on a number of factors,[18] some researchers have problems conceptualizing language "dominance" outside of a particular context, topic, situation, and experience. However, as Baetens-Beardsmore (1982) argued, the fact that in many studies the directionality of the scores on one indirect measure correlates with scores on other such measures suggests that some assumptions about the value of such dominance measures may need reappraisal. Nevertheless, for the moment, many students of bilingualism would agree with the same author when he came to the following conclusions about indirect measures as used to determine bilingual dominance:

> Their major achievement seems to be the confirmation of what can be assumed from the bilingual subject's case history, namely, the greater the contact with two languages the greater the likelihood of balance and the smaller the effect of dominance. . . .It should not be thought that dispensing with attempts at dominance measurement could be advocated in favour of language background questionnaires since these, too, have been shown as poor in predictive power. (p. 76)

Comparing bilingual performance with monolingual norms. As an alternative to comparing a bilingual's performance on parallel measures in each of his languages in order to determine language dominance, a number of researchers have elected to compare this performance with that of monolinguals. For the most part, researchers who take this approach tend to focus on linguistic features, that is, on pronunciation, syntax, or vocabulary. Taking the position that an "ideal" bilingual will be two monolingual speakers in one, these researchers collect samples of bilinguals' speech in both languages and then subject the samples to a rigorous analysis the object of which is to identify all features that are not typical of the

---

speed or speededness as an index of or component of bilingualism or verbal interaction in general.
[18]The reader is directed to Note 13 for a review of Dodson's position on this ever-shifting functional ease.

monolingual standard. The language that appears to be closest to the monolingual norm is then designated the dominant language.

Using Norms Obtained with the Same Instrument or Procedures. In some cases, the identification of the monolingual norm is made using the same instruments or procedures which are then used to elicit a language sample or a performance from bilinguals. This is what was done, for example, in the study conducted by Doyle, Champagne, and Segalowitz (1977) in which the Peabody Picture Vocabulary Test was used to compare the vocabulary development of 60-month-old bilingual children with their monolingual peers. These procedures have been criticized because the assumption that a bilingual person's vocabulary should equal or nearly approximate that of a monolingual is problematic. Because of the context(s) in which circumstantial bilinguals acquire their two languages, it is highly likely that lexical measures will merely reflect the areas and domains of experience that a bilingual has had contact with. Although an individual might appear to have a larger vocabulary in Language A than in Language B when particular topics or domains are tested, this may not indicate that he/she is dominant in Language A. It may be that, if other areas were sampled, it would become evident that such apparent dominance is superficial and that the individual's larger lexical inventory is instead available in Language B.

Using Idealized General Monolingual Norms for Comparison An alternative approach to determining language dominance by comparison with a monolingual norm involves the use of an idealized, grammar-textbook standard, which is fundamentally prescriptive in nature. When this approach is used, the language samples collected from bilinguals are subjected to an analysis which seeks to identify the language in which there is a greater total amount of "interference," transfer, or borrowing (phonological, morphological, syntactic, and lexical).[19] Interference is defined as the use of elements by bilinguals when speaking Language A that are not part of the idealized monolingual norm for that language. For example, lexical items that may be commonly used by all members of a bilingual community – such as *troca* (truck), *brecas* (brakes), and *yonke* (junk) that are used in Mexican-American communities – are considered to be "interference" from English because they are not part of the monolingual, standard, prescriptive Spanish norm. On the other hand, Spanish-

---

[19]*Interference* has been defined in different ways by various researchers. For the most part, however, it has been considered to be an involuntary transfer of elements or features from one language to another. (For a discussion of various definitions of interference, borrowing, and other code "mixing," the reader is directed to Valdés, 1980).

influenced pronunciation in English, which may be typical of an entire region or area and thus characteristic of a legitimate variety of English, is also labeled "interference" because it does not mirror the pronunciation of monolingual speakers.

As might be expected, the conclusions to be reached about bilingual dominance in the case of a large number circumstantial bilinguals in this country may be predictable, particularly for adult bilinguals. If pronunciation is the focus, the language displaying the greatest amount of interference when compared to the idealized norm will be English, that is, the language acquired in adulthood.[20] If, on the other hand, vocabulary is the focus, the language displaying the greatest amount of interference will be the ethnic or immigrant language particularly in those areas that have been experienced exclusively in this country. Given the predictability of these results, it would appear that the use of this strategy for determining bilingual dominance is less than useful. Not only does it not take into account the fact that bilinguals may speak a contact variety of both of their languages, but it also takes a narrow view of what constitutes language strength.

Current Views about Language Dominance. In spite of the difficulties surrounding the measurement of language dominance that were described earlier, the notion of dominance itself appears to be an enduring one. For most bilinguals who are themselves aware of different functional strengths in their two languages, the view that one or the other of their languages may be more dominant appears to be a common-sense one. The problem is: (a) how to determine what that dominant language might be, and (b) how to ascertain whether this dominance is a stable one or one that shifts according to contexts and domains of activity.

To date, most of the approaches that have been used or proposed for measuring language dominance have focused on the first problem: how to determine what a bilingual's dominant language might be. Whether this involves the development of a "dominance configuration" in which various facets of the bilingual's ordinary use of language are examined for instances of interference (Baetens-Beardsmore, 1982; Weinreich, 1974), or whether it involves the complex series of measurements including background questionnaires, rating scales, indirect measures, and measures of achievement in reading, writing, and so on, as proposed by Macnamara (1969), the tendency has been to view dominance as a condition that is generally stable. To our knowledge, studies have not been carried out with circumstantial bilinguals that have sought to trace the gradually changing

---

[20]For a summary of eventual attainment of immigrants in L2 in natural settings, the reader is referred to Harley (1986).

nature of language dominance in response, for example, to increased frequency of use, isolation from colinguals or political circumstances, nor have studies been carried out that view dominance as a dynamic and possibly ever-shifting condition.

Problems in Assessing Bilingual Dominance and Bilingual Proficiency: An Example from the Field of Bilingual Education

The concepts of language dominance and language proficiency, as opposed to other theoretical constructs, have been used for different purposes by persons only superficially familiar with bilingualism and its complexity. A key example of such use and of the problems surrounding such use is found in the area of bilingual education. As a result of federal statutes (e.g., Title VI of the Civil Rights Act of 1964; the Bilingual Education Act of 1968), judicial decisions (*Lau V. Nichols* 414 U.S. 563), consent decrees (e.g., 72 Civ. 4002 entered into between the Board of Education of the City of New York et al. and ASPIRA of New York, 1974), and state legislation that focused on the education of non-English-speaking children, educators were faced with a need to determine the "appropriate" language of instruction for children from non-English-speaking backgrounds. Because of this need, a number of different procedures and strategies for assessing children's language were quickly developed. Specifically, what was called for in the variously worded mandates was that schools determine whether or not children were proficient enough in English to profit from exclusive instruction in this language. Although this was not a problem when children were in fact non-English speakers, problems arose when children appeared to have knowledge of both English and a non-English language. In these cases, it became crucial to determine whether the amount of English ability of a particular child was enough to allow him to participate meaningfully in school, or whether this ability was merely incipient and insufficient to permit the child to learn through this language.

In the broadest sense, the questions raised by these "bilingual" children, that is, by children who had some knowledge of two languages, touched upon a number of key issues confronting the study of bilingualism in general. For example, they focused squarely on problems of: (a) establishing standards against which to measure bilingual competence, and (b) measuring large numbers of individuals. They also focused on the connection between a bilingual's two languages and the relationship between language proficiency and language dominance.

The first issue, the development of standards against which to measure bilingual competence, is directly tied to the very concrete question of "how much ability in Language A is needed to carry out activity x, to profit from activity x, and to obtain the benefits from activity x normally available to native speakers of A?" In the area of bilingual education – in spite of what individuals might have claimed to be interested in measuring – what needed to be decided was whether a given child's English language ability was enough to permit him to learn through this language in a school context. This question presupposed that one could discover and describe exactly what kinds of demands on language are made by the instructional context, by the subject matter to be covered, by instructional materials, and so on. One could argue that such a description was no more difficult to obtain than were descriptions of language demands made by other contexts and activities, and that problems involved in developing such a description were not insurmountable.

, In general, it can be said that the problems of describing the language demands made by classroom contexts on young children fell directly within the realm of assessing language for special purposes. In the same way, for example, that one can carefully study the demands made on an airline stewardess in order to determine what types of language skills might be required to carry out the job, one would also be able to carefully investigate and describe the instructional context. One could then identify the levels of demand made by such contexts and the types of language ability typical of native, monolingual, English-speaking children who generally succeed in such contexts. From these observations, one could derive a set of criteria against which to measure the abilities of nonnative, English-speaking children in order to decide whether to educate them in English or in their home language.

For example, one might have discovered that, in the first grade, most mainstream English monolingual children could understand: (a) classroom directions, (b) explanations about sounds and letters when concrete objects/ materials were used in such explanations, and (c) stories read by the teacher from children's books well enough to retell such stories. One would then have to develop procedures for determining whether or not, or to what extent bilingual English-speaking children might have these same abilities. One would need to develop means for assessing such comprehension abilities either directly (by observing to what degree children followed directions) or indirectly (by assessing other abilities or dimensions of language competence that might be indicative of the ability to understand oral directions).

Interestingly enough, a procedure such as this was, in general, not followed. Even though deciding which of two languages was the appropriate language for instructing young bilingual children had to do with a specific domain and with a relatively narrow set of functions, the measurement of language ability within the field of bilingual education was undertaken from an entirely different perspective. Perhaps because of familiarity with work carried out in measuring foreign languages or perhaps because of superficial knowledge that many of its language assessment instrument developers had about bilingual measurement, language assessment procedures used for placement in bilingual education claimed to measure proficiency or dominance in general and broad terms. Rather than asking, for example, Does the child understand explanations about first-grade number concepts given in English?, they asked: How proficient is the child in English? Is he more or less proficient in English than in the minority language? and Is the child dominant in one language although he may be fluent in both?

For reasons that are not entirely clear, early trends in language assessment sought to identify children's "dominant" language rather than their most proficient or their most fluent language. These "so-called dominance tests," as they were referred to by Shuy (1978) in his criticism of their development and use, were primarily utilized for administrative purposes. This means that they were used in order to quickly and efficiently classify large numbers of students and to make decisions about whether children should be placed in bilingual or monolingual programs. They were, however, not designed to offer information about individual children's specific language strengths or weaknesses. In Shuy's (1978) words:

> Efforts to carry out the bilingual legislation requirement for an administrative decision include the New York City *Language Assessment Battery*, the Chicago Public Schools' *Short Test of Linguistic Ability*, the *James Dominance Test* and many others. These measurements do not profess to be individually diagnostic. They offer only to determine whether a child needs to have bilingual education or whether he does not. How the threshold is determined for such decision making is, at best arbitrary and, at worst, dangerous. (p. 376)

Adding to Shuy's statement and also criticizing the entire concept of language dominance as operationalized in bilingual education placement, Peña and Bernal (1978) argued:

> Some language dominance tests, for example, do not sample the receptive and productive domain of the two languages adequately, and do not cover a broad enough range of syntactic structures, or rely excessively on vocabulary-related skills. Most of these measures, furthermore, utilize neither validated criteria nor standard scores for their operational definitions of language dominance; instead the comparative determination of language dominance is based on raw scores, and no assessment of individual language proficiency need be made.
>
> Language dominance assessments made without an examination of language proficiency have, in my opinion, fostered two related and tacitly held beliefs

which desensitize educators to individual differences. One is that a child cannot be proficient in the language which is not dominant; and the other is that the child must be competent in the dominant language. (p. 107)

What is particularly interesting about these criticisms is that both make the assumption that, as opposed to dominance, language proficiency can be measured meaningfully. Given our prior discussion about the complexities of measuring degree of bilingualism and/or proficiency in a broad overall sense, this assumption can, at best, be considered optimistic.

In point of fact, even though the concern for measuring "dominance" was recast over time in the field into a concern for measuring "proficiency," the problem of defining proficiency was not solved. New instruments were developed. The term *proficiency* was used conspicuously in the names of these instruments or in their supporting literature, but very little progress was made in terms of developing diagnostic instruments that could move beyond mere labeling of groups of children to the identification of key language areas in which individual children needed instructional support.

As might be expected, instruments developed to assess the language proficiency of "bilingual" students borrowed directly from traditions of second and foreign language testing. Rather than integrative and pragmatic, these language assessment instruments tended to resemble discrete-point, paper-and-pencil tests administered orally. In spite of certain similarities, however, instruments used to measure such proficiency differed in important ways and were based on often contradictory views about the nature of language competence. So different indeed were they that even the three instruments most widely used in California (i.e., the Bilingual Syntax Measure [BSM], the Basic Inventory of Natural Language [BINL], and the Language Assessment Scales [LAS] were found by Ulibarri, Spencer, and Rivas (1981) to classify a very different proportion of students as Non-English-Speaking (NES), Limited English-Speaking (LES), and Fluent English-Speaking (FES). All three of the measures, moreover, placed the very same students in different categories.

So great indeed were the discrepancies between the numbers of children included in the NES and LES category by different tests that cynical consultants often jokingly recommended one "state-approved" instrument or another to school districts depending on whether administrators wanted to "find" large or small numbers of LES children.

The result of the perceived inability of bilingual educators and supporters to establish precise criteria for measuring language proficiency and their failure to develop instruments able to serve both diagnostic and administrative needs was seen not as a symptom of the fact that the measurement of bilingualism is extraordinarily complex, but as a failure. Those who argued against bilingual education (e.g., Baker, 1986; Baker & de Kanter, 1981) strongly criticized the use of English oral-proficiency instruments and another frequently used standard (scores on standardized achievement tests) as adequate measures for determining selection for bilingual education. Arguing that using low scores on CTBS tests should not be used as indices of command of English, Baker (1986, p. 134) also cited numerous studies that confirmed that language proficiency tests themselves were both unreliable and invalid.

In the meantime, other individuals who were also critical of existing measures of "bilingual proficiency" (e.g., Slaughter, 1988) sought to develop procedures for measuring children's language production that might more accurately reveal their true strengths. Fundamentally, the group of researchers and practitioners who worked within this perspective produced integrative and pragmatic tests of communicative competence. They selected testing situations in which children might actually use language because their goal was to get as accurate a sample as possible of a child's functional ability in each of his languages. Many such assessment procedures included a number of different measures to include teacher assessments, home surveys, classroom observations, and language samples collected in a context in which the child would be likely to interact naturally.

The excitement that might have been generated by this framework was dampened by work carried out by Cummins (1979, 1981). Concerned that "superficial" or "basic" communicative skills (those normally responded to by teachers and tapped by the new pragmatic procedures) were only one dimension of the type of language strengths required by the school context, he cast serious doubts about the usefulness of communicative assessments in general. For Cummins, what needed to be assessed was a broad generalized ability to process decontextualized language, which he considered to be essential to succeeding in the educational context. This broad ability he believed to be obtainable only in a bilingual's first language and then transferrable to an acquired second language.

He argued that in spite of superficial functional skills such as the ability to function in everyday face-to-face interactions, bilingual children who have not acquired the generalized, academic-like ability to make sense out of language when it is used without supporting context and in carrying out a cognitively demanding task, will not preform well academically. For this reason, then, the use of communicative tests or other cognitively undemanding and contextualized procedures for placement purposes was, according to Cummins, problematic. This was the case because the use of such instruments frequently led to children being placed in monolingual

English language programs and given no support in the development of the generalized academic language abilities that, according to Cummins, could only be developed in their first language.

To date, these differences of opinion and theoretical dilemmas have not been resolved. Children potentially in need of mother-tongue support are still being assessed at entry level using one of several instruments that many scholars have questioned, and some years later they are being exited from bilingual programs using another of such instruments which is in no way comparable to the first. The field is no more close to developing means for assessing whether a child can or cannot "perform" satisfactorily in an all-English program than it was in 1964. Given our discussion here, however, the reasons for this "failure" should be obvious. Language ability, proficiency, and even dominance are difficult to measure. Whether we want to establish which of two languages is stronger or whether we want to describe the exact range of abilities and functions available in one or both of two languages, to date, because of the complexity involved, an attempt to simplify the task of measurement will ultimately be inadequate. In the case of bilingual education, the possible effects of this inadequacy are unfortunately quite serious and can easily be construed as engendering irreparable educational harm for thousands of children.

The Measurement of Bilingualism: Summary and Conclusions

Measuring bilingual ability and bilingual proficiency is both complex and problematic. As Macnamara (1969) so aptly expressed, "Obviously the complexity is such that it would take a team of psycholinguists and sociolinguists several years to study even a limited number of bilinguals" (p. 81). The fact of the matter is that there is no simple way of measuring language ability, language proficiency, or language competence in even one language. There is no exact set of procedures that can be used to determine how bilingual an individual is across a broad range of contexts and settings, and there are no strategies or instruments that can economically and easily assess either the language proficiency or the language dominance of large groups of individuals. Because of the nature of language itself and because of the fact that its use varies with time, place, interlocutors, setting, purpose, topic, and so on, language use involves performing one's competence in ways which are fundamentally different from demonstrating other kinds of acquired knowledge. Revealing how much and at what level one controls a range of language functions (e.g., asking for explanations, hedging, apologizing) is not entirely parallel to revealing how much one has learned about American history or how well one can add and subtract. Although one might indeed be able to construct an instrument that would reveal which of two individuals knew more vocabulary items in their common native language, it is doubtful that one could construct an instrument or even a set of procedures that would meaningfully assess the differences in articulateness between two adult native speakers of English. The point here is that procedures for measuring the range of abilities and skills that are involved in being a native speaker of a language have not been developed. They have not been developed for very good reasons. First, it is a difficult task, and second, it is doubtful that we need precise information about native speaker abilities (e.g., the nature of native fluency) except to carry out certain kinds of linguistic research.

The result of this is that there are no models for assessing the language ability or proficiency of circumstantial bilinguals in two languages. Whether we view bilinguals as native speakers of one or both languages or as near-native speakers of one or both languages, the best we can do is to use a series of measures that together might provide guidance for describing an individual as more like or unlike other bilingual individuals. Using, for example, a language background questionnaire, self-rating scales for which precise criteria have been defined, language samples in both languages, language-related achievement tests designed for native speakers (e.g., measures of reading comprehension), and a series of indirect tasks (word naming, rapid reading, etc.), a researcher could construct a profile of some characteristics of individual bilinguals. Such a profile may allow him or her to group bilinguals into different types and categories and to comment about the performance of different groups on various other tasks or measures. These procedures, however, may not yield acceptable indices of validity. At present, this is an open emprirical question that waits further research.

What is most important is that it be recognized that measuring bilingualism is not simple and that even checking for "balance" involves much more than the use of instruments that may have been designed for entirely different purposes. Much caution is needed in using standardized instruments in order to test for language ability. It is particularly important that unless it can be determined by other means that a circumstantial bilingual is still a language learner who can appropriately be tested with instruments designed for use with elective bilinguals, such instruments should not be used.

3

Bilingualism and Cognitive Difference

**THE REVIEW AND EXAMINATION OF EXISTING
RESEARCH THAT HAS FOCUSED ON THE
RELATIONSHIP BETWEEN BILINGUALISM AND
COGNITIVE DIFFERENCE**

As was made clear in our discussion of bilingualism, bilingual individuals share with each other the fact that they have *more than one language competence*, that is to say, they are able to function (i.e., speak, understand, read, or write) even to a very limited degree in *more than one* language. As this definition of bilingualism makes obvious, there are many different kinds and types of bilingual individuals. At one end of the continuum, there are bilinguals who may indeed be accepted as native speakers of each of their two languages by other native speakers, and, at the other end of the continuum, there are bilinguals whose only ability in L2 may be limited to reading with the aid of a bilingual dictionary.

The individuals who concern us here would be placed in the middle of the continuum, somewhere between the "perfect ambilinguals" and the "almost totally monolingual" individuals. The question is are these bilingual individuals, these circumstantial bilinguals of various backgrounds and origins, different from monolinguals in "important" ways, that is, in ways that might directly affect their performance on standardized tests? How might these differences be discovered? How might these differences be manifested?

To date, a number of different areas of research on bilingualism and bilingual individuals suggest that bilinguals may indeed be different from monolinguals. Indeed, research on what may be the unique processing characteristics of bilingual minds (e.g., the psychological verbal storage systems of bilinguals and their possible neurological representations, the nature of bilingual information processing, and the nature of the greater cognitive flexibility of bilinguals) implies that bilingual persons are cognitively different from monolinguals.

What is not known is of what this cognitive difference consists. Is cognitive difference a simple by-product of becoming bilingual? To date, a number of different areas of research on bilingualism and bilingual individuals suggest that bilinguals may indeed be unlike monolinguals. These areas are: (a) the investigation of cognitive development in bilinguals, (b) the neuropsychological work on hemispheric involvement in the learning and processing of first and second languages, and (c) current work on language and information processing in bilinguals. In this segment, we include a brief review of each of the three areas mentioned, as well as an analysis of each area's limitations.

The Investigation of Cognitive Development in Bilinguals: A Brief Summary

From its inception, work in the investigation of cognitive and intellectual development in bilinguals has been carried out with the expectation that there are differences between individuals who know or function in two languages and monolinguals who only know or function in one. Indeed, although the research on such differences has shifted from viewing bilingualism as a negative condition to viewing bilingualism as an advantage, what underlies this entire area of inquiry is the assumption that bilingualism itself will result in measurable contrasts in performance between these two groups.

At first glance such a position seems obvious and logical. Given the fact that, as Carroll (1971, p. 97) stated, "language use is central to many kinds of intellectual operations," it might seem reasonable to assume that there is an intimate connection between growth in a first language and the development of intellectual processes. For researchers who have this perspective, the development and use of two languages would of necessity also be expected to impact on cognitive development. Given this expectation, the conclusion that bilinguals and monolinguals are cognitively different might also seem to follow logically.

As Hakuta, Ferdman, and Diaz (1986) have argued, however, some theories of cognitive development and/or some dimensions of these theories have not predicted effects of bilingualism on cognitive development at all. Reviewing some of the commonly used typologies (i.e., nativism vs. empiricism, modularity vs. commonality of functions, and context and cultural sensitivity vs. independence) Hakuta et al. (1986) pointed out the following:

1. With regard to the nativistic–empiricist dimension, "any theory of cognitive development that subscribes to primarily innate factors . . . would not predict bilingualism to have any effect on the course of cognitive growth" (p. 5). This includes both the Chomskian orientation and the hereditarian interpretation of individual differences in intelligence. Theories that emphasize the role of learning, however, could predict that bilingualism would have on effect on cognitive development. These would include traditional learning theory, and Piagetian constructivism.
2. With regard to the modularity versus commonality of structures dimension, extreme modular approaches would reject claims of broad-sweeping effects of bilingualism and would confine such effects to those aspects of cognitive function involving language. Learning theory and theories of general intelligence as well as Piagetian operational theory, however, "would expect generalized effects since all cognitive functioning share a common source and are interrelated" (p. 6).[1]
3. Theories that view context and/or culture as central in the development of cognition (e.g., Vygotskian theory) "hold the strongest promise for relating cognitive development with the social psychological and societal levels of bilingualism" (p. 6).

What this means, in sum, is that views concerning differences between bilinguals and monolinguals will depend on theories of cognitive development and on their various interpretations of how and whether language development and/or language experience impact(s) on this process.

Unfortunately, however, the relationship between theories of development and the study of the "effects" of bilingualism on cognitive development and/or intelligence have not been explicitly discussed by most researchers. Early work, focusing on the relationship between intelligence and bilingualism, for example, did not make clear the fact that, as Hakuta et al. (1986) stated: "the primary definition of what we now call cognitive development was a psychometric one, defined on the basis of differential performance of individuals within a defined population on IQ tests" (p. 5). This early research on bilingualism and cognitive development sought to account for the differences in performance on IQ tests by monolinguals and

---

[1]The authors noted, however, that Piagetian theory, "though a theory of general intelligence, is characterized by its ascription of a marginal role for language in structuring intelligence" (p. 6).

bilinguals. Given the fact that these tests were administered to bilinguals in an attempt to demonstrate that there was a significant difference between new immigrants of southern European backgrounds and northern Europeans of "better" stock, it is not surprising that many explanations about differences in performance centered around language.

From the perspective of this chapter, however, this early work contributes little to answering our fundamental question: Are bilinguals different from monolinguals in significant ways? What we can gather from this work (much of which is now considered to be methodologically flawed) is that large numbers of bilinguals (about whose bilingualism we know little) scored below monolinguals on standardized tests of intelligence. In light of the methodological problems alluded to earlier, we can conclude little from the early research about *how* and *why* and *to what degree* individuals who appear to be identical except for their experience in two languages also differ in terms of their cognitive development.

Later research on the impact of bilingualism on cognitive development has itself been based on the assumption of difference. In this case, however, researchers have sought to select their bilingual subjects carefully and to design tasks (often language related or language based) that might demonstrate the hypothesized superiority of the bilingual group. Nevertheless, the fact that the narrow view of cognitive development against which their findings are directed has itself been found wanting, has not been emphasized by these later researchers. To date, reviews of the impact of bilingualism on cognitive development (e.g., Diaz, 1983) discuss this early work and compare it with more recent work on the impact of bilingualism on cognitive development as if there were no widely differing theories underlying early and later research.

Indeed, one of the first studies to question the negative impact of bilingualism (Peal & Lambert, 1962) was based on a view of expected and assumed differences between bilinguals and monolinguals. Without focusing on what is being defined here as a key question—the limitations of the theory underlying previous research (i.e., the limitations of the psychometric definition of cognitive development)—Peal and Lambert worked within the boundaries of this very definition and yet sought to cast doubt on the way in which bilingualism and its "effects" had been viewed until that time.

In essence, Peal and Lambert did not quarrel with the perspective that held that bilinguals had lower IQs than did monolinguals based on their scores on standardized tests. Instead, they argued that *pseudobilinguals* (individuals who know one language better than the other) performed poorly on certain tasks because they were not *true* bilinguals (individuals who master both of their languages at an early age). As opposed to what others had done, Peal and Lambert described two distinct types of "bilinguals" who in contrasting ways were still significantly different from monolinguals when their performances on standardized instruments were compared. Specifically, pseudobilinguals were different from monolinguals in that their bilingualism was a problem that could lead to intellectual retardation. True bilinguals were also different from monolinguals, but in this case, "genuine" bilingualism was seen as an asset. According to Peal and Lambert, because of their bilingualism, "true" bilingual children performed significantly higher on tests of both verbal and nonverbal ability. Moreover, further analyses of their scores revealed to Peal and Lambert that bilinguals were superior to monolinguals in concept formation and in mental flexibility.

What is significant about this research is not only the fact that it established that there were important positive differences in performance in favor of bilinguals, but also that it sought to explain these differences by focusing on the degree of bilingualism (i.e., dual language mastery) of the individuals studied. Perhaps more important is the fact that it led to a new direction in the study of the effects of bilingualism, a direction which has focused on the "advantages" of bilingualism with regard to a series of dimensions.

Following the perspective of bilingual "advantage," recent interest in the cognitive development of bilinguals has centered on determining whether and to what degree bilinguals have particular advantages in performing different cognitive tasks. Some researchers have argued that bilinguals are more "cognitively flexible" than monolinguals.[2] Others have claimed that bilinguals are superior to monolinguals in the development of metalinguistic abilities, to include the capacity to compare words on the basis of semantic features (Ianco-Worrell, 1972), the awareness of the conventional nature of words and language (Ben-Zeev, 1977; Feldman & Shen, 1971), and metalinguistic awareness (Cummins, 1978; Hakuta & Diaz, 1984). Still other researchers (Liedtke & Nelson, 1968) have investigated differences between monolinguals and bilinguals on concept formation tasks (e.g., conservation of length, measurement of length), differences in discovery learning (Bain, 1974), the relationship between bilingualism and creative abilities (Torrence, Wu, Gowan, & Aliotti, 1970), and the influence of bilingualism on cognitive style (Duncan & DeAvila, 1979; Ramirez, Castaneda, & Herold, 1974; Ramirez & Price-Williams, 1974).

---

[2]According to Diaz (1983) this construct has been poorly defined and has been used to describe a number of different cognitive tasks such as performance on measures of general intelligence (Peal & Lambert, 1962), attention to detail and structure (Ben-Zeev, 1976, 1977b), performance on perceptual and "set changing" (Balkan, 1970), and divergent thinking skills as measured by tests of creativity (Landry, 1974).

Even though theories of cognitive development underlying the above research vary, it can be said that, in general, this research direction has provided evidence that there are differences between certain kinds of bilinguals and monolinguals. While because of the narrowness of the criteria or because of the special type of elective or circumstantial bilingualism involved, we might still want to quarrel with the way in which bilingualism has been defined within this research tradition and with the manner in which subjects have been selected; we nevertheless agree that these studies argue strongly that bilinguals may indeed be different from monolinguals in significant ways. Even though it is our position that there is insufficient evidence to claim, as Peal and Lambert (1962) did, that bilinguals' greater "flexibility in thinking" develops from their experience in switching languages as well as from their verbal manipulation of visual symbols, we do agree with these researchers that bilingualism may lead to key differences in the use of information processing strategies between bilinguals and monolinguals. Although it is implied by the work of several investigators, there is nothing in the literature that can provide support for the position that because bilinguals approach experimental language-related tasks differently than monolinguals, these bilinguals might approach other tasks (e.g., those normally found on standardized tests) quite differently also. At best, one can view the literature on the relationship between bilingualism and cognitive development and conclude that there is some evidence that certain kinds of bilinguals, whose bilingualism is not always well described, are different from monolinguals.

The Neuropsychological Work on Hemispheric Involvement in the Learning and Processing of First and Second Languages: A Brief Overview

Beginning with early work on aphasia in bilinguals,[3] it had been suspected that the languages of bilingual individuals might be located in different areas of the brain. With bilingual aphasiacs, the fact that one language has been found to be more impaired than the other and that one language has been found to recover whereas the other did not, has led to the conclusion that there might be significant differences between a language first learned and a language acquired subsequently in terms of its localization in the brain. This early work, although inconclusive, has offered some support for the position that bilingual individuals are more neuropsychologically complex than are their monolingual counterparts.

Currently, the question of whether bilinguals' languages are localized differently is viewed as a simplistic question. As Genesee (1988) argued,

---

[3]See Albert and Obler (1978) and Paradis (1977) for a discussion of this work.

researchers today are concerned instead about describing and explaining hemisphere involvement, that is, about understanding how and when the two hemispheres contribute to language learning and/or to language processing. Specifically, this research is based on the view that, according to Schneiderman (1986), is now widely accepted. This view is that "in normal, right-handed adults, the majority of language functions are governed by the left cerebral hemisphere" (p. 233). Schneiderman also added, however, that there is evidence that the right hemisphere may play an important role during the acquisition of the first and second languages.

Recent interest in hemisphere involvement is also based on current thinking about hemispheric specialization. As Genesee (1988) made clear, whereas in the past it was thought that different types of stimuli were processed in the left versus the right hemisphere, it is now thought that the hemispheres differ "not so much in the types of stimuli that they process, but rather, in the manner of processing stimuli given certain task requirements" (p. 85). What this means is that what are lateralized are different *modes* of processing. However, each of the hemispheres is thought to be able to engage in some of the processing modes normally thought typical of the other. For example, the left hemisphere may also be able to engage in some holistic/parallel processing, and the right hemisphere may also carry out serial or analytic processing. Because neither hemisphere can be considered to be limited to a specific processing mode, it is now generally thought that both hemispheres can contribute to language processing to some extent.

For the most part, research relating to bilingualism in this general area has focused primarily on the role of the right hemisphere in both first and second language acquisition. Based on research conducted by a number of researchers on the role of right hemisphere participation in first language acquisition,[4] researchers focusing on this same involvement in second language acquisition have focused on three areas: (a) age of second language acquisition, (b) level of second language proficiency, and (c) manner of second language acquisition.

With regard to age and second language acquisition, it is generally hypothesized that the earlier the second language is learned, the more left hemisphere involvement there will be, and that the later the second language is learned, the more right hemisphere involvement will take place. Work carried out on this question by Albert and Obler (1978), Galloway (1981) Genesee, Hamers, Lambert, Mononen, Seitz, and Stark, (1978), Soares and Grosjean (1980), Vaid (1981a), Vaid and Lambert (1979), has produced mixed results.

With regard to level of proficiency, it is generally expected that late-

---

[4]For a discussion of this research, the reader is referred to Schneiderman (1986).

rality differences will decrease as proficiency in the second language increases; and with regard to manner of acquisition, it is expected that there will be greater right-hemisphere involvement when the second language is learned formally than when it is learned informally. Work in these two areas has been conducted by: Albert and Obler (1978), Carroll (1978), Hamers and Lambert (1977), Obler, Albert, and Gordon (1975), Rupp (1980), Schneiderman and Wesche (1980), Vaid (1981b), Walters and Zatorre (1978), Zatorre and Piazza (1979).

Although the research in all three areas is contradictory (see Galloway, 1982, for a concise and graphic summary), what is important about this area of inquiry for this chapter is the fact that its very existence provides support for the position that bilinguals may, in fact, be significantly different from monolinguals.

Recent Work in Language and Information Processing and Bilinguals

Recent work in bilingual information processing has focused on such aspects as the psychological verbal storage systems of bilinguals (Arnedt & Gentile, 1986; Glanzer & Duarte, 1971; Johnson, 1986; Kolers & Gonzalez, 1980; Mack, 1986; Paivio, Clark, & Lambert, 1988; Soares & Grosjean, 1984; Vaid, 1988;), automatic and controlled processes in bilinguals (Segalowitz, 1986), and the effect of environmental variables on processing speed (Blair & Harris, 1981; Dornic, 1979; Hoosian & Salili, 1987; Magiste, 1979, 1980; Navaeh-Benjamin & Ayers, 1986; Soares & Grosjean, 1984).

Since the 1960s a rich experimental research program surrounding this topic has emerged, providing an unprecedented amount of scientific studies on both qualitative and quantitative issues on bilingual mentation. However, none of the theoretical and applied issues and findings from this research program have been substantively considered by tests and testers, particularly in the most relevant field of psychometrics, intelligence testing.

On the qualitative/theoretical dimension, the scientific study of bilingualism has focused on the psychological verbal storage systems of bilinguals and on their possible neurological representations. Three models exist. Some posit dual storage systems accommodating L1 and L2 and linked by translation referents (Arnedt & Gentile, 1986; Paivio, Clark, & Lambert, 1988; Vaid, 1988). These language-dependent systems manifest themselves in low cross-lingual transference and inhibition on certain learning tasks (recognition and recall of words in massed presentations; data-driven tasks where lexical decisions and recognition of surface of written codes are involved) as well as in higher learning rates when both linguistic systems are used to process information (Kardash, Amlund,

Kulhavy, & Ellison, 1988). Neurological evidence which supports this language-dependent perspective reports greater right-hemisphere activity in bilinguals (particularly at the early stages of L2 acquisition) and language-specific aphasic damage and recovery following neurological injury in bilinguals (Chernigovskaya, Balonov, & Deglin, 1983; Galloway, 1982; Jungué, Vendrell, Vendrell-Brucet, & Tobeña, 1989; Solin, 1989; Sussman, Franklin, & Simon, 1982; Vaid & Lambert, 1979).

Diametrically opposed is the model that posits a single storage system. The psychological evidence for this position comes from studies which have found that repetition regardless as to whether it is done in L1, L2, or L1/L2 leads to greater recall (Glanzer & Duarte, 1971; Johnson, 1986; Kolers & Gonzalez, 1980; Mack, 1986; Soares & Grosjean, 1984). Also, data on retrieval of conceptually driven tasks (where image formation is required, or where semantic processing is necessary) show that languages, per se, do not affect recall. Clearly, for a single storage model, transference and inhibition intervene. Here too, neurological evidence is available (Albanese, 1985; Zatorre, 1989).

The third model posits separate but overlapping storage models. The demands of various learning tasks as well as metacognitive and volitional factors determine whether the single, overlapping part of the system or the separate, independent systems switch on (Durgunoglu & Roediger, 1987; Kolers & Brison, 1984). Neurologically, recent studies suggest that bilinguals as well as monolinguals process linguistic information in the left-cerebral hemisphere. However, the left-cortical area of L1 and L2 representation for bilinguals shows separate, overlapping topological characteristics (Rapport, Tan & Whitaker, 1983; Whitaker, 1989; Zatorre, 1989).

Notwithstanding the theoretical debate about single, overlapping, and separate storage models with their own decoding, storage, and encoding characteristics, data on key parameters that quantitatively differentiate monolinguals from multilanguage speakers are available. These involve speed, memory (Dornic, 1979), and strategy factors. In this chapter, results on two of these are reviewed—speed and strategy factors.

For bilinguals, encoding and decoding in the weaker language (which might the either the first of the second) are carried out at a slower processing speed (Blair & Harris, 1981; Dornic, 1979; Mack, 1986; Soares & Grosjean, 1984). Further, both operations are more susceptible to the effects of environmental variables (stress, load, noise) to the point of a shut down. This occurs even after L2 has become dominant (but where L1 is still in the home; Magiste, 1979, 1980). Also, the greater the number of languages, the slower the speed for successive "weaker" languages (L1 < L2 < L3, etc.; Magiste, 1980).

Slower processing in the weaker language(s) means that in situations in which subvocal naming speed (such as in reading), subvocal rehearsal, or aural comprehension are important, bilinguals may be put in a distinct disadvantage, particularly when psychological pressure is present. Some studies even suggest that where the pronunciability rate of L2 is more difficult (takes longer) than L1, short-term memory space, or working memory, may be significantly affected in carrying out digit naming tasks or executing arithmetic operations (Hoosian & Salili, 1987; Naveh-Benjamin & Ayres, 1986). Also, when bilinguals are exposed to mixed language presentations, as often happens in supposedly bilingual education programs in which teachers do inter- and intrasentential code switching, processing latencies increase, potentially affecting comprehension (Grainger & Beauvillain, 1987). This speed factor may even affect reaction-time tasks (Johnson, 1986).

As was pointed out previously, some 30 years ago, Peal and Lambert (1962) summarized the empirical results of well-controlled studies on bilingual children and concluded that the data demonstrated a strategic advantage of bilinguals over monolinguals in that the former showed greater cognitive flexibility involving mental tasks. These results, although replicated, have been challenged. Recently, a more rigorous, experimental set of studies has suggested that when bilinguals are asked to consciously process learning tasks bilingually (through translation), they learn better and they learn more (Durgunoglu & Roediger, 1987; Kardash, Amlund, Kulhavy, & Ellison, 1988; Paivio, Clark, & Lambert, 1988).

Limitations of Existing Research

Important as the research in these areas summarized has been, and tempting as it might be to build on this research without examining it closely, it is imperative that researchers working to develop a coherent research agenda on the relationship between bilingualism and testing consider this work carefully. Both the implications and the limitations of this work must be understood clearly.

For example, taking only one perspective and examining the types of bilingual individuals studied by each of the three research thrusts, the following limitations soon emerge.

Limitations of the Research on Cognitive Development. The work carried out in the area of bilingualism and cognitive development has either not concerned itself with measuring and describing the bilingual individuals studied, or it has endeavored to be extraordinarily strict in its selection of subjects. Recent work on the advantages of bilingualism, for example, has led to the use of a narrowly defined group of bilingual subjects (e.g., children who are being raised in a one-parent, one-language household), or to the study of only those bilinguals who by some definition are considered "balanced." Unfortunately, because of the various definitions given to the notion of bilingual balance,[5] it is not at all clear that the same types of bilingual subjects have been examined by different researchers. The results of this research, therefore, must be interpreted with great caution.

Without minimizing the importance of the differences in definitions of bilingual balance, in our opinion, the most important limitation of the research carried out to date on bilingualism and cognitive development is that it has focused almost exclusively on elective bilinguals. The very fact that circumstantial bilinguals have not been studied (except to suggest that theirs may be the wrong kind of bilingualism) indicates that attempts have not been made to understand how circumstantial bilingualism might affect cognitive development. In other words, we know very little about the cognitive development of circumstantial bilinguals and particularly about how and whether their bilingualism also has consequences on cognition.

Given what appears to be a lacuna in the existing research, it would appear that before it can be used to structure the direction of future research on bilingualism and testing, the work on bilingualism and cognitive development must be subjected to a rigorous examination. Questions such as the following might be expected to inform such an examination:

1. What kinds of bilinguals have been used as subjects in each study?
2. To what degree have circumstantial bilinguals been used as subjects?
3. How was circumstantial bilingualism defined?
4. What were the characteristics of these circumstantial bilinguals?
5. To what degree is there an implication that the same research replicated with circumstantial bilinguals would lead to very different results?
6. Is there an indication that this research could or should be replicated with circumstantial bilinguals?

---

[5]For example, researchers such as Lambert have, in practice, defined bilingual balance as that condition that is present when individuals are found to perform similarly on a set of experimental tasks. Other researchers (e.g., Hakuta & Diaz, 1986) consider that a balanced bilingual child "is a child that can function, age appropriately, in his or her two languages" (p. 14). The first definition is linguistic and psycholinguistic in nature, whereas the second definition is sociolinguistic and pragmatic. One would expect different strategies to be used in determining the presence or absence of "balance." One might also logically expect to find two very different groups of "balanced" bilingual individuals.

7. What are the implications of this existing research for circumstantial bilinguals whose language processing is assumed by standardized tests to be identical to that of monolinguals?

Limitations of the Research on Hemispheric Involvement Research on lateralization and hemispheric involvement has, as a body, been concerned with two different types of subjects: (a) bilingual aphasiacs, and (b) second language learners.

For the most part, research on bilingual aphasiacs has been carried out on different kinds of bilinguals and includes the study of circumstantial bilinguals who have used both a minority and a majority language in the course of their daily lives. Generally such studies (e.g., Galloway, 1978; Wulfeck, Juarez, Bates, & Kilborn, 1986) make specific mention of the subject's life history and take into account the periods in his or her life when one or the other or both languages were used. The differences in rates and types of recovery experienced by different aphasiacs have been interpreted as evidence of the fact that bilinguals may not store or process languages in the same way as do monolinguals.

It is important to note that research on polyglot aphasia is perhaps the only area of research on bilingual cognition that has taken into account the fact that individuals who live in the real world use their languages in different ways over time. To the degree that it has done so, this research is clearly relevant to the study of languages in the brains of circumstantial bilinguals. On the other hand, the fact that the individuals studied are those who have suffered cerebral lesions of different types does raise the question of how similar or dissimilar they are to "normal" circumstantial bilinguals.

By comparison with the work on bilingual aphasia, research conducted on the relationship between language learning and lateralization and hemispheric involvement has used bilinguals of different types. It has, however, shown a strong tendency to focus primarily on elective bilinguals and/or "balanced" bilinguals.

Studies concerned about lateralization and the age of second language learning/acquisition generally appear to the exception in their choice of subjects. These studies have included different types of bilinguals such as early and late bilinguals balanced bilinguals, incipient elective bilinguals, and incipient circumstantial bilinguals. Unfortunately, as is often the case with other studies, researchers have included very little information about the nature of their subjects' bilingualism in the presentation of their work.

On the other hand, studies seeking to examine the relationship between hemispheric involvement and level of second language proficiency have focused almost exclusively on elective bilinguals or on circumstantial bilinguals within a formal classroom setting. This same focus has characterized the research on the manner of second language acquisition. In this latter case, classroom instruction and course methodologies have been the subject of investigation. For example, degree of hemispheric involvement has been studied in students enrolled in second language courses using deductive methods and compared with that of students enrolled in courses using inductive methods.

Although these studies are interesting and valuable in what they can reveal about second language processing, it must again be argued that there is little in this work that can be said to describe the language processing of circumstantial bilinguals. Specifically, the existing research does not attempt to examine the processing characteristics of individuals who acquire or learn their second language over the course of a lifetime without benefit of either classrooms or teachers. Because of the implications of this research, however, particularly because of its potential ability to offer serious evidence about the differences between bilinguals and monolinguals, the implications of these investigations must clearly be incorporated into the questions which will be included in a final research agenda on bilingualism and testing.

In order to understand these implications fully, especially as they contribute to our understanding of bilingual minority children, the following types of questions should be used as guide for reviewing this literature:

1. Were circumstantial bilinguals included in each of these studies?
2. Was circumstantial bilingualism defined explicitly?
3. Were researchers aware that there are differences between elective and circumstantial bilinguals?
4. Was there an attempt to account for or explain these differences?
5. When researchers were not aware of such differences or not interested in such differences, did the discussion of their research suggest that they considered their results to be generalizable to all bilinguals?
6. To what degree is there an indication that the same research replicated with circumstantial bilinguals would lead to different results?
7. Should this research be replicated with circumstantial bilinguals?
8. What are the implications of this research for circumstantial bilinguals whose language processing is assumed by standardized tests to be identical to that of monolinguals?

Limitations of the Research on Information Processing. As compared to research on cognitive development and hemispheric involvement, research on information processing has tended to include bilingual subjects of different types. Although the concern for "balance" is still present, a number of key researchers (e.g., Dornic, 1977; Segalowitz, 1986; Bain &

Yu, 1984) have specifically stated their interest in studying individuals who are not two perfect monolinguals in one. Their interest, rather, is in one-eighth of the inhabitants of industrialized countries who, as Dornic (1977) expressed it, "receive, store, organize and use information in languages differing from their dominant language" (p. 3).

Dornic and his research associates, in particular, have been concerned about understanding circumstantial bilinguals, that is, people who have moved to another country where a different language is spoken. Bain and Yu (1984) have carried out cross-cultural studies in which the difference between middle-class elite bilingualism (here termed *elective bilinguals*) and working-class immigrant bilingualism (here termed *circumstantial bilinguals*) is directly taken into account.

Segalowitz (1986), on the other hand, studied "fluent" bilinguals (i.e., persons who have "for all practical purposes rapid and accurate ability to use the vocabulary and syntax of a second language, at least when required to perform under normal speaking and listening conditions, and are also generally skilled at reading the second language") (p. 4). He argued that such bilinguals are interesting from a theoretical point of view because "they are both relatively fast and slow readers at the same time, depending on the language being read. Their slow reading is not easily accounted for in terms of some general reading skills deficit (skills that would affect reading any language), nor in terms of some fundamental weakness in the second language such as unfamiliarity with vocabulary or syntax" (p. 4).

Enlightened as these three positions are, they are unfortunately not representative or reflective of how most subjects have actually been selected for specific studies. Problems of selection, definition, and measurement are very much evident across this area of inquiry. For example, even Dornic (1978a) in his study on noise and language dominance stated that his subjects were individuals whose proficiency or ability in one language was 85% of that in the other. However, no information was included in the report about the measures used to arrive at such a determination.

A number of other researchers have used only self-report data (e.g, Myers et al., 1974; Rose, 1980) as a criterion for selection, whereas others (e.g, De Avila, & Duncan, 1985;[6] Vaid, 1984)[7] have used a combination of

---

[7]In this study, Vaid (1984) utilized the following combination of strategies for selection: (a) self-rating, (b) background questionnaires focusing on language histories, (c) telephone or face-to-face interviews, and (d) a speeded reading measure adapted from the Stroop Color Naming Test. Using this set of measures, bilinguals were classified as belonging to one of three different groups of bilinguals.

[6]De Avila and Duncan (1985) used a family background questionnaire, cognitive-style measures (The Children's Embedded Figures Test and The Matching Familiar Figures Test), the Language Assessment Scales (LAS), the Cartoon Conservation Scales, a teacher questionnaire, and standardized achievement tests.

methods. For the most part, however, the same difficulties that have plagued other research on bilingual individuals are evident in the work on information processing.

The work on memory, for example, has tended to focus on elective bilinguals considered to be "balanced." As in other areas, the notion of "balance" has been poorly defined, and measures designed to assess bilingual proficiency itself differ widely. This is true of early studies such as Kolers (1963, 1966) which are frequently considered to be fundamental to the study of bilingual storage. In the first of these studies, Kolers used foreign students whose first language was German, Spanish, or Thai. All of the subjects were fluent in English and were interviewed after the testing in order to determine whether their English "was good enough for them to be successful students here in college classes conducted in English." In the second study, Kolers used English-speaking natives who had spent at least 9 months in France at some time, and French-speaking natives who had lived in the United States for 9 months. As will undoubtedly be obvious, the groups of bilingual individuals studied by Kolers—even within the same study—were conceivably quite different.

In the light of what these facts suggest, the research on information processing and bilingualism must be carefully examined and interpreted after taking into account the possible contradictions stemming from the various kinds of bilingual individuals studied. The following questions may be of help to researchers who attempt to synthesize this area of research:

1. What kinds of bilinguals have been used as subjects for each study?
2. How were bilingual subjects selected?
3. What definition of bilingualism was the researcher using?
4. Was the same definition and/or the same types of bilingual subjects used in different studies conducted by the same researcher?
5. Did the researcher select different types of bilinguals deliberately, or did he/or she assume that all bilinguals are fundamentally similar?
6. Were differences in performance by different kinds of bilinguals discussed by the researcher?
7. To what degree did such differences impact on the researcher's attempt to account for differences in information processing found between bilinguals and monolinguals?
8. To what degree was the researcher aware of differences between middle-class elective bilinguals and working-class immigrant bilinguals?
9. How was this distinction used?

10. Is there an indication that this research could or should be replicated with circumstantial bilinguals?
11. What are the implications of the existing research for circumstantial bilinguals whose language processing is assumed by standardized tests to be identical to that or monolinguals?

Tests, Bilingualism, and Cognitive Difference. As previously noted, the experimental literature on bilingual information processing has not been considered by tests or testers. The literature on bilingual information processing, in spite of existing caveats or debates, does make an unequivocal assertion: Bilingual persons are cognitively different from monolinguals. Tests fail, are found wanting, and are biased with bilingual groups insofar as they do not assess this difference. Their content and methodology mitigate against bilinguals, but just as importantly, so does what the tests do not measure.

L1 tests, such as the standardized Spanish versions of intelligence tests, administered in conjunction with their L2 versions, may seem to address the complex phenomena involved with bilingualism. But this technique is inadequate. In an outstanding article recently published, Grosjean (1989) outlined the reasons for this inadequacy.

To begin with, bilinguals have traditionally been viewed from a "monolingual bias" (p. 4), that is, as if a bilingual is the "sun of two complete or incomplete monolinguals" (p. 3). This monolingual model used to explain the bilingual hearer/speaker has led to descriptions of bilinguals in terms of L1/L2 "balance," "dominance," "proficiency," "semilingualism," "alingualism," and so on. Inherently, such a perception assumes a standard: The real bilingual is equally and thoroughly competent in L1 and L2. Language proficiency tests work from such a standard by defining bilinguals on a 0–5 continuum for each language. The same applies to cognitive and developmental tests. Their standards come from monolingual norm groups – and "deficits" or "substandard" performance are derived from single language yardsticks. The fact that most circumstantial bilinguals throughout the world vary in L1/L2 use, proficiency, and literacy according to need, social circumstance, volition, opportunity, SES, personality, and so on, does not seem to compel researchers to take the phenomenon on its own terms:

> Tests rarely take into account the situations and domains the languages are used in, the skills covered by these languages, or the amount and type of code mixing normally produced by the bilingual. . . . much of what we know about bilingualism today is tainted – in part at least – by a monolingual, fractional, view of the topic. (Grosjean, 1989, p. 5)

Bilinguals are unique hearer/speakers who are put at an artificial disadvantage when held to monolingual standards. A holistic view of bilingualism, according to Grosjean (1989), includes recognition of the unique organizational, structural, and processing characteristics of bilingual and mixed-language competencies, as well as the unique environmental and contextual linguistic demands for L1, L2, and L1/L2 hearing and speaking:

> The bilingual is NOT the sum of two complete or incomplete monolinguals: rather, he or she has a unique and specific linguistic configuration. The coexistence and constant interaction of the two languages in the bilingual has produced a different but complete linguistic entity. (p. 6).

From a measurement perspective, bilingualism is not the sum of a score in L1 plus the sum of a score in L2. As the information processing literature suggests, much more is cognitively involved. For example, taking some of the empirical findings and applying them to tests and testing, the following "principles" may apply:

1. For mental tests that require conceptualization during massed multiple items, the use of L1 and L2 (either in requiring translation or in providing item presentations in L1 and L2) enhances cognitive performance. The reasons – "extra processing" (Durgunoglu & Roediger, 1987).
2. When a test item requiring associative recall (e.g., vocabulary) is given in L1 and repeated in L2 (with or without an interitem lag), the bilingual repetition may have "summative effects that are additive or even superadditive relative to once-presented items, or to a same-language repetition of a single item" (Paivio, Clark, & Lambert, 1988).
3. "The retrieval requirements of different memory tasks must be considered" (Durgunoglu & Roediger, 1987, p. 387) in determining whether the independent (single storage) or dependent (dual storage) systems help or inhibit.

Hypothetically, bilingual testing may equal a test score in L1, weighed by the individual's proficiency in L1, the information-processing demands of the test, exposure to L1 test's content, and an ideographic random (chaos?) factor that includes content available to the individual in L2 but outside the universe sampled by the test in L1, the sociopolitical affect attached to L1 and personality factors (Hakuta, 1986; Ruiz, 1988), as well as a test score in L2 weighed by similar intervening variables attached to L2 (though potentially varying in the value of such weights).

The inclusion of "bilinguals" in norming samples, in and of itself, does nothing. Such norming studies are quite common (e.g., Kaufman & Kaufman, 1983; Mercer, 1979). Usually these groups are distinguished by ethnicity with little, if any, consideration given to bilingualism. In such studies, individuals who are limited-English-speaking are excluded (Mercer, 1979), but bilinguals are not. Follow-up studies of tests normed on these populations show a marked bilingual language-background effect on virtually every type of test (cognitive, social, and even "medical") (Figueroa, 1987). Often, these tests exacerbate the existence of nonrandom error variance by providing L1 translations of instructions for "nonverbal" items (e.g., Kaufman & Kaufman, 1983) or L1 versions of entire tests (Mercer, 1979) even though the norm tables treat the groups as monolingual English speakers.

Bilingual norming studies (i.e., where the language factor is controlled) essentially do not exist. At least three reasons account for this. First, the technology for measuring language proficiencies is primitive and incapable of capturing the multifactorial, unique aspects of bilingual linguistic skills. Second, the large primary language groups such as Hispanics and Asian Americans are exceedingly complex encompassing a broad range of nationalities, dialects, and semantic characteristics. Third, the economics involved in sampling even the largest of these groups, Hispanics, are prohibitive if the various types of bilingual skills, dialects, and vocabularies are to be taken into account.

Summary: Bilingualism and Cognitive Difference

Seen as a body, research on bilingualism and cognitive difference suggests that bilinguals are not identical to monolinguals at a number of levels. Indeed, this literature makes a strong case for the position that bilingual persons are quite distinct from monolinguals. Summarizing briefly, the literature on information processing and bilingualism offers a view of both "nonbalanced" and "balanced" bilinguals that suggests that a "bilingual factor" may indeed be operating when bilingual individuals are engaged in the process of test taking itself. This factor, which might be manifested in a number of different ways, may directly contribute to the poor performance of bilingual minorities on standardized tests.

The two chapters that follow examine this question in some detail. Chapter 4 reviews the area of intelligence testing and the problems and questions raised by the use of such tests with bilingual individuals. It also includes a discussion of achievement, personality, and vocational testing. The focus of this chapter is the performance on tests by bilingual individuals and the assumptions made by this practice about the nature of bilingualism itself.

Chapter 5, on the other hand, is concerned with diagnostic testing and the impact of this testing on the placement of minority children in special education. Court cases deriving from questionable practices are discussed at some length and the results of a recent study of decision-making accuracy are presented as an illustration of existing difficulties in measuring the abilities of bilingual children. This study, conducted over a 10-year period, empirically demonstrates the hidden effects of decisions based primarily on "objective" predictive scores.

CHAPTER 4

The Testing of Bilinguals

When a bilingual individual confronts a monolingual test, developed by monolingual individuals, and standardized and normed on a monolingual population, both the test taker and the test are asked to do something that they cannot. The bilingual test taker cannot perform like a monolingual. The monolingual test cannot "measure" in the other language.

Ironically, single-language tests deceptively measure the "monolingual" part of the bilingual (one or the other of the bilingual's two languages), irrespective of proficiency in that language, and they do so reliably. But these tests fail insofar as they may exclude mental content that is available to the bilingual in the other language, and mental processes and abilities that are the product of bilingualism (Hakuta & Garcia, 1989; Hakuta, Ferdman, & Diaz, 1987).

The unique American tragedy of bilinguals has been that over the last century both test makers and testers have generally ignored the psychological robustness of bilingualism. The result has been a waste of human potential. Bilingual persons have needlessly been misled and misdiagnosed, especially children. This section examines the empirical bases for these assertions.

INTELLIGENCE TESTING

Psychologists are relatively latecomers in the study of intelligence. Their earliest attempts at measuring intelligence were dismally ineffective because the initial focus was on differences among individuals on reaction-time tasks. Given the instruments available for measuring time to react and the tasks used to measure "intelligence" at the turn of the century, it was found that individuals were very similar in their ability to respond quickly to stimuli. This was undesirable for measurement purposes and also contrary to the experience of most children and adults (i.e., that there are large differences in how much people know and how well people learn).

Alfred Binet, a French psychologist faced with the practical task of finding a way to identify very slow learners in the Paris schools, took a different direction in the measurement of intelligence. He concentrated on mental tasks that required more complex forms of information processing. These mental tasks were typically of the sort encountered in schools, although not exclusively curriculum centered. He tested for social knowledge, vocabulary, numerical understanding, ability to detect similarities and differences, amount of retained knowledge, comprehension of linguistic puzzles (adages, proverbs, metaphors) and so on. Purposely, he "calibrated" his tests by making them harder and harder to pass within and across different ages. He came up with the concept of "mental age" to describe how "old" a person was in his or her ability to solve mental problems. If an 8-year-old passed all the items of a test for 10-year-olds, but not for 11-year-olds, then that child's mental age was 10, or 2 years above most of his chronological peers. By age-norming mental tests of varying difficulty levels, Binet was able to succeed where others had failed. He produced a way to measure "intelligence" that differentiated among individuals, and he achieved a modicum of prediction by identifying those children who were failing and would have failed in school.

Several points need to be noted. Binet's tests began because of a school problem and were developed on school populations. The content of the tests, although not predominantly academic, relied on mental operations that are most typically used and observed in schools. The goal of the tests was to *predict* academic learning. The tests were empirically grounded, that is, their various degrees of difficulty and age-appropriateness were determined from the actual performance of norming samples.

Interestingly, the success of Binet's work was greatest in the United States. Gottsman and Goddard at Stanford University, after adapting and renorming Binet's scales, launched a success story that remains unparalleled in American psychology. Thanks to the critical need for sorting and classifying army recruits during the two world wars, and to the relatively successful job done by tests in this regard, differential/correlational psychology developed into a virtual "school." As Cronbach (1957) pointed out, however, the separation between correlational psychology and experimental psychology has worked to the detriment of both "schools." For "intelligence," the results of this separation have been critical: Although the tests have been useful for modestly predicting educability, they have not helped to explain the meaning, development, and variations of "intelligence."

From an explanatory and definitional perspective, "Intelligence" has been one of the most elusive constructs in American psychology. In spite of considerable discussion and debate in the psychometric literature, agreement on the definition of intelligence has been unattainable (*"Intelligence and its measurement,"* 1921; Sternberg, Conway, Ketron, & Bernstein, 1981). As Sternberg et al. (1981) noted, however, some common themes run through most of this literature: among experts in the 1920s, intelligence was typically seen as "the ability to learn from experience and to adapt to one's environment" (p. 6); among laypeople and experts in the 1980s, three factors describe the commonalities among behavioral descriptions of "intelligence" – "problem-solving, . . . verbal ability, . . . and social competence" (p. 53).

The Logic of Intelligence Tests

IQ tests supposedly measure the amount of learning and learning skills an individual has acquired in the curriculum of a culture or society. The "classroom" is the national environment (the home, neighborhood, national language, public schools, media, institutions, etc.). The test samples information bits extant in the society and presents them as items arranged in an empirically determined order of difficulty. Age norms taken from a representative sample in the national population map out a sequence of information acquisition at various ages within the national "classroom." When a person takes an intelligence test, he or she is measured relative to the amount of incidentally acquired knowledge and learning skills in the national school and in comparison to others of the same age.

The assumptions behind all this have been clearly explained by Mercer (1979). It is assumed that the person taking the test comes from the same "classroom," has had the same relative exposure to the curriculum, has acquired the same general motivation towards solving the test items, and has had about the same types of experiences with test taking. When these factors "apply," the IQ score supposedly informs as to learning ability and "intelligence."

One of the most enthusiastic defenders of IQ, Arthur Jensen (1977), made an interesting set of observations about the empirical relationships found between intelligence (IQ) and learning: Intelligence is critical for *learning* that is intentional, that requires use of hierarchically arranged knowledge, that requires comprehension, that relies on transference, that is insightful, that is complex, that must be done within a specified and limited time frame, that presents a new problem, and that is keyed to chronological age. Of course, the critical issue in these relationships is the applicability of the assumptions about an individual's background and his or her experience with the national classroom. If Hmong children, recently arrived in the United States, demonstrate the same empirical relationships between IQ and school learning, the critical question becomes whether in their regard IQ is a measure of intelligence.

Bilingual Populations and Intelligence Tests

The Historical Literature. In a recent review of the historical, empirical literature (1920s to 1950) on testing bilingual populations in the United States, Figueroa (1990) identified four key parameters that describe most of this literature. First, the majority of language minority (circumstantial bilingual) groups show the same, ubiquitous low verbal IQ, high nonverbal IQ profile. Table 4.1 gives a representative sampling of these results. Associated with these results, there emerged a widespread opinion that nonverbal measures of intelligence were free of primary language effects. However, it was widely recognized that such performance IQs could not be substituted for verbal IQs and that the former typically had lower predictive validity to schooling. With respect to circumstantial bilinguals' verbal IQs, the earliest large studies (Brigham, 1923) showed that length of residence in the United States was positively associated with increases in verbal IQs. Perhaps because of these findings, rate of English language acquisition came to be considered an index of intelligence, even though the empirical data tended to show that VIQ increases were extremely modest even after many years in this country. Brigham's foreign-born army recruits, for example, showed an increase in VIQ (Army Alpha) of.66 raw-score points per every 5 years over a 20-year span of time (Brigham, 1923, p. 91).

Second, testing psychology came to perceive bilingualism as a "language handicap" that retarded intelligence (low VIQs) and handicapped English-language acquisition. Anomalous data were usually ignored. For example, the fact that bilingualism in middle-class groups enhanced intelligence scores was passed over. So was the fact that older, educated (in the ethnic language) test takers from circumstantial bilingual backgrounds showed no appreciable retardation in their intellectual ability.

Third, psychometric properties, by and large, came to be seen as robust indices of test appropriateness for use with circumstantial bilingual populations. Reliabilities were universally as good for monolingual English speakers and for speakers of other languages. The same applied to most measures of validity. The one unattended and occasional exception was predictive validity. Its record was not so universally consistent. In fact, predictive validities were often attenuated (Davenport, 1932; Feingold, 1924; Paschal & Sullivan, 1925; Wheeler, 1932; Wood, 1929; Yoder, 1928).

TABLE 4.1
Compilation of Verbal and Nonverbal Intelligence Score Means for Diverse Language
Background Groups on Widely Used Measures of Intelligence, 1920–1950

Nationality	Verbal IQ		Nonverbal IQ	
Alaskan Indians	78.88	B* 14**	91.55	J* 14**
Aleut	80.27	B 14	93.29	J 14
Armenians	94.28	D 1		
"			92.3	J 16
Austrians	94	B 4		
"	99.5	B 13		
Bohemian	93	B 8	123	C 8
Bulgarians	96.0	D 1		
Chinese	96.5	B 14		
"			107.4	C 2
"	108	B 3	108	C 3
"	79.8	R 15	104.1	J 15
"			92.1	E 15
"			98.0	M 15
"			107.8	C 15
"			100.2	U 15
"	97.0	B 24		
"			104.1	J 16
Croatian	86	B 4		
(Assyrian, Slovanian and Serbian)			92.8	J 16
Danish & Swedish	100	A 12		
(Danish, Swedish and Norwegian)			103.5	J 16
East Indian	93	B 4		
Eskimo	73.67	B 14	89.56	J 14
Finnish	94	B 4		
"	90.0	B 13		
French	98.0	A 12		
"	95.4	B 13		
(French & Swiss)			94.5	J 16
Foreign Speaking			103	K 4
	87.8	P 19		
German	91	B 4		
"	102.0	A 12		
"	102.3	B 13		
"	91.0	B 16		
"			101.1	J 16
Greek	83	B 4		
"	92.63	D 1		
Gypsy	74	B 4		
Hawaiian	92.76	B 6	101.92	E 6
Hawaiian Chinese	97.4	B 6	104.5	E 6
Hawaiian White	100.5	B 6	106.0	E 6
Hawaiian White Chinese	103.0	B 6	108.0	E 6

(*continued*)

TABLE 4.1 (*continued*)

Nationality	Verbal IQ		Nonverbal IQ	
Hispanic	82.4	I 9		
"			92.0	J 10
"	80.5	B 9		
"	83.5	B 16		
"			88.5	J 16
"	88.5	R 23		
"			111.5	J 11
"	79.1	G 20	76.4	Q 20
"	78.0	B 24		
Hungarian	89	B 4		
Irish	98	A 12		
Italian	84	B 4		
"	85	B 5		
"	105.5	F 8		
"	77.5	B 13		
"	85	B 8	109	C 8
"	88.5	R 8		
"	98.0	A 12		
"	90.85	B 17	97.4	N 17
"	84.0	B 16		
"			89.1	J 16
"	84.0	B 24		
(Sicilian)			92.5	J 11
Japanese	95	B 7		
"	89.5	B 18	77.5	0 18
"	91.2	B 15	101.9	J 15
"	98.2	L 15	99.4	E 15
"	97.61	T 23		
"			114.2	C 2
Jewish	128.5	F 8		
"	98.0	B 8	102	C 8
"	105.7	R 8		
"	105	B 8		
"	106.1	Q 8		
"	103.19	R 8		
"	88.04	H 8		
"	100.6	A 12		
"	101.8	S 22	102.14	K 22
Polish Jews	102.8	G 8		
Russian Jews	99.5	G 8		
Lithuanian	87	B 4		
Norwegian	103.8	B 16		
Polish	85	B 4		
"	97.0	A 12		
Portuguese	86.0	B 16		
"			94.5	J 16

(*continued*)

TABLE 4.1 (continued)

Nationality	Verbal IQ		Nonverbal IQ
Portuguese	84.0	B 24	
Roumanian	97	B 4	
Russian	89	B 4	
Slavish	85	B 4	
"	85.6	B 13	
Swedish	101.9	B 13	
Syrian	80	B 4	
Turkish	95.50	D 1	

*A = Army Alpha; B = Stanford Binet; C = Pinter–Patterson Tests; D = Otis Self-Administered Test of Mental Ability; E = Porteus Maze Test; F = Pressey Group Intelligence Test; G = Pinter–Cunningham Primary Mental Test, Dearborn Group Test of Intelligence, Examination A and B, combined; H = Thorndike Intelligence Examination; I = Stanford Binet, Spanish Translation; J = Goodenough Intelligence Test; K = Pintner Nonlanguage Group Tests; L = Japanese Binet; M = Porteus Form and Assembly Test; N = Atkins Object-fitting Test, Form A; O = Army Beta; P = Otis Classification Forms A and B; Q = Meyers Pantomine Group Intelligence Test; R = National Intelligence Tests, Scale A, Form B; S = Pintner Intelligence Test; T = Hennmon–Nelson Tests of Mental Ability; U = Goddard Binet.

**1 = Wood, 1929; 2 = Sandiford & Kerr, 1926; 3 = Luh & Wy, 1931; 4 = Pintner & Keller, 1922; 5 = Arlitt, 1921; 6 = Louttit, 1931; 7 = Fukuda, 1923; 8 = Brill, 1936; 9 = Manuel, 1935; 10 = Manuel, 1932; 11 = Lamb, 1930; 12 = Feingold, 1924; 13 = Brown, 1922; 14 = Eels, 1933; 15 = Hung Hsiao, 1929; 16 = Goodenough, 1926; 17 = Darcy, 1946; 18 = Darsie, 1926; 19 = Haven, 1931; 20 = Garretson, 1928; 21 = Garth, 1923; 22 = Pintner & Arsenian, 1937; 23 = Portenier, 1947; 24 = Yeung, 1921.

Interestingly, some studies on test items produced results that were extremely unusual. Bilinguals, for example, had a harder time recalling digits forward than digits backward, exactly the opposite of what occurred with English speakers (Darsie, 1926; Hung Hsiao, 1929; Luh & Wy, 1931; Manuel, 1935). Again, researchers ignored these data.

Fourth, most studies were flawed in their designs. Specifically, they not only failed by ignoring SES and the effects of inadequate and segregated schooling, they also ignored L2 proficiency as a mediating factor in circumstantial bilinguals' test scores. Typically, "Jews," "Italians," "Indians," "Chinese," "Japanese," or "Mexicans" were all treated as an entity devoid of individual differences in English language proficiency.

Fifth, politics more than data often determined researchers' interpretation of results (e.g., Saer, 1923).

The Contemporary Professional Literature. Textbooks on the psychometric measurement of intelligence have changed very little from the historical treatment of bilingualism (e.g., Aiken, 1987; Cronbach, 1984; Jensen, 1980, 1984; Kamphaus & Reynolds, 1987; Kaufman, 1979; Reynolds & Gutkin, 1982; Salvia & Ysseldyke, 1988; Sattler, 1988, 1992).

Although the attribution for the verbal/nonverbal IQ discrepancy in bilinguals' scores has changed from a language handicap to "bilingualism," the critical problem of inadequate research designs persists. There are still only a few studies controlling for proficiencies in the bilingual's two languages. This allows for citing psychometric studies on monolithic groups such as "Hispanics" and "Mexican Americans" to tout high reliabilities and high validities. In spite of the fact that 20% of the population in the United States comes from potentially "bilingual" homes, two or three pages are the most that are usually devoted to "bilingualism" in these texts, and usually not as an independent factor but rather as a practical consideration for testing Hispanics; for example, do not use the verbal IQ to get a full-scale score; beware that many Hispanic children have two "underdeveloped" languages; test in Spanish if that is the stronger language; the longer subjects have been in the United States, the more likely it is that they will do better in English; if you translate a test, make it like the dialect used; nonverbal tests are relatively free of language and can be pantomined if necessary; and so on.

Kaufman (1979) is the only text reviewed that suggests more research in order to explicate the VIQ/PIQ discrepancy found in circumstantial bilingual groups. Some of the impetus for this recommendation, regrettably, comes from Kaufman's own ignorance on language acquisition as it pertains to circumstantial bilingual groups in the United States. The fact that English speakers from bilingual "cultures" also demonstrate the VIQ/PIQ discrepancy, and that ethnic language speakers also show it on ethnic language tests perplexes him. Parsimonius explanations related to the fluctuating linguistic experiences of some circumstantial bilingual groups and how such experiences essentially are not comparable to those of the monolingual normative populations in each of the language groups in question seem to escape him. Interestingly, Sattler (1988, 1992) was sensitive to these facts and even included evaluative reviews of language proficiency tests for bilinguals. But even he failed to appreciate the gap in the existing psychometric literature when it ignores the possible covariation of such linguistic variables with internal and external indices of bias.

Jensen (1984), in spite of earlier work suggesting the attenuation of psychometric test properties due to bilingualism, regressed back to the early "scientific" literature and espoused a rather outlandish proposition that the VIQ/PIQ discrepancy may be due to factors other than bilingualism for specific circumstantial bilingual groups. Specifically, he hypothesized that the lower VIQ may be due to "lower verbal aptitude per se" (p. 535). He commended Gordon's article (1980) for this particular insight. What makes his regression so interesting is the lack of empirical data for such an extreme position. Basically, in siding with Gordon (1980) on the possibility that some groups have fewer "verbal ability genes" (p.

96), Jensen relied on the anomolous fact that in a very, very few circumstantial bilingual groups their verbal IQ is higher than their nonverbal IQ (see Table 4.1) and on Gordon's analysis of the 1966 Coleman data to substantiate "the fairness of ability tests with Mexican Americans" (p. 98). Apparently unaware of the historical literature on circumstantial bilingual groups, Gordon rediscovered that (group) ability tests predict as well (if not overpredict) for Mexican-American (representing "bilinguals") as for Anglo children. As with the historical literature, language proficiency in the societal language – English – plays no part in his research design.

Cultural Bias. The psychometric study of bias with circumstantial bilingual groups has changed even less than the professional literature on this topic, although promising trends are in evidence in some studies published in the 1980s and 1990s (Armour-Thomas, 1992; Clark, 1987; Miller-Jones, 1989; Tharp, 1989). Both with respect to culture and language proficiency (in the ethnic and societal languages), the psychometric literature has failed to adequately control for these independent, robust variables.

With respect to culture, for example, the investigation of bias has relied on a strange definition. "Culture" is something that is supposed to be manifested in the group score when it is contrasted to the group score of the Anglo (cultural) group. It is a unitary trait inherent in a sampled group, and usually "packaged" as a monolithic, group, statistical effect (Weisner, Gallimore, & Jordan, 1988). It is also assumed that this "variable" will somehow interact with the "Anglo cultural variable" and that the interaction will produce bias in the Anglo test. Transposing this logic to another context, this is like saying that cultural bias in a curriculum developed in the United States will be found if Hispanic culture, as defined by the Hispanic children receiving the curriculum, somehow changes the curriculum. The fact that Hispanic children do poorly in the curriculum is immaterial in terms of demonstrating cultural bias. The critical index for bias is if the curriculum is changed by the "other" culture.

A good example of this type of research on cultural bias in tests comes from studies on item difficulty levels. Jensen (1980) is one of the most influential researchers in the area of item bias and Hispanic children. In fact, some of the models he has proposed (Jensen, 1974) have been quite influential in subsequent studies (Sandoval, 1979; Sandoval, Zimmerman, & Woo, 1980) in which bias has not been found.

Using the *Peabody Picture Vocabulary Test* (PPVT) and the *Raven's Progressive Matrices* on 700 Mexican-American and approximately 600 Anglo-American children of elementary school age from one California school district, Jensen (1974) calculated the indices of item difficulty, or p values, for each item on both tests and for each ethnic group. Rank-order correlation coefficients for both groups showed that the items behaved in essentially the same manner for both groups. That is, the "staircase effect," showing that from the first to the last item of each test progressively fewer and fewer children passed the items, was similar for both Anglo- and Mexican-American children. Jensen calculated the differences in p (p decrements) for each pair of contiguous items in both the Raven and the PPVT. That is, differences in p values between Items 1 and 2, 2 and 3, 3 and 4, and so on, were calculated.

According to Jensen (1974), p decrements are extremely sensitive indices of item bias with regards to the internal consistency of tests. Even when the rank order of p values of two groups is highly similar on a given test and correlates accordingly, p decrement correlations may not yield the same results.

This model for evaluating bias is supposedly quite powerful. Clearly, if the items perform very similarly in two groups regardless as to which one was over- or underrepresented in the norming sample, the argument of bias falls short. It is also worth noting that if the items have the same "deep structure" in both groups, almost every other measure of internal consistency will fall in line, be these p decrements, Group X item ANOVA interactions, reliability coefficients and factor structures. This is essentially what Jensen (1974) found.

A more recent study by Sandoval (1979) verified Jensen's (1974) findings. Using a subset of the SOMPA sample (approximately 351 Anglo, 350 black, and 349 Hispanic children), he examined some of the item characteristics suggested by Jensen (1974) in the WISC-R across the three ethnic groups. An essential aspect of this study involves testing the notion that, according to Sandoval, has been argued by black psychologists such as Williams (1970, 1971), that is,

> The minority child's experiences with concepts and vocabulary are different from the majority child's and that a number of items on the WISC-R are unfairly difficult for children experiencing a common minority culture. Because their experience is different, it follows that the *pattern* of responses for minority children is quite different from the pattern for majority children. (p. 920; emphasis added)

Sandoval's analyses are very powerful, going quite beyond those proposed by Jensen. In Sandoval's (1979) analyses, the WISC-R proved to be reliable and consistent (high p value correlations, high p decrement correlations, minimal item X ethnic groups interactions, and minimal item X SES interactions) for all groups. The analyses of the items generally did not demonstrate a different pattern of difficulty levels for the groups, rather, "the differences in scoring between groups [was] spread across the items and subtests" (p. 923).

Sandoval's (1979) analyses also provided a list of those items that were the most difficult for Hispanic children and that contributed "to the observed differences in ethnic group performance" (p. 922). Overall, these findings, as Jensen's (1974), showed that:

> The pattern of children's responses to the test is very similar regardless of the children's cultural background. Despite the fact that the black and Mexican American cultures are different from each other, as well as from the general Anglo-American culture, the same items (59 or 34% of WISC-R items) tended to be difficult for the black and Mexican American groups. The lack of a clear pattern of difficult items and the fact that there exist a large number of items (76 for Hispanics) just slightly more difficult for minority children spread throughout the entire test suggest that general factors rather than specific item content contribute to differences in means. (p. 925)

Sandoval leaves open the question as to what this "general factor" might be, citing various possible background or developmental deficiencies in minority children and in the examiner–examinee relationship. Nothing is mentioned relative to acculturation or linguistic differences.

In a very related study, Sandoval, Zimmerman, and Woo (1980) again examined the item difficulties in the WISC-R of 7- and 11-year-olds from Hispanic ($N = 95$), Anglo ($N = 108$), black ($N = 93$), and Bermudan ($N = 94$) groups on the verbal, culture-loaded items and subtests of the WISC-R. Again, the results were similar to those found by Jensen (1974). The p values and the rank-order correlations between the Anglo group and each of the other groups fairly consistently showed that the patterns of item difficulty levels were very similar. The Bermudan children's responses showed the greatest variation in pattern, though again, not sufficient to indicate pronounced and consistent evidence of bias.

There are many other studies examining bias in the item difficulty levels (Cleary & Hilton, 1968; Miele, 1979; Scheuneman, 1975) similar to Jensen's (1974), Sandoval's (1979), and Sandoval, Zimmerman, and Woo's (1980). The results from these usually come from black-Anglo test results. In these as well as those where Hispanic children are involved (Cotter & Berk, 1981; Scheuneman, 1978), the findings are essentially the same. The item-difficulty levels established from the norming group's responses (again, predominantly the Anglo, middle-class) on the whole remain fairly invariant for Hispanic children.

As noted, the critical assumption in this line of investigation is that non-Anglo cultures will interact with established item-difficulty levels. That is, that a different pattern of item difficulties should be obtained because of exposure to different cultures. This is a very strange and unusual expectation. Why should the U.S. item-difficulty levels be changed if there is cultural bias? Should cultures, in effect, *interact* in a "disruptive" manner? Anglo acculturation for circumstantial bilingual groups proceeds in as uniform a manner as for the Anglo majority. One is acculturated, more or less, to a given culture in proportion to the degree of exposure to that setting. Accordingly, test results may not show disruptive, discrete (items) effects, but rather total, proportional effects.

In Sandoval's studies (1979, 1980), just as in Jensen's (1974), it was found that Mexican-American children did not show much indication of altered p values and hence, of internal test evidence of bias. Figueroa (1983) replicated part of Sandoval, Zimmerman, and Woo's (1980) study, using the total (not half) of the 7½-year-old and 10½-year-old Hispanic and Anglo SOMPA children. He conducted the same p value analyses and item rank-order correlations for the most culturally loaded subtests of the WISC-R: Vocabulary, Information, and Similarities. However, he divided the Hispanic group into three subgroups: those who came from homes in which the mother spoke only Spanish, in which the mother spoke English and Spanish, and in which the mother spoke only English. These groups provide an excellent way to test not so much the questions of item bias as the expectation that cultures, particularly linguistically different cultures, will interact with the English item structure of the WISC-R in a "disruptive" manner. The results showed that in none of the subtests or age groups did the Hispanic subgroups differ much from the Anglo group's sequence of p values and rank orders.

It would appear that cultures do not affect each other in such a way as to disrupt each other's developmental order of verbal and knowledge presentation and acquisition. Properly normed tests of vocabulary or information essentially map out an age-linked order of a culture's verbal and knowledge "curriculum" that is learned by the children and that is representative of the frequency with which words and information bits appear in that culture. Jensen (1974) himself demonstrated that the normative sequence of words in the PPVT is very closely correlated with the mean, Thorndike–Lorge frequency of the items. The linguistic, incidental learning in Anglo society proceeds in the same sequence or order for the child whose parents speak another language, both languages, and only English. Cultural bias will not be found as Jensen (1974) and Sandoval (1979) expected. Rather, it might be found throughout the test depressing all or most items (the entire sequence of the incidental "curriculum") in direct proportion to acculturation or exposure to the Anglo, English incidental "classroom." This, of course, is speculative because the study of how culture affects U.S. tests awaits several developments, (e.g., Valencia & Rankin, 1986).

To begin with, some consensus has to be reached that "culture" cannot be treated as a monolithic factor inherent in a circumstantial bilingual sample. When "culture" comes to be recognized as a dimensional factor, the next step will be to measure it accordingly. At that juncture, several considerations will have to be addressed: Will the content of any such measure focus on the anthropological traits of the given cultural group in its own national setting, or in the United States among those who are in the process of acculturation?

The most well-known effort in this regard was carried out by Mercer and Lewis (1977) in the development of the System of Multicultural Pluralistic Assessment's (SOMPA) *Sociocultural Scales* (Mercer, 1979). In 11 questions that generate some 24 pieces of information, these scales can gauge the distance between a family and U.S. middle-class families. In effect, the Sociocultural Scales are a unique measure of acculturation on sociological factors (family size and stability, SES, and urbanization) that correlate with U.S. IQ scores. They measure the acculturation end of the possible circumstantial bilingual cultural continuum. In this sense, they constitute a unique departure from the treatment of culture as a unitary dimension. However, they are silent on any anthropological content unique to a given culture. As Figueroa and Sassenrath (1989) noted, this omission may well have determined their impotence in discovering unaccounted ability in the measurement of minority children's intelligence. "Foreign" content and cognitive skills, when not accessed by U.S. IQ tests, can function as subtrahends in any determination of intelligence. The test could measure a lower range of a bilingual's ability because the test may not have sampled cultural content that is part of the cognitive repertoire and processes available to the bicultural individual (Conroy, 1992; Hakuta, Ferdman, & Diaz, 1987; Pearson, 1988).

Linguistic Bias. Over the last 70 years, the data on linguistic bias in tests of intelligence have been consistently perplexing though seldom acknowledged as such by those conducting the studies. Part of the problem stems from the fact that "bilingualism" or "English language proficiency" continues to be ignored as a critical independent variable. Since the 1920s, psychometric studies on circumstantial bilingual groups do not gauge the levels of L1 and L2 linguistic proficiencies in "Mexican-American," "Hispanic," "Chinese," "Japanese," or "American-Indian" subjects. Bilingualism is virtually nonexistent in the psychometric literature. Mishra's (1981a) work is one of the most incredible examples in this regard. He selected Mexican-American subjects partly on the basis of the use of Spanish in the home. Then he ignored this fact and proceeded to show that psychometric tests are reliable (Mishra, 1981a; Mishra & Hurt, 1970), valid (Mishra, 1981b), and not biased with these children.

Researchers have seldom noted the perplexing aspects of circumstantial bilinguals' test data. Aside from the VIQ/PIQ discrepancy described in Table 4.1, not even the unusual subtest profiles of bilinguals have succeeded in alerting researchers to the possible importance of the bilingual factor. Figure 4.1 is an excellent example. The 700 Hispanic children, whom Mercer (1979) randomly selected in 1972 from among 5–11-year-olds in the public schools of California, were all chosen after it was determined that they were all English proficient. Yet, as Figure 4.1 shows, their WISC-R subscale profile showed a marked difference in their verbal-factual subtest scores (Information, Similarities, Vocabulary, Comprehension).

However, even more interesting was the fact that these "English fluent" children actually came from homes in which only Spanish was spoken (32%), in which English and Spanish was spoken (30%), and in which only English was spoken (38%). Further, their WISC-R subscale profiles were identical to those in Figure 4.1 but lowest for those from the Spanish-only homes and highest for those from the English-only homes (Figueroa, Delgado, & Ruiz, 1984).

The profile sketched in Figure 4.1 is anomolous enough to warrant some sort of attention. The fact that it is a duplicate of what had already been reported (Brigham, 1923) and what continues to be reported (Cummins, 1984a), is perplexing particularly in light of findings about psychometric bias with Hispanic school-age children.

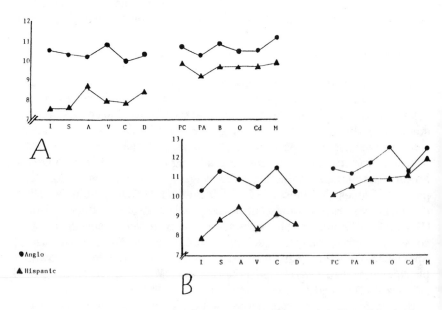

Figure 4.1.   1972 (A) and 1982 (B) WISC-R Subtest scores (x = 10, SD = 3) for Anglo (N in A = 699, B = 485) and Hispanic (A = 690, B = 382) pupils (data from Vukovich & Figueroa, 1982).

Item analyses. As already discussed, the empirically established difficulty levels in psychometric test items are not altered by cultural differences. Neither are they because of proficiencies in the societal language.
Other than in the case of Spanish-English cognates (Schmitt, 1988), the
empirical literature has not found anything to the contrary (Argulewicz &
Abel, 1984; Mishra, 1982). But in assuming that culture (or knowledge of a
non-English language) would also affect English item structures, the
results substantiate an artificial conclusion of "no bias." As Figueroa (1983)
has argued, expecting item structures to change would be tantamount to
having Salvadoran children receive a different form of English language
acquisition than that encountered by Anglo children. This is ludicrous. The
linguistic menu extant in a society is fairly invariant, the easy words are
those that occur most often and that are learned earliest, the grammatical
structures are the same, and even some of the acquisition behaviors are
the same (Ruiz, 1989). The Salvadoran child would score lower on an
English-based test, but the item difficulties would be the same because the
linguistic menu would have been the same.

Reliability. If a test measures an individual's output with approximately the same accuracy over several repetitions, the test is said to be
reliable. Reliability in this sense refers to total test scores, not to item
scores. By correlating total scores from repeated testings or from different parts of a test (odd-even items, for example), one can numerically
describe how reliable a given test actually is. Note again, that consistency
is the main focus.

Reliability studies across ethnic groups on the principal psychometric
tools used in school assessment are very uniform in their results, showing
that tests are as reliable for Hispanics as for Anglos; for example, Ortiz-
Franco (1990) with The National Longitudinal Study of Mathematical
Abilities; Valencia (1983) with the *McCarthy Scales*; Powers, Rossman,
and Douglas (1986) with the *Boehn Test of Basic Concepts*; Jensen (1974)
and Argulewicz, Anderson, and Bingenheimer (1983) with the *Peabody
Picture Vocabulary Test* and the *Raven Progressive Matrices*; Sandoval
(1979), Elliot et al., (1985), Elliot and Boeve (1987), with the *WISC-R*;
Arnold (1969) and Hurt and Mishra (1970) with the *Metropolitan Achievement Tests*; Valencia (1985a, 1985b) with the *Kaufman Assessment Battery for Children*; Dean (1977) with the *WISC-R*; Henderson and Rankin
(1973) with the *WPPSI*; Karabinus and Hurt (1969) with the *Van Alstyne
Picture Vocabulary Test*; Valencia (1984) and Powers, Barkan, and Jones
(1986) with the *Raven Progressive Matrices*; and so on. Rarely (e.g.,
Mishra & Hurt, 1970, with *Metropolitan Readiness Tests*; and Elliot,
Piersel, Witt, Argulewicz, Gutkin, & Galvin (1985) with the WISC-R) does
one find a study showing ethnic differences in reliabilities.

Factor Structures.   A popular approach for determining how test items related to each other is to do a factor analysis procedure. The item interrelations are statistically made manifest from data collected on (ideally) large numbers of subjects. Factors, or the associational clusters to which items converge, appear. A test that purports to measure five distinct psycholinguistic abilities through five subtests, for example, should exhibit five clusters that emerge from the items of each subtest. In terms of fairness, if the five clusters do not appear across different ethnic groups, an argument for bias can be made.

Again, this factor approach to investigating bias empirically looks at the internal consistency of a test. As already mentioned, a test which does not demonstrate ethnic differences in indices of item difficulty will in all probability not demonstrate differences in factorial structure. The results with Hispanics are, once again, consistent. Studies show that for many tests, factor-analytic investigations seldom demonstrate ethnic differences in the factors measured (e.g., Corman & Budoff, 1974, with the *Raven Progressive Matrices*; Gutkin & Reynolds, 1980, Reschly, 1978, Taylor & Richards, 1991, Barona, 1989, Geary & Whitworth, 1988, and Taylor & Ziegler, 1987, with the *WISC-R*; Mishra, 1981a, with the *McCarthy Scales*; Valencia & Rankin, 1986, with The K-ABC).

Prediction.   As already noted, the classic work of Cleary, Humphreys, Kendrick, and Wesman (1975) on the use of tests with minority populations focuses heavily on how well tests predict to school-related criteria, particularly academic achievement. The regression model described there supposedly provides a powerful set of indices from which questions of bias can be addressed. All of these essentially compare the percentage reduction in original error effected by using a test and whether there is comparable reduction between ethnic groups. If there is, then, the tests behave in essentially the same manner for both groups and, therefore, are not biased. The fact that one group generally scores below the other on the test does not indicate bias. The crux is whether the test is as predictive for both.

Tests of linguistic abilities, mental aptitudes, and general intelligence predict academic achievement with moderate accuracy for Anglo children with few important exceptions (e.g., Goldman & Hartig, 1976; Goldman & Hewitt, 1975). Many would argue that the same applies to Hispanic pupils (Cantwell, 1986; Dean, 1979; Elliott, Argulewicz, & Turco, 1986; Glutting, 1986; Henderson & Rankin, 1973; Karabinus & Hurt, 1969; Oakland, 1980, 1983; Reschly & Reschly, 1979; Reschly & Sabers, 1979; Schroeder & Bemis, 1969; Worthington & Benning, 1988). The fact is, that just as the historical literature suggested otherwise, current studies indicate that predictive validity is not consistently found when language proficiency is controlled for (Figueroa, 1990; Gandara, Keogh, Yashioka-Maxwell, 1980; Pilkington, Piersel, & Ponterotto, 1988) or when its impact is allowed to emerge either through translating tests (McGowan, Johnson, & Maxwell, 1981; Sattler, Avila, Houston, & Toney, 1980; Valencia, 1984; Valencia & Rankin, 1983, 1985) or selecting bilingual samples with potentially strong L1 backgrounds (Emerling, 1990; Glutting, 1986; Hiltonsmith, Hayman, & Kleinman, 1984; Johnson & McGowan, 1984; Kaufman & Wang, 1992; Mishra, 1983; Nielson & Fernandez, 1981; Stone, 1992; Valdez & Valdez, 1983; Valencia, 1982; Valencia & Rankin, 1988).

Concurrence. Unbeknownst to him, Jensen is probably one of the best sources of empirical support for Mercer's (1979) argument that if the inferential model assumed by tests does not hold, then diagnostic inferences are not possible. His classic study on bias (Jensen, 1974) included one extremely important analysis that has not been replicated or given much attention (e.g., Reynolds, 1982). This analysis essentially examines bias not from the usual perspective of p values or prediction, but rather concurrence of construct scores on tests that measure cognitive ability through two channels (i.e., linguistic and perceptual). He designated the former (Peabody Picture Vocabulary Test [PPVT]) as being culture loaded, the latter (Raven Progressive Matrices) as culture fair.

The sample consisted of 700 Mexican-American and 600 Anglo-American children of elementary school age from a California school district. First, he generated comparable forms of the PPVT and the Raven tests for the male Anglo group by matching the p values of 35 items on each test. He then checked to see if mean test scores between the PPVT and the Raven were as equal for the Anglo female, Chicano male, and Chicano female subsamples as they proved to be for the Anglo male group. There were no significant differences between the Anglo male and Anglo female average scores on the PPVT and Ravens,[1] indicating that in terms of measuring the construct of intelligence, both the culture-loaded and the culture-fair tests were operating in the same fashion. In other words, the incidental learning was essentially being measured with the same degree of precision by both tests. But with the Mexican-American group, this did not hold. The mean score on the Raven was significantly greater than on the PPVT. In other words, children with varying degrees of exposure to another culture (though supposedly proficient in English) and probably with a lesser degree of exposure to Anglo culture, achieved lower (less fair) scores on the culture-loaded test. Thus, the PPVT that loads quite significantly on the "g" factor and predicts as well as other tests of general ability to school achievement fails to measure linguistic incidental learn-

---

[1]Same for black male and female subsamples.

ing. Jensen's conclusion is crucial both to the study of bias and how it may operate in Hispanic test scores and to the support given to Mercer's argument about the distinction between prediction and diagnosis:

> The fact that the Mexican group is very similar to the white in rank order of p values and p decrements on both the PPVT and the Raven, yet has lower scores on the PPVT than on the Raven, suggests that some factor is operating to depress the PPVT performance more or less uniformly for all items and that this factor does not depress Raven performance, at least to the same degree. It seems plausible to suggest that this factor is verbal and may be associated with bilingualism in the Mexican group. (Jensen, 1974, pp. 239–240)

Referring to the same analysis in another publication, Jensen (1976) further stated: "Thus, there is some evidence that a vocabulary test in English may be a biased test of intelligence for Mexican-Americans" (p. 342).

This type of study on test concurrence is rare. Most psychometric studies examine intertest correlations or compare predictive coefficients of tests to a given criterion. Concurrent validity is closely related to construct validity, although its methodology tends to rely more on factor analysis. Most psychometric studies of both types of validity when conducted on bilingual subjects (principally Hispanic) find that tests are valid (Argulewicz, Bingenheimer, & Anderson, 1983; Argulewicz & Kush, 1983; Piersel & Reynolds, 1981; Teuber & Furlong, 1985; Valencia, 1984; Valencia & Rankin, 1986; Valencia & Rothwell, 1984; Whitworth & Chrisman, 1987). However, researchers in these studies universally seem unfazed by the consistently low verbal scores of potentially bilingual subjects (most studies provide little or no valid evidence of "English dominance"). In cases in which low sequential processing scores are involved (Fourqurean, 1987), researchers do not even discuss the possible involvement of bilingualism. Also, in some studies in which L1 is potentially strong (Hays & Smith, 1980; Hiltonsmith, Hayman, & Ursprung, 1982; Mishra, 1981a), the finding of concurrence is not always clearly supported (however, exceptions have been published, e.g., Argulewicz, Bingenheimer, & Anderson, 1983).

Bias and Test Translation. Scientific journals routinely accept studies in which a well-known test (e.g., the McCarthy Scales) has been translated into another language, administered to experimental subjects who speak that language, and the scores used for data analyses and reporting "results" (e.g., Chavez, 1982; Fourqurean, 1987; Lynn, Hampson, & Bingham, 1987; McGowan, Johnson, & Maxwell, 1981; Oplesch & Genshaft, 1981; Sattler & Altes, 1984; Sattler, Avila, Houston, & Toney,

1980; Valencia, 1979, 1983, 1984, 1988; Valencia, Henderson, & Rankin, 1981; Valencia & Rankin, 1983, 1985). This is an old tradition in psychometrics (Manuel, 1935) and one that seems impervious to the well-known fact that although words can be translated psychometric properties cannot (Thorndike, 1973). In its milder, contemporary form, this tradition is manifested in translating instructions for nonverbal tests (e.g., the K-ABC) or in translating surveys (e.g., the SOMPA). In its worst form, it includes selling direct translations of U.S. tests with U.S. norms to foreign countries or selling experimental translations without normative data (Psychological Corporation, 1982).

Translating a test assumes that the items in one language arrange themselves in the same order of difficulty as in another language. In 1983, an opportunity for studying the effects of translating on psychometric properties appeared with the publication of the normed and standardized Mexico City WISC-R (Gomez-Palacio, Padilla, & Roll, 1983). The test began with a straight translation of the WISC-R (with other items added on). The WISC-RM appeared in its final form with many of the original U.S. items intact. Table 4.2 presents the subtest rank-order correlations for the items that appear in both the U.S. and Mexican WISC-R. Two points are worth noting. First, the rank-order correlations are lowest for the verbal subtests, particularly for those subtests where the SOMPA Hispanic children scored lowest (see Figure 4.1), a point to which we return later. Second, the verbal tests had the greatest number of item substitutions. More Mexican items were added to the Information, Vocabulary, and Comprehension subtests than to the nonverbal items where there were virtually no items and little if any rearranging from the U.S. item sequences. These data clearly indicate that translating U.S. verbal test items (and perhaps some nonverbal as the Picture Completion subtest indicates) to another language either produces a new sequence of item difficulties or introduces content that is not part of the societal curricula and hence inappropriate for gauging the "intelligence" of individuals with no exposure to this knowledge base.

TABLE 4.2
Reliability of Cross-Lingual Versions of the WISC-R Subtests

Verbal			Nonverbal		
Information	[66%]*	−.82**	Picture Completion	[89%]	− .82
Similarities	[94%]	−.91	Picture Arrangement	[100%]	− 1.0
Arithmetic	[100%]	−.997	Block Design	[100%]	− 1.0
Vocabulary	[78%]	−.68	Object Assembly	[100%]	− 1.0
Comprehension	[76%]	−.69	Coding	[100%]	− 1.0
Digit Span	[100%]	− 1.00	Mazes	[100%]	− 1.0

*Percent of U.S. items in Mexican version of WISC-R
**Rank-order correlation coefficient

The literature on test bias does not even acknowledge the practice of using direct translations of U.S.-normed tests of intelligence, in spite of long-standing warnings in this regard (Manuel, 1935; Sanchez, 1934). A translated test is a different test, an unknown test, an unfair test. Researchers who use translated tests may well find that their results are anomalous if not spurious (e.g., McGowan, Johnson, & Maxwell, 1981; Sattler, Avila, Houston, & Toney, 1980; Valencia & Rankin, 1983, 1985).

Closely related to the practice of using translated tests is the use of interpreters (e.g., McLoughlin & Lewis, 1990). Again, this is an old practice that occurs on a daily basis in clinics, schools, and offices. Unlike translating, however, this practice is virtually unacknowledged in the scientific literature and to date there is no substantive data on the prevalence, reliability, and validity of this procedure.

Twomey, Gallegos, Anderson, Williamson, and Williamson's (1980) study in California is unique in actually providing some limited empirical data on this process. They report that for limited-English-proficient, Hispanic pupils, only 37% of their case files indicate that an interpreter was needed. Other language groups (Portuguese and Pilipino) fare even worse. Only Asian limited-English-proficient children do better (50%). Whether these data generalize to other regions of the country is unknown.

There are no substantive data on the reliability of test scores generated through the use of interpreters. The same applies to validity. In great part this may be due to several factors. Perhaps the most important of these is the tests. Comparably developed and equally robust tests have not been available in L1 and in English.

The professional literature has also been simplistic and wrong about how and when to use an interpreter. Watson, Grouell, Heller, and Omark (1980, pp. 47–52), for example, present a few highly questionable principles for using interpreters among a list of general recommendations on the topic. They begin by downplaying the tester's need for extensive second language competence in order to do assessment in the child's primary language: "Learning to present and interpret some tests in a foreign language should require a given but limited vocabulary. The practitioner does not have to have complete fluency in order to begin, and fluency increases with practice" (p. 47).

They imply that straight translations are all right so long as the interpreter has been trained. They recommend that when an interpreter cannot be found, a parent or an older sibling can be used (p. 51). However, before using a parent, they seem to suggest that the child should be immersed "in a classroom where no one else speaks the child's language" (p. 51) and that the testing should "not occur until the second year" (p. 52).

Models for training and using interpreters are becoming more numerous and popular (e.g., Figueroa, 1987; Langdon, 1986). These generally have one thing in common: lack of any empirical basis for their suggested procedures. Although it is quite likely that interpreters will always be needed for low-incidence language groups, some sort of study and validation of this procedure is urgently needed.

Testing Bilinguals and Bilingual Tests. Testing bilinguals' intelligence occurs most frequently in school settings and with Hispanic pupils. A unique aspect of testing Hispanic children is that there exist several psychometric versions of U.S. tests available in Spanish and with Spanish norms. "Bilingual testing," in effect, has supposedly become possible (e.g. Wilen & Sweeting, 1986; Prewitt-Diaz, 1990; Bracken, Barona, Bavermeister, Howell, Poggioli, & Puente, 1990). But there are two considerable problems attendant on this process and which serve to illuminate the dilemma of psychometrics when confronted by individuals with two language systems.

First, although the Spanish language tests (e.g., the WISC-RM [Gomez-Palacio, Padilla, & Roll, 1983], Kaufman Bateria de Evaluación Intelectual [Gomez-Palacio, Rangel-Hinojosa, & Padilla, 1985], Bateria Woodcock Psico-educativa en Español [Woodcock, 1982], and Test de Vocabulario en Imagenes Peabody [Dunn, Padilla, Lugo, & Dunn, 1986]) have acceptable psychometric properties, they were not normed on individuals who live with two language systems,[2] and the question of their equivalence remains unanswered.

Concerning the latter (test equivalence), data from the WISC-RM clearly indicate that because its norming sample is not comparable in SES to the WISC-R norming sample, it takes fewer raw-score points per scale score in the WISC-RM norm tables than in the WISC-R's. Similar problems exist for most Spanish versions of U.S. tests, such as The Escala de Inteligencia Wechsler Para Adultos (EIWA) (Lopez & Romero, 1988). However, these problems are seldom acknowledged, as in the case of the Woodcock Johnson Psycho-Educational Battery (Fletcher, 1989).

Concerning the former (norming with nonbilingual populations), a Mexico City child who has migrated to Los Angeles and its school system a year ago is no longer like his sister who stayed in the public schools of Mexico City (from which the WISC-RM sample was drawn). He is in the process of L2 acquisition and more than likely experiencing primary language loss, particularly if he is in an English-immersion classroom. Also, he has developed domain-specific linguistic codes in L2 which may not be as readily available cognitively in L1. This type of child when tested

---

[2]The New York version of The Escala de Inteligencia Wechsler para Niños (EIWN) is the one exception. Unfortunately, its "bilingual" norming population is not operationally defined, and its psychometric properties are inadequate (Canner, 1989).

on the WISC-RM may find certain questions easier to answer in L2 or may even be able to answer them correctly only if asked in L2. When asked for the definition of *diamante*, he may respond with "diamond" leaving the tester with the problem of deciding whether such a response is equivalent to a synonym (1 point) or a repetition (0 points). If the WISC-R is administered to this same boy in English (and assuming his English proficiency allows him to comprehend the test questions), testers may also find that on items previously answered correctly in Spanish incorrect or no answers are often given.

Historically, the role of testers in bilingual testing has received relatively little attention in the professional literature even though the 1985 testing Standards (American Educational Research Association et al., 1985), in standard 6.10, comes close to requiring bilingual skills in order to test bilingual individuals. Recent publications have begun to advocate on behalf of bilingual testers (Ambert, 1986; Martinez, 1985; Plata, 1985; Rosado, 1986). However, studies directly measuring the effect of bilingual versus monolingual testers on bilingual populations are vitually nonexistent. This may reflect the fact that there are no "bilingual" tests, per se, even though there are many tests in L1 and L2. On the larger issue of bias due to ethnic differences between test takers and test givers, the data are equivocal (Fuchs & Fuchs, 1989; Rappaport & McAnulty, 1985), albeit flawed insofar as bilingualism is, once again, not taken into account.

In "bilingual testing," on the other hand, anomalies are not uncommon. In fact, on digit naming subtests, bilinguals always seem to have performed in peculiar ways. In 1931, for example, Darsie (1926) found that whereas digits forward in English for Chinese bilingual pupils (age 11) had a passing rate of 41%, digits backward had a rate of 86% (versus 80 and 86, respectively, for American children). Similar results have been reported by Manuel (1935), Hung Hsiao (1929), Jensen and Inouye (1980) and Pearson (1988). Figueroa (1987), in fact, in studying the LVL I–LVL II theory of intelligence posited by Jensen, found that on Mercer's (1979) Hispanic SOMPA sample ($N = 700$), backward digit-span items behaved more like a Level-I test and forward digit-span items more like a Level-II test, or completely the opposite from what is predicted by Jensen's (1969) theory. A subsequent, more detailed analysis of these data show that the more bilingual the linguistic experience, the more likely it is that backward digit-span tasks are easier than forward digit-span tasks (Figueroa, 1987).

These and other anomalous psychometric outcomes associated with bilingual populations (such as the ubiquitous and intractable low-VIQ, high-PIQ bilingual profile) are curious in and of themselves, but not quite as perplexing as psychometricians' lack of interest about why such outcomes occur. In point of fact, however, such ennui extends to test users and administrators, particularly in educational settings and in matters concerned with academic achievement.

ACHIEVEMENT TESTING

The national concern with educational excellence has raised the status of educational achievement testing to an unprecedented level of importance. Achievement test results, in fact, are often accepted on face value (Ebel & Frisbie, 1986). The predominant uses for these tests are ideographic. They affect the student more than the system. For all pupils, achievement tests have always functioned under a specific set of assumptions. These have never been as explicitly enunciated as in the 1975 report commissioned by the American Psychological Association (APA):

> It is recognized that three assumptions are basic to this report. The first assumption is acceptance of a single society, heterogeneous though it may be, rather than a divided one. The second assumption is that few radical changes are expected in curriculum content or methodology of instruction in our educational establishment. . . . The third assumption accepts the importance of evaluation in education. Diagnosis, prognosis, prescription and measurement of outcomes are as important in education as in medicine. If these assumptions are rejected, the research on which this report is based could become more or less irrelevant. (Cleary, Humphreys, Kendrick, & Wesman, 1975, p. 18)

As candid as this last caveat might seem, the assumptions are presented in a most slanted manner. In the first assumption, the issue is posed as a choice between a single or a divided society. Such a choice is contrived. The real issue is whether there is a single heterogeneous society or a single homogeneous society. If the former is true to a significant linguistic and cultural degree, the research on test validity in the APA report "could become more or less irrelevant." The second assumption, particularly as it might apply to many Hispanic students, is wishful thinking. ESL and bilingual instructional programs are very different from English-only programs, if not in content, certainly in methodology. The third assumption lumps together diagnosis, prognosis, prescription, and measurement without acknowledging the differences among these or the fact that the report concentrates almost exclusively on one aspect of evaluation: bias in prognosis (prediction). Further, although evaluation might be as important in education as in medicine, in the former it is not as diagnostic, predictive, prescriptive, or accurate. This is and has been particularly true for bilinguals.

The Past

Historically, the American school has never been an easy place for circumstantial bilingual students (First & Carrera, 1988; Reynolds, 1933). Besides being economically poor, bilingual children from virtually every linguistic background, such as Italian (Goodenough, 1926), Chinese (Yeung, 1921), American Indian (Garth, 1925, 1926), and so on, have had to cope with teaching that is incomprehensible for many months if not years, and have been ordered to stop talking in their primary language in school. Knowing another language has never been seen as an asset or an avenue for enhanced academic achievement. Quite the opposite. The other language has invariably been seen as an academic handicap, to be left behind as quickly as possible in order to do well in school.

It is quite likely that, at some point in their American experience, most circumstantial bilingual groups have been perceived as dumb and incapable of much academic learning: "with regard to more purely intellectual traits, the Japanese are judged as inferior. This is shown in the [teacher] ratings of general intelligence, desire to know and originality" (Darsie, 1926, p. 76).

Tests of academic achievement have usually validated these perceptions. In a recent review of circumstantial bilingual groups and the achievement testing literature, Figueroa 1990 underscored the similarities between the historical literature on intelligence testing and achievement testing with respect to bilingualism. Just as with verbal IQ, bilingualism was directly and proportionally associated with low academic achievement (Garrettson, 1928; Pratt, 1929; Smith, 1942; Yeung, 1921). It would seem, also, that in varying and unknown degrees, English achievement tests also functioned as tests of English. This was particularly true where the L2 linguistic demands were strong in the achievement test (e.g., reading comprehension, analogy, metaphor, composition) and curiously less so where the linguistic demands were more orthographic (spelling) or arithmetic (Johnson, 1938; Livesay, 1936; Manuel, 1935; McElwee, 1935; Pratt, 1929). This is a variation of the PIQ profile of bilinguals.

Anomalies also surfaced. Grades were not as sensitive to linguistic background as were achievement test scores (Bell, 1935; Smith, 1942). Also, some studies even reported slight positive correlations between bilingual proficiency and grades, and slight negative correlations between achievement test scores and bilingual proficiency (Smith, 1942).

The context in which achievement testing took place for bilingual students included poverty at home and poverty at school. Their schools were economically disadvantaged (Manuel, 1935), segregated (Bell, 1935; Haught, 1934; Koch & Simmons, 1926), and had more retentions and higher drop-out rates (Darsie, 1926; Garth, 1920; Reynolds, 1933). In effect, they were similar to the schools that typically educate some present-day linguistic minorities (Arias, 1986; Kozol, 1991; Oakes, 1985; U.S. Commission on Civil Rights, 1973).

The Professional Literature

Contemporary texts on achievement testing seldom, if ever, consider bilingualism as a problem or as an important independent variable badly in need of research (Cunningham, 1986; Ebel & Frisbie, 1986; Mehrens & Lehmann, 1987; Nuttal, 1986). The major theoretical and methodological developments in achievement testing, most notably in item-response theory, essentially ignore the possible effects of two linguistic codes on tests (e.g., McArthur, 1987). However, some of the mathematical models for analyzing qualitative differences in response characteristics of students (e.g., Harnisch & Linn, 1982; McArthur, 1987; Sato, Takeya, Kurata, Marimoto, & Chimura, 1981) seem potentially useful for studying the interaction between achievement test outcomes and bilingualism. Schmitt's (1988) work with SAT test items' interaction with true and false English-Spanish cognates is a particularly promising example in this regard.

Textbooks on academic achievement tests and testing treat the issue of bias as an outcome of court cases and minority complaints or as a topic narrowly defined by systematic error in prediction. Some texts suggest that bias in achievement tests is less likely to occur than in intelligence tests because the former are so closely linked to construct validity. Ebel and Frisbie (1986) were particularly convinced of this and even maintained:

> That students who do poorly on a particular test written in English might do better if the test were in Spanish, or if the questions were presented orally, does not mean that the original test is biased against them. It simply means that they have not learned enough of what that particular test measures. Its linguistic context is part of the test. The particularity of what the test measures does not constitute bias. (p. 6)

For Ebel and Frisbie, it would seem that reading, writing, and math ability only happen in English. This modern version of what is usually called nativism, a polite description of the political positions upheld by psychometrics in the name of science in the early part of this century, is quite in sync with the APA report, "The Educational Uses of Tests with Disadvantaged Students" (Cleary, Humphreys, Kendrick, & Wesman, 1975). It is not, however, quite in keeping with what the National Research Council (Wigdor & Garner, 1982) or the major professional organizations (American Educational Research Association, American Psychological Association, National Council on Measurement in Education, 1985) are finally, if not modestly, beginning to acknowledge. The National Research Council, for example, in the two pages (out of more than 600) it devotes to "Testing Bilingual Students" asserts that" an English-language test is not sufficient to assess a bilingual child's performance . . . because the child's pattern of language development is likely to be mixed, with varying degrees of command of listening, reading, writing and thinking in English and in the native language" (p. 158). A more emphatic set of statements can be found in the *Standards for Educational and Psychological Testing* (American Educational Research Association et al., 1985). These will be reviewed in the last section of this chapter.

Textbooks also do not adequately treat the achievement testing needs or directives on bilingual pupils. One of the most important textbooks on the topic, *The Eighth Mental Measurements Yearbook* (Buros, 1978), failed to review the available tests in other languages which purport to have a valid role in bilingual achievement testing in the United States. Often, serious flaws in such instruments place bilingual children at risk in terms of tracking and misdiagnosis (Figueroa, 1989).

Psychometric Properties and Bias

The psychometric studies on achievement tests with bilingual samples, in general, support the assertions that these tests have good psychometric properties (Knudson, 1993; Mishra, 1981b; Powers & Jones, 1984). However, these studies ignore any variation of English-language proficiency in the samples used.

Just as in the literature on intelligence, however, achievement tests are open to criticism with respect to predictive validity (Alderman, 1982; Duran, 1983; Goldman & Hewitt, 1975; Maspons & Llabre, 1985; Nielson & Fernandez, 1981; Powers, Escamilla, & Houssler, 1986; Whitworth & Barrientos, 1990). For example, in a comprehensive review of tests used to predict college aptitude, Duran (1983) found compelling evidence that for Hispanics, there is evidence of bias. Similar conclusions are reached for Asian American students (Asian American Task Force on University Admissions, 1985; Lucero, 1985; Vernon, 1982), particularly because of the lower verbal scores these students get on SAT-like tests.

As Ulibarri (1985) noted, the issue of bias for bilinguals must extend beyond purely psychometric considerations. "Linguistic contamination" is a further issue in achievement tests if the wording of the tests systematically favors monolingual English speakers independent of the achievement content being measured. An additional set of concerns deal with the qualitative differences in the educational experiences of some circumstantial bilingual groups in the United States. For many, as the National Academy of Sciences has suggested, the curriculum and its application may be devoid of evidence of validity (Heller, Holtzman, & Messick, 1982). Contemporary data on achievement testing and language background, using the SOMPA Hispanic sample of 15- to 21-year-olds tested in 1982 (Figueroa, 1987), also indicate that achievement tests, unlike grades, are hypersensitive to language background. They demonstrate differential levels of association with grades according to language background. Tables 4.3 and 4.4 present these data.

Finally, if one assumes that the oldest solution to measuring bilingual intelligence—nonverbal tests of intelligence—has some degree of construct validity with bilingual pupils, a serious anomalie emerges when such scores are found to have a near-zero correlation with achievement test scores for English-speaking children from Spanish-speaking homes (Figueroa, 1990). If other studies with groups that differ either in home language background or English-language proficiency corroborate these results, achievement tests may seriously be called into question for packaging in the scores something other than the homogeneous or comparable

TABLE 4.3
Mean Achievement Scores and GPA's by Language Background

| | GPA's | | | | | Scores | |
	Acad.	Pract. Arts	Creat.	Athle.	Total	Reading	Math
English (N = ±154)	2.08	2.41	2.47	2.68	2.29	101.5	99.7
Eng/Span (N − ±102)	2.01	2.39	2.49	2.57	2.20	96.8	96.5
Spanish (N = ±102)	2.10	2.47	2.55	2.71	2.30	92.7	94.9

TABLE 4.4
Correlations between Reading and Math Achievement Scores and GPA's by Language Background

| | | GPA's | | | | |
		Acad.	Pract. Arts	Creat.	Athle.	Total
Reading	Eng	.46	.48	.34	.42	.48
	E/S	.29	.34	.23	.29	.36
	Span	.31	.37	.15	.26	.35
Math	Eng	.53	.52	.42	.50	.54
	E/S	.49	.39	.32	.45	.53
	Span	.59	.52	.28	.39	.59

curriculum assumed by tests (Cleary, Humphreys, Kendrick, & Wesman, 1975).

Bilingual Achievement Testing

Achievement tests in other languages are available and with Hispanic children the Spanish versions of many tests (Figueroa, Delgado, & Ruiz, 1984) are widely used in educational settings. Most of these have been standardized and normed abroad and assume that the monolingual educational and sociocultural experiences in Mexico, Latin America, or Spain are comparable to those in the United States. Some, like the *Brigance* (Brigance, 1983), rest on word counts or curricula that are so outdated that, were they meant for English speakers, they would not be accepted.

The vast majority of U.S.-developed achievement tests for some U.S. bilingual groups, according to reviews conducted in 1978 (Pletcher, Locks, Reynolds, & Sisson, 1978) on tests for Chinese, French, Italian, Navajo, Portuguese, Spanish, and Tagalog speakers, are inadequate because of unavailable psychometric data, or because the norming samples are too regional.

In many, many cases, U.S. achievement tests are locally, if not extemporaneously, translated. Among these, the *Wide Range Achievement Test* appears to be a favorite because of its few items, ease of administration, and popularity. As already noted, translations of this sort produce unknown tests.

As with the measurement of intelligence in ethnic and societal languages, "bilingual" achievement testing is exceedingly problematic and anomolous (Ortiz-Franco, 1990). Valid tests in the ethnic language are relevant for children in the United States if the educational experiences of the norming samples are congruent with curricula in the United States. Their most appropriate use would be for pupils in bilingual education programs. But even in these special circumstances, the tests should reflect the unique academic learning and classroom information processing of children in classes where two language systems are appropriately used. Such tests would have to meet a unique set of criteria. These are seldom adequately explicated in the research literature (e.g., Fletcher, 1989).

Using the most popular model for bilingual academic learning (Cummins, 1984b), for example, these criteria might include norms in the ethnic and the societal language that would covary directly with Cognitive Academic Language Proficiency (CALP) in the ethnic language and with the development of a common underlying academic proficiency that would be accessible in both languages only after reaching a critical stage in bilingual language proficiency. Technically, these type of controls may be possible (Baker, 1988).

The bilingual learner and the manner in which he or she "achieves" is currently not addressed in tests that are available in ethnic and societal languages. A circumstantial bilingual learner's achievement may not equal the sum of achievement test scores in ethnic language norms and societal language norms. The process of academic learning for these students is far more complicated than for a monolingual learner. Even over short periods of time, educational "change" for them is more complex and dynamic (as when children commute between countries or are immersed in environments with fluctuating proportions of ethnic and societal languages).

The National Assessment of Educational Progress

The well-known rates of underachievement of some bilingual groups is inadequately being investigated at the national level. The National Assessment of Educational Progress (NAEP), now housed at Educational Testing Service, has yet to adequately explore the impact of bilingualism on the measurement of academic achievement. In fact, the NAEP's treatment of circumstantial bilingual children can be characterized as an exercise in error. The relatively inaccessible reports on bilingual children are amateurish, naive, and lacking much evidence of scholarship on the topic of bilingualism. The following are the specific reasons for this strong indictment.

The NAEP has never even been able to correctly identify the ethnicity of Hispanic, Asian, and American Indian children. As Rivera (1986) noted, pre-1972, the available categories were: White, Black, and Other. In 1973, Mexican-American and Puerto Rican students were identified by Spanish surname. In 1980, "visual identification" was the primary way by which children were categorized. However, it was later found that when this method was checked against a self-identification procedure, large discrepancies appeared. Agreement rates ranged from a low of 7% for American-Indian pupils to a high of 85.9% for Asian-American students (the Hispanic range was 45.8% to 74.5%). Since 1989, self-identification procedures have been used with Hispanic pupils (Asian and American-Indian students generate samples that are too small for separate reporting, except in specific, small substudies). However, even this method of self-identification is suspect. Younger children are not as accurate in self-identification procedures and, as Rivera and Pennock-Roman (1987) reported, this procedure may entail hidden error "possibly because of lower reading proficiency, less experience with multiple choice forms, . . . [and] less familiarity with terms such as Hispanic" (p. 36). In fact, in a study on child–parent agreement rates on a background questionnaire administered to a circumstantial bilingual subsample, Baratz-Snowden, Pollack, and Rock (1988) cast serious doubt on the overall validity of the self-reporting procedures of the NAEP when these are used with bilingual groups. On questions dealing with home language usage and English language competence, parent–child agreement rates are between 60% and 76%, a range that these NAEP researchers consider "high" (p. 32) but that by any standard of reliability would be considered unacceptable.

The NAEP reports are also suspect because of the manner in which students from linguistically different backgrounds are chosen. In spite of advancements in sampling procedures, random selection seems to be precluded in the manner that pupils from Hispanic, Asian, and American Indian backgrounds are ultimately chosen. Local school personnel determine which of these pupils should be excluded because of limited English proficiency and which should be included because they are judged competent in English. The decision to exclude pupils who are judged limited-English-proficient not only disenfranchises these pupils from the "national report card," it also precludes investigating the limits of English-only testing and the longitudinal merits of primary language instruction. This decision, in effect, can be viewed as part of a political tradition in the education of bilingual populations.

By far the most disappointing activity of the NAEP is the one major study that could have made a difference because it specifically addressed *The Educational Progress of Circumstantial Bilingual Children: Findings From the 1985-86 Special study*, (Baratz-Snowden, Rock, Pollack, & Wilder, 1988). This study was conducted on a national sample of third, seventh, and eleventh graders from Mexican-American (N = 3, 944), Puerto Rican (N = 1, 742), Cuban (N = 1, 226), Other Hispanic (N = 1, 993), Asian American (N = 1, 661), and American-Indian (N = 426) students. The independent variables included: (a) ethnicity; (b) self-reports on non-English-language use and competence, home-educational supports, competence in English-language skills, attitudes about school, locus of control, behaviors at school; and, (c) teacher/school characteristics. The dependent variables were the scores achieved in NAEP tests of reading and math and the grades that the students self-reported.

Anyone reading this study should first turn to the "limitations" (p. 40) section where the researchers acknowledge the following: The sample is not random because school personnel chose the subjects; self-reported information constitute much of the data investigated; it is assumed that reading ability does not "contaminate" the results; there is evidence that on some parent-background information, the children were poor reporters; there was no direct measurement of the subjects' language proficiency; and "This report does not address issues relating to the relationship between native language and English proficiency of students whose first language is not English" (p. 40). The researchers could also have added that no attempt was made to control for SES or to demonstrate any sort of knowledge or scholarship on the extensive literature on bilingualism and testing and bilingualism and learning.

Three broad sets of outcomes are reported by this study. First, that Asian children have higher academic achievement grades and scores (and, interestingly, that these and self-perceived English competence are positively correlated with ethnic language usage in the home). Second, that:

> There is little or no consistent relationship between any of the achievement outcomes and frequency of use of a non-English language in the home. Competency in English, however, shows positive relationships with academic grades and also with important mediating variables such as locus of control. . . . It would appear that whether or not one comes from a home where a second language is spoken is not the critical issue, but rather the central question is whether or not one is competent in English. (Baratz-Snowden, et al., 1988, p. iii)

And third, that the more academic the courses taken in school, the higher the measured and reported achievement.

The second finding, for the purposes of this chapter, is the most critical. Contrary to what the NAEP researchers maintain, however, the central question is not that *self-reported* English competence rather than degree of exposure to the ethnic language is most critically linked to achievement. The central questions are why the researchers failed to reconcile the contrary findings in their modest literature review, why in another place in the report they mention that "the amount of native language use in the home was negatively related to English competency" (p. 144), and why on the self-reported English competency data they fail to realize the discordant nature of a subsequent, major caveat: "Thus, the validity of the present interpretation as well as the succeeding interpretations must assume that the scale points [on ratings from "very well" to "not at all"] are being interpreted in the same way by all ethnic groups, an assumption for which we have no data, and for which there is not widespread support in the literature" (Baratz-Snowden, 1988, p. 144).

Until the National Assessment of Educational Progress and new efforts at creating national assessment systems, such as The New Standards Project (Resnick & Resnick, 1992), demonstrate more competence in the matter of measuring circumstantial bilingual pupils' academic achievement and address the issue of bilingualism in schooling and achievement testing, any policy considerations attached to empirical findings on circumstantial bilingual pupils are open to accusations of ignorance and nativism. What is known, in a black-box experiment sort of way and independent of the NAEP, is that if children are left in academic bilingual programs for prolonged periods of time, achievement tests in English show enhanced levels of achievement (Ramirez, Wolfson, Talmadge, & Merino, 1986; Willig, 1985).

PERSONALITY TESTING

Personality tests are used in many contexts: in employment agencies and businesses, in schools, and in mental health institutions. Their primary purpose is to identify or diagnose emotional or character pathology. A list of the 10 most widely used tests in the United States (Lubin, Larsen, & Matarazzo, 1984) includes 7 "personality" tests: the Minnesota Multiphasic Personality Inventory (MMPI), the Visual Motor Gestalt Test (Bender-Gestalt), the Rorschach, the Thematic Apperception Test (TAT), Sentence Completion tests, the House-Tree-Person Test, and the Draw-a-Person Test. Generally, these illustrate two broad types of such tests: the survey-like instruments (MMPI), wherein the test taker responds to written test items; and the projective tests (e.g., TAT, Rorschach, Sentence Completion), wherein a client is instructed to respond to ambiguous stimuli either orally or in writing. Another popular category of such tests is the rating scale wherein an informant evaluates another person. The greatest use of personality tests occurs in mental health settings in which their use is integrally related to therapy.

Bilingualism, as an independent variable, is seldom taken into account in textbooks on personality assessment and personality tests (Barnett & Zucker, 1990; Kestenbaum & Williams, 1988, Vol. I, Vol. II; Knoff, 1986; Spielberger & Butcher, 1985, 1987, 1988; Woody, 1980).

There are, however, quite a few empirical studies that touch on bilingualism and personality testing that, although miniscule in comparison with the corpus of published, clinical investigations, raise many important issues and also suggest an emerging realization about the importance of language in personality assessment. As Church (1987) noted:

> Reports of research in other cultures highlight the important role of language in personality research and description. This role has received little attention in American psychology, where the English language is so dominant. In multilingual cultures, however, the optimal language of conceptualization, data collection, and personality description is a central concern. With the increasing number of multilinguals in the United States, this issue will likely increase in importance for American psychology as well. (p. 273)

The "optimal language" in the personality assessment of bilinguals may well turn out to be the optimal languages. As an analog to intellectual assessment, this could also mean a formula comprising a score from a personality test in the ethnic language, plus a score from an equivalent personality test in the societal language plus moderator variables such as proficiencies in: L1, L2, the first culture, and the second culture. Some of the issues raised in the small but intriguing literature on personality testing and bilingualism would tend to support this. These issues fall into two broad categories: comprehension and expression.

Comprehension

When a bilingual patient is being given a personality test, several linguistic assumptions apply. At a surface level, it is assumed that when a test requires that the test items be read and then answered (as with the MMPI), the test taker has reading skills commensurate with those of the monolingual standardization group. As the reviewed literature on the reading achievement of bilinguals showed, this assumption may be flawed. At a deeper level, it is assumed that for the bilingual patient, the English meanings and nuances are similar to those of a monolingual English speaker. Regrettably, studies on the connotative and denotative dimensions of words (Brizuela, 1975; Collado-Herrell, 1976; Diaz-Guerrero, 1988; Guttfreund, 1990; Rastogi & Singh, 1976) and even tachistoscopic studies of taboo words in the ethnic and societal languages (Gonzalez-Reigoza, 1976) fail to support this assumption. Also, more compelling dimensions of meaning can intervene. In the classic, longitudinal study on "Personality Development in Two Cultures," Holtzman, Diaz-Guerrero, and Swartz (1975) demonstrated that on something as straightforward as the three simple locus-of-control questions, Mexican middle-class respondents opted for the more "meaningful" cultural canon of not disagreeing with the tester at the expense of scoring "fatalistic" or with an "external locus of control" (a finding that is apparently unknown to NAEP researchers [Baratz-Snowden, Rock, Pollack, & Wilder, 1988], although they used the same three locus-of-control questions).

Tangential, though important, in considerations about comprehension, is the tendency among personality testers to use translations and interpreters in this type of diagnostic assessment. Cross-cultural testers and researchers are particularly impressed by translating techniques (back-translating, "decentering") (Brislin, Lonner, & Thorndike, 1973) that may yield equivalence in meaning but not necessarily in psychometric difficulty. Psychiatrists and clinical psychologists in the United States seem also content to use interpreters. The assumption in both procedures, of course, is that a translation without restandardization or renorming and the use of an interpreter in testing both "work" in a manner wholly equivalent to the monolingual test and tester with the monolingual client. These assumptions are presently gratuitous.

Expression

In an interesting study that gets cited in virtually every publication that focuses on bilingualism and personality testing, Ervin (1964a) found that English–French bilingual respondents to the TAT produced personality profiles that varied according to the language in which the test was answered. Although subsequent replications of Ervin's heuristic study (Ervin, 1964b; Faniband, 1976) failed to support his findings, other, similar results on various bilingual groups have been reported, all in varying degrees asserting that the assessment-based expression of personality may be language dependent. Chinese–English bilinguals when tested in the societal language exaggerated their affiliations to Chinese values (Bond & Yang, 1982; Yang & Bond, 1980). Affective responses are often richer and more revealing in the ethnic language (Gonzalez, 1978; Gonzalez & Bautista, 1986; Guttfreund, 1990; Ruiz, 1975). Ratings of bilingual patients on a psychiatric rating scale have often shown more psychopathology in the societal language than in the ethnic language (Grand, Marcos, Alpert, Urcuyo, Kesselman, 1973; Freedman, & Barroso, 1977; Kesselman, & Alpert, 1973; Westermeyer, 1987), although ironically, the opposite has also been reported (Price & Cuellar, 1981; Del Castillo, 1970). Finally, the perception of mental illness may have a language-dependent component (Edgerton & Karno, 1971).

One researcher in this field, more than 20 years ago, suggested that some of the findings on bilingual personality studies may be attributable to separate storage systems (Marcos & Alpert, 1976). Regrettably, it would appear that such a bilingual information processing stance has received little, if any, attention. In part, this may be due to the influence of cross-cultural studies of personality. Until recently (Clark, 1987) the legacy from this field does not include concerns with bilinguals' expression of personality. Instead, it has included a simplistic tradition of translating tests (Brislin, 1986); using U.S. norms; assuming equivalence in existence, saliency, and manifestation of personality constructs (e.g., "person," "conformity," "fatalism"); ignoring, until recently, what U.S.-developed tests may not be capable of measuring, that is, cultural or *emic* (Brislin, 1983; Jones & Thorne, 1987; Laosa, Swartz, & Diaz-Guerrero, 1974) personality factors; using research designs that define "culture" in terms of the sample used; and ignoring intraculture linguistic factors (e.g., Malgady, Constantino, & Rogler, 1984; Montgomery & Orozco, 1985). For circumstantial bilingual populations in the United States, even the salutary and laudable accomplishments of cross-cultural psychology in the development of culturally appropriate personality tests (e.g., the Japanese MMPI, the Holtzman Inkblot Technique developed for Mexican children) may find limited applications. Biculturalism and bilingualism, and their ideographic expressions in people in the United States present a different set of construct and measurement considerations. Certainly, the "bilingual" and "bicultural" development of the Tell-me-a-story (TEMAS) test (Costantino, Malgady, Casullo, & Castillo, 1991; Malgady, Costantino, & Rogler, 1984) underscores this.

VOCATIONAL TESTING

Generally, there are two broad uses for this type of test: job placement and career planning. In the former, many tests can be used (intelligence, academic achievement, personality), depending on the congruence between the nature of job and the ability being measured. In the latter, vocational interest tests (such as the Strong Interest Inventory, Strong Vocational Interest Blank–Strong-Campbell Interest Inventory, the Vocational Preference Inventory, the Kuder General Interest Survey, etc.) are used in K–12 schools, colleges, and job placement agencies to determine the most "appropriate" career in terms of a tester's configuration of interests. These tests, in effect, set up profiles of interests of individuals in various careers. A test taker is advised as to her or his most "appropriate" career choice on the basis of congruence with the interest structures of various job holders in the United States.

The pre-eminent standard for the use of job-placement tests with linguistic minorities is:

Standard 13.5. In employment, licensing and certification testing, the English language proficiency level of the test should not exceed that appropriate to the relevant occupation or profession. (American Educational Research Association et al., 1985, p. 75)

However, as with other areas of testing, bilingualism, as an independent variable, does not appear in the professional literature on job placement tests and testing (e.g., Gottfredson, 1986). Studies on employment-related decisions for linguistic minorities or bilinguals based on such tests do not exist. The question of test fairness in job selection and promotion for linguistic minorities has yet to be adequately addressed. Some evidence does exist, however, suggesting that the use of some psychological tests for job screening with Hispanics may engender considerable risks for both test giver and test taker (Campos, 1989).

The literature on vocational interest tests does reflect a concern for their application cross-culturally and with national ethnic minorities (Fouad & Bracken, 1986; Fouad, Cudeck & Hansen, 1984; Fouad & Hansen, 1987; Hansen, 1987; Haviland & Hansen, 1987). But, bilingualism, as an independent issue, seldom exists in these published studies. However, this literature does focus on techniques borrowed from cross-cultural psychology on how to translate vocational interest tests to produce seemingly semantically equivalent versions (with no concern for psychometric equivalence). There is also a strong emphasis on demonstrating construct equivalence across international and national (ethnic) groups (Hansen, 1987). However, there are critical gaps and limitations in these endeavors (Lauver & Jones, 1991). Construct concurrence is not convincingly demonstrated and, more importantly, empirical studies showing "evidence for the validity of the test as a determinant of major factors of job performance" (American Educational Research Association et al., 1985, p. 1), or satisfaction across diverse national, cultural, and linguistic groups have yet to be done.

The literature is also flawed in that it fails to substantiate two critical assumptions: that work and employment are organized and stratified in some universal way and that the relationship between clusters of interests and jobs manifests itself in a fairly universal configuration for entire nations and cultures (not just university students). With respect to claims about bilingually equivalent test versions, the published studies suffer from considerable methodological limitations. "Culture" (e.g., Hispanic) is defined by the group studied. "Bilingualism" is never operationally defined. The samples are selected without much concern for representativeness or randomness. Socioeconomic status is seldom controlled for.

The optimism expressed by researchers in this field about the cross-national and cross-ethnic use of translated versions of these instruments, and the validity of U.S. norms for such populations is unwarranted (e.g., Candell & Hulin, 1986; Levin, 1991) and in many instances unsupported by the statistics reported (e.g., Fouad & Hansen, 1987).

CHAPTER 5

Diagnostic Testing

DIAGNOSTIC TESTING

Special Education Testing

In no other context are intelligence tests as widely used nor as critical in determining the course of individual lives than in special education. This is particularly true for those handicapping conditions that are invisible such as mild mental retardation, learning disabilities, and behavioral problems. For these "handicapping conditions," IQ tests often play the pivotal role in diagnosis and educational placement (Berk, Bridges, & Shi, 1981; Knoff, 1983; Mehan, Hartweck, & Meihls, 1986). With bilingual pupils, the results of this quasimedical use of intelligence tests are exceedingly harmful.

Data collected by the United States Office for Civil Rights (1978) indicated that schools in various states tended to be overrepresented with Hispanic children in classes for the mentally retarded, underrepresented in classes for the learning disabled, and very underrepresented in gifted classes. Almost the opposite type of representation rates occurred with Anglo children in most states. Figure 5.1 shows this for states where the Hispanic representation was 10% or more.

These phenomena have a long history in the United States. It is not unique to Hispanic children. As early as 1916, the Cleveland School Board of Education heard:

At the present time such cases are often handled in a most unsatisfactory manner. The non-English-speaking child cannot keep up with his companions

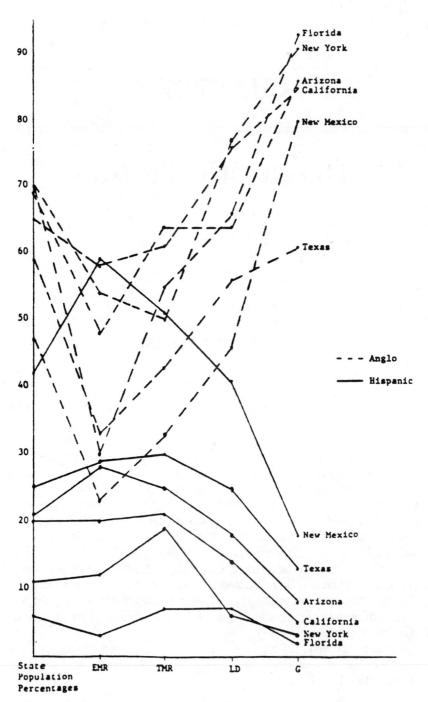

Figure 5.1. Hispanic and Anglo representation in four special education programs (Educable Mentally Retarded, Trainable Mentally Retarded, Learning Disabilities, Gifted) in six states (Brown, Rosen, and Hill, 1980, p. 62, Reprinted by permission).

in the regular grades. For this reason he is sent to a special class. . . . This is not because the backward class is the right place for him, but rather because it furnishes an easy means of disposing of a pupil, who, through no fault of his own, is an unsatisfactory member of a regular grade. (Miller, 1916, p. 74)

In recent times, the unique manifestation of special education misplacement has been widely reported (Chandler & Plakos, 1969; Palomares & Johnson, 1966). How it applies to Hispanics and other minority children has been investigated by Professor Jane R. Mercer. In a series of studies documenting the referral, testing, and placement outcomes that befall Mexican-American and Hispanic children (whose sociocultural characteristics are ignored), she has shown that school personnel and tests fail in that they misplace and misdiagnose large numbers of Hispanic students in special education classes.

In one investigation (Mercer, 1973, p. 113) she showed that though minority children in the Riverside (California) School District were referred for pupil personnel services and for testing in proportions that were equal to their numbers in the school population, they were overrepresented in the number that failed IQ tests, in recommendations for special class placement and in the numbers that actually did get placed in classes for the educable mentally retarded. This was particularly true for Mexican-American children. Of the 66 Chicano children who were tested, 48% were eventually diagnosed as mentally retarded. Of the 717 Anglo children who were tested, only 3% were so diagnosed.

In another study, Mercer (1971) tested 1, 298 children on the WISC and found that an IQ score below 80 was "a necessary but not sufficient" condition for being placed in an EMR class since there were many children among those whom she tested that were "eligible" but not actually placed (however, 15.7% of the Chicano children were eligible vs. only 1.2% of the Anglo children).

Further analysis of the data from this study failed to yield significant relationships between eligibles and labeled in terms of attitudes about self, school, or occupational aspirations. There were negligible differences in SES levels and in the standardized achievement test scores of the two groups. But, there were significant differences in the teacher comments found in the children's school folders. Mercer concluded that a minority child, in order to be labeled, must have the following profile: low IQ, low academic competence, poor adjustment, *low competence in English* [our emphasis], and few friends in order to be perceived as having low mental capacity, and to be referred for IQ testing and possible placement in special education.

An early, influential investigation relative to minority misdiagnosis was in the Riverside study (Mercer, 1973). There were two parts to this study:

1. A comprehensive survey of all the community organizations in Riverside that had anything to do with the mentally retarded, and
2. An epidemiological study on a representative sample of the Riverside population on the incidence of mental retardation.

The survey of community organizations indicated the following:

1. Organizations had varying standards for defining and diagnosing mental retardation.
2. Schools did the greatest amount of labeling, principally using IQ test results, and were the institutions responsible for the largest number of labeled persons in the 5–20 age range.
3. Mexican Americans were more vulnerable, regardless of SES, to being labeled mentally retarded.

The epidemiological study compared the effects of various IQ cutoff levels on the proportions of minority people labeled mentally retarded. It examined the effects of utilizing a preliminary form of an adaptive behavior scale (see Heber, 1961, for the original definition of adaptive behavior) in conjunction with IQ on these population proportions. Also, it examined the linkage between sociocultural variables and ethnic groups' mean IQs. The study led to a set of conclusions that have had considerable impact on special education testing.

1. "The cut-off level for subnormality should be the lowest 3 percent (IQ below 70)" (Mercer, 1972, p. 46).

This not only reflects the standards of a sound medical epidemiology, it also lowers representation of Anglos in the mentally retarded range to 4.4/1000, of African Americans to 4.1/1000, and of Mexican Americans to 60/1000 (Mercer, 1973). For Mexican Americans this is still very high, yet better than using a 9% cutoff where mental retardation "occurs" at the following rates: 238.4/1000 for Mexican Americans, 53.1/1000 for African Americans, and 9.6/1000 for Anglos.

2. "Both IQ and adaptive behavior must be used together to define mental retardation" (Mercer, 1972, p. 47).

This reflects professional guidelines (Herber, 1961) and yields a better typology of mental retardation. It also distinguishes between children who have few learning problems and those who have considerable learning problems (or between the quasi-retarded and clinically retarded). Likewise, adaptive behavior, when used with IQ, provides for a greater chance of not being penalized by a label. "Fully . . . 60 percent of the Chicanos with IQs below 70 passed the behavior test" (Mercer, 1972, p. 47).

3. "IQ tests that are now in use are culture-specific and therefore biased" (Mercer, 1972, p. 47).

This is based on a critical finding in her research: A child's particular sociocultural characteristics are significantly correlated with his IQ score. If a Chicano child, for example, lives in a house where there are less than 1.4 persons per room, where the mother expects the child to go on to college, where the head of the household has completed at least nine years of education, where the family speaks English, and where the family owns rather than rents its housing (Mercer, 1972, p. 47), he or she would generally be indistinguishable from Anglo children on the WISC full-scale IQ. According to the results of one study, involving 590 Mexican American children (6–14 years), Chicano youngsters with all five of the sociocultural characteristics listed above achieved a full-scale IQ of 104.5 (Mercer, 1972, p. 95). Those with fewer of the above characteristics received proportionally lower IQs.

Mercer's work has not been free of criticism (Gordon, 1977; Jensen, 1973). For Hispanic children, however, her work has been unparalleled in documenting how the school-based diagnostic process presents two alternatives. Either Hispanic children are less intelligent and hence should be overrepresented in classes for the mentally retarded, or the process, particularly the testing, fails with Hispanic children.

Disparities in the special education representation of Hispanic children continue to challenge special education throughout the United States (U.S. Commission on Civil Rights, 1974; Staff, n.d.; Tucker, 1980). The entire question as to what constitutes a disparity has also evolved into a full-blown debate. One can, for example, look only within the total number of handicapped, ethnic children to see if the proportions of children in handicapping conditions are similar across ethnic groups. Using this method, for example, the U.S. Comptroller General (1981) can assert:

The proportions of Hispanic special education students in specific programs are similar to those of the white special education students. When compared with white children, Hispanic children appear slightly underrepresented in the educable mentally retarded and speech impaired program. (p. 63)

Similarly, looking at the proportion of Hispanic students in all special education categories across the United States, the Comptroller General (1981) can document that though white children comprise 75% of the entire student population, they make up only 71% of the special education population; Hispanic students who made up 7% of the United States student population in 1981 only accounted for 6% of the special education population (p. 32). The problem of *criteria* for defining over-and underrepresentation has become a major issue. Disparate results are appearing more and more and will undoubtedly continue to confound the topic so long as an aggregation of data is carried out without concern for intervening variables and so long as meaningful, straightforward comparisons are made. It is this text's contention that overrepresentation and underrepresentation vary by Hispanic concentration, state, rural-urban setting, availability of bilingual instructional settings, and local policies. Large aggregations of data will bury meaningful information. In some locations, for example, Mexican-American children, as a matter of policy, are not placed in EMR programs (Twomey, Gallegos, Anderson, Williamson, & Williamson, 1980). In others, they are overplaced in such programs.

One of the more sophisticated studies on this matter has been carried out under the auspices of the National Academy of Sciences by Finn (1982). Using the 1978 OCR *Elementary and Secondary Civil Rights Survey* of 6, 040 school districts in the United States (54, 082 schools), Finn applied a series of statistical procedures that permitted him to examine the questions of over- and underrepresentation of minority pupils in special education by various indices of disproportion (long-linear analyses, Q-statistics and straight percentages across and within geographical location, school district size, Hispanic student representation, and, in the case of Hispanics, availability of bilingual options). His findings are among the most instructive on the topic.

According to Finn (1982), across the United States, minority children tend to overpopulate mentally retarded classes (EMR and TMR), as well as classes for the seriously emotionally disturbed (SED). Minority students are at parity in specific learning disabilities classes and slightly underrepresented in speech impaired (SI) classes. Smoothed estimations of log-linear values of disproportions indicate that the most overrepresented states in EMR minority enrollments, in descending order, are: Alaska, Florida, Georgia, South Carolina, Alabama, North Carolina, Delaware, Louisiana, Maryland, Texas, Mississippi, Virginia, New Mexico, Rhode Island, Tennessee, and Utah. The most underrepresented (very significantly so) are West Virginia and Iowa. On the whole, however, Finn concludes that "while the magnitude of the difference varies from state to state, as does the degree of consistency among districts within states, EMR disproportion by race or ethnicity is a nationwide phenomena" (p. 338).

Also, the larger the EMR program in each district, state, or geographical area of the United States, the higher the minority overrepresentation in EMR classes. The OCR data, unfortunately, do not allow for determining which caused which. Large districts with large percentages of minority enrollment tend not to have EMR disproportions. Small districts with large minority enrollments, on the other hand, do have increasingly larger disproportions. The more economically depressed the district, the more likely that disproportions will occur. Districts with 1, 000 to 30, 000 students showed a positive, significant correlation between minority student suspensions and disproportions in EMR placements.

For Hispanic children the data are particularly instructive. In districts where they represent 1% or more of the student population (31 states), their mean EMR representation is greater than that for Anglos in 26 states. In many such areas, the greater the Hispanic district representation, the greater the EMR overrepresentation. In the 765 districts with EMR programs and with 5% or more Hispanic student representation, there are unpredictable disproportions in over- and underrepresentation. However, in large districts with large black enrollments, the Hispanic EMR representation declines proportionally, to the point where when 75% of the student district population is black, there is Anglo EMR overrepresentation compared to Hispanics.

In districts where there were small or nonexistent bilingual programs, the highest EMR Hispanic disproportions appeared. In SLD classes, Hispanics tend to be overrepresented in states with high Hispanic concentrations (not including California). Although Finn (1982) does not see the SLD classes an an emerging alternative to EMR misplacement, his data are not convincing (cf. Tucker, 1980).

> In summary, the apparently similar EMR placement rates for Hispanic and nonminority students disguise enormous variation in practices among school districts. There are a number of districts in which Hispanic students are assigned to EMR programs in large proportions. They are distinguished from other districts by having small enrollments that are often—but not always—largely Hispanic; furthermore, they have small black enrollments, small or nonexistent bilingual programs and high percentages of Hispanic students in SLD classes as well. Among large districts with the greatest pool of resources, low EMR and SLD disproportions occur where many Hispanic students participate in bilingual programs. (Finn, 1982, p. 374)

Amidst all these issues about special education overrepresentation, the role of *testers*, of those who assess and recommend placement in special education, has remained essentially unexamined by judicial and legal bodies. Tests have not been so ignored, particularly by the courts.

THE COURTS AND INTELLIGENCE TESTING IN SPECIAL EDUCATION

There is a considerable amount of law related to the assessment of culturally and linguistically different children. Much of this is directly attributable to the influence of the courts. Judicial intervention through testing cases has significantly influenced federal and state law as well as professional guidelines. However, all this progress has had a modest impact on professional practices (Kirp, Kuriloff, & Buss, 1975). Practitioners, the users of tests, have remained essentially untouched by judicial, legal, or administrative sanctions. Circumstantial bilingual children continue to be tested in the wrong language and with inappropriate tests and procedures. Misdiagnoses that lead to Hispanic overrepresentation in some categories of exceptionalities continue to occur on a national basis.

This section reviews some of the most relevant court cases concerning the testing of Hispanic children. Particular attention is given to *Diana v. California State Board of Education* (1970) for three reasons: (a) it covers most of the issues involved in Hispanic testing cases – cf. *Arreola v. Board of Education* (1968), *Guadalupe v. Tempe School District* (1978), *Ruiz v. State Board of Education* (1971), *Covarrubias v. San Diego Unified School District* (1972), *Jose P. v. Ambach*, 1979, *Lora v. Board of Education of the City of New York*; (b) it is a case that is still evolving and that may yet change the predominant overconcern of the courts with just *tests*; and (c) it is a case that typifies the resistance extant in many who are charged with the responsibility of executing court mandates, federal laws, and state regulations concerning Hispanic testing.

Brown v. Board of Education (1954). This is undoubtedly the most critical supreme court case dealing with education. Its influence extends to all facets of schooling. Testing is no different in this regard. The facts of the case are well known: Black children were systematically and deliberately segregated in southern schools in a separate (and as contended by the defendants) but equal educational system. The United States Supreme Court, however, held that the denial of access to peers foreclosed any possibility of equality. Even if children had comparable teachers, school buildings, and textbooks, segregation denied a critical educational component: peers.

Decades after *Brown v. Board of Education*, the unique meaning of *equal educational opportunity* espoused by the supreme court has yet to see full implementation. Yet *Brown's* influence, particularly during the 1960s and early 1970s, has been extensive. Many ardently hold to the belief that public education should be the same for all, and should in no way and under no circumstances treat any group or person substantially different. For Hispanic children, this position, unfortunately, has been used to argue against linguistically appropriate instructional and testing procedures.

In the area of psychoeducational assessment, *Brown v. Board of Education* has had a pronounced, albeit indirect, impact. Because of one of the earliest applications of *Brown*, tests came to be linked with bias, prejudice, segregation, and unfairness.

Hobson v. Hansen (1967). In 1954, 43% of the schools in Washington, DC were Black. One year after *Brown v. Board of Education*, 73% of the schools were racially mixed. But by 1967, the school district was segregated by academic tracks. What happened was that with desegregation the school district became aware of the educational underpreparation of African-American children. Superintendent Hansen and his staff decided to remediate the educational problems that black children were experiencing in integrated classes by: (a) testing children's aptitudes, and (b) placing children in different academic tracks based on their tested aptitudes. There were three tracks in the elementary grades and four in the secondary schools. Children were to receive special help and counseling so that movement from track to track would be possible. By 1967 and 1969 when *Hobson v. Hansen* came before courts, the Washington, DC school district had its lower tracks populated by African-American children and the upper tracks by Anglo children. Desegregation had, for all intents and purposes, failed.

The testing program, the courts found, was at the heart of the tracking segregation. School personnel assumed that the tests could measure children's maximum educational potential and that the tracking program with its auxiliary services could actualize it. The court found that the tests were completely inappropriate for predicting black children's academic potential. The tests relied on the use of standard English. Tests assumed that children had equal opportunities provided in their diverse (SES) environments. Tests were not as predictive for black children. The tests were normed on white, middle-class pupils. Further, the lack of auxiliary services that were to provide children with the opportunity to move across different tracks were, in fact, not operating. The net effect was a segregated school system and a perception that African-American children had low potential.

Many would argue (Jensen, 1980) that the court's "findings" in *Hobson v. Hansen* relative to test predictions are not supported by available data. It is doubtful, however, whether as many would argue that tests measure "potential" or that a rigid tracking system, regardless of racial impact, is justified. Superintendent Hansen's decision to use tests that were meant to measure "potential" through the use of standard English and through reliance on the norms established by a white, middle-class sample is a clear misguided use of "the same for all" principle of *Brown v. Board of Education* (1954).

Hobsen v. Hansen (1967) is an extremely important case for tests and testing. Though the problems associated with tests and their use with minorities were known before *Hobsen v. Hansen* (Cronbach, 1975), this court case is the first major, legal review on the topic. The association of testing with segregation, bias, denial of equal educational opportunity, and prejudice, all judicially begin in this case. It is also the first time that a court tried to arbitrate among opposing professional positions on such complex issues as test validity, the measurement of "potential," and culturally appropriate testing. The opinion that Judge J. Skelly Wright wrote in *Hobsen v. Hansen* (1967) echoes in every major testing case to the present.

Diana v. State Board of Education (1970). The parents of nine Mexican American children who had been placed in EMR classes in Monterey County in California sued the State Board of Education in 1969. They alleged that the EMR placement was incorrect and caused irreparable harm. Further, they complained that the manner by which the "EMR" diagnosis was arrived at was invalid. The children spoke predominantly Spanish, yet they were given an IQ test in English. The results of the IQ tests were anomalous in themselves since the nonverbal IQ's of the children were never under the "normal" criterion. The verbal IQ's of the children, however, produced ludicrous results (a 30 IQ for one child) because of the level of English language proficiency of the children. The IQ tests also failed to tap the cultural experiences of these pupils.

Diana never went to court. To a large extent this was because the nine plaintiffs typified what was happening throughout the state. EMR classes were heavily overrepresented with Hispanic pupils. The out-of-court settlement arrived at before Judge Robert Peckham of the U.S. Ninth Circuit Court in San Francisco established a unique set of precedents relative to testing LEP pupils: testing was to be done in the primary language and in English, nonverbal IQs could be used, all previously diagnosed EMR, Chicano children had to be retested paying particular attention to their nonverbal scores, an intelligence test appropriate for Mexican-American children had to be developed, and the representation of EMR Hispanic students in each school district throughout the state had to be monitored to make sure that there were no ethnic disparities of Chicano pupils in EMR classes.

This agreement proved to be problematic. Two issues were especially difficult. The California Rural Legal Assistance (CRLA) agreed that a test of intelligence appropriate for Mexican American children could not be developed (although Governor Reagan had already appropriated the funds for it). Also, many difficult issues came up surrounding the monitoring of EMR Hispanic representation in California public school districts. First, this monitoring agreement began to be perceived as a quota. Second, the manner in which a district was judged to be overrepresented became contentious. Though on June 18, 1973 the court set forth a stipulation wherein an "E Formula"[1] was proposed as the vehicle for determining when a district was overrepresented, on July 26, 1973, the California State Department of Education (SDE) in a letter from one of its consultants (Mr. Simmons) to counsel for the plaintiffs (Mr. Jourdane) recommended the use of two new formulas for determining which districts were out of compliance. One was for small districts, that is, those with less than 500 EMR pupils. It would have set the maximum Chicano EMR enrollment at ten pupils over the straight district percentage of Chicano students. The one for large districts would set the maximum at the percentage of Chicano district enrollment plus 2% of the Chicano EMR enrollment. Both formulas were directly keyed to the population of Chicano students in the districts. The greater the percentage, the greater the number allowed before constituting a significant variance. The SDE suggested this definition of "significant variance" so as not to penalize small districts that did not have "other (non-EMR) instructional resources." It is well known that for limited-English-proficient (LEP) children, EMR classes offer a seemingly desirable pupil–teacher ratio and a solution to the dilemma of instructing children whose primary language skills are not programmatically addressed (Finn, 1982).

At an August 30 meeting in 1973, the SDE rejected the plaintiffs' E Formula for determining "significant variance." The reason for the Department's objections to the plaintiffs' formula was the *Larry P.* case:

> Perhaps the most compelling consideration which made it clear to the Department that a flat significant variance figure would not work in this case was the intrusion of the *Larry P.* case and the complications posed by counsel's position in that case. (Rubin, 1973, p. 17)

The "complications" referred to *Larry P.* counsel's goal to obtain relief for his client in a manner similar to that required in the *Diana* Settlement and Stipulation. Such relief would require the removal of misplaced black children from EMR classes. If the EMR enrollments declined because of *Larry P.*, then the percentages of Chicano children in EMR classes would increase.

On May 24, 1974, Judge Peckham settled this dispute. In a Memo-

---

[1]

$$E = A + \sqrt{\frac{A(100 - A)}{N}}$$

where A represents the percentage of Spanish surnamed pupils in a district, N represents the total number of all pupils in the EMR classes of a district, and E represents the maximum percentage of Spanish surnamed pupils permitted in EMR classes.

randum and Order, he reiterated that the 1973 Stipulation's "E Formula" was to be used.

The 1973 Stipulation was important not only in terms of the "E Formula" and the district monitoring provision of the original *Diana* settlement, it was also relevant to the perception that many school officials had of *Diana* that is, that it set forth a *quota* of Hispanic EMR pupils. Sections 5, 6, and 7 of the 1973 Stipulation clearly set forth a process of reviewing districts overrepresented with Hispanic EMR pupils:

5. When a significant variance continues or occurs after the three-year period, the State Department will cause a thorough audit of the district's program to be conducted, including the reevaluation of pupils if necessary. The audit shall be by persons other than district employees and shall have a professional person representing the Chicano community as a member of the audit team.

6. In addition, in the event that significant disparities still exist or reoccur after the three-year period or if the disparity increases during any school year, the State Department may investigate by sending a monitor or review team to the district or such other investigative methods as it may deem appropriate.

7. In any year in which a significant variance appears in a school district which did not have such disparity when this stipulation was reached, the district will be contacted in accordance with Paragraphs 5 and 6 of this stipulation.

Later, in the 1974 Memorandum and Order, Judge Peckham again underscores the procedural (vs. quota) aspects of *Diana*:

In its present form, however, the STIPULATION does not require or provide for any orders of the court which would operate directly against individual school districts. At the direction of the Board of Education, designated districts will be instructed to develop a plan to eliminate overrepresentation of Chicanos in EMR classes, and will be required to make certain annual reports. Before any punitive or remedial sanctions will be imposed upon any district by the court, however, *the STIPULA-TION provides for a review hearing at which an opportunity can be given to the district in question to present any unique factors which might affect the appropriateness of the nature of such sanctions.* (pp. 3–4; emphasis added)

Judge Peckham was clearly sensitive to the meaning of chance variation and flexibility required in its regard. The implication is that in some instances of overrepresentation, there may not be any sanctions brought against a district. This would, in effect, foreclose the possibility that some child would not receive an appropriate educational placement because of the fortuitous possibility that a district was over the standard deviation ("E") guideline.

On June 7, 1974, the California State Superintendent of Schools, Dr. Wilson Riles (1974), echoed these provisions in a letter to overrepresented districts:

> The court order requires the development of a district plan for the next two years. If, at the end of the two-year period a significant variance continues or reoccurs, the State Department is required to cause an audit to be conducted. The audit is to review the conditions under which such overrepresentation is continuing. Following such efforts, the Court will review the progress of compliance with this order. At that time, the Court may order such further relief as it deems appropriate. (p. 2)

> This order does not require the precipitous removal of pupils from the educable mentally retarded program. Adjustments in enrollments must be planned so as to minimize any problems for individual pupils. In assessing enrollments among ethnic groups, consideration must be given to the overall effect of under or overrepresentation of each group upon the total. *The Court has indicated in its order that, if there is substantial basis for a percentage exceeding the Court's formula, a review hearing can be provided for each district to present any unique factors which might affect the appropriateness of the district's EMR enrollments.* (p. 3; emphasis added)

The "quota" issue, in effect, was a nonissue, a misperception of what *Diana* required relative to determining and correcting overrepresentation.

On February 4, 1977, the plaintiffs filed a motion to compel the SDE to update its data on the ethnic representation in EMR classes. Questions had arisen as to whether the SDE would present up-to-date information on the ethnic composition of EMR classes in 1978 when both sides were to return to Judge Peckham's court to review the progress in the case.

In 1978, the California State Advisory Commission for Special Education, at the request of Commissioner Figueroa, convinced the California State Board of Education to renegotiate the *Diana* settlement. Lawyers for *Diana* agreed. The California State Department of Education then set up a special committee of Hispanic consultants to review the *Diana* case and to propose new directions and new guidelines. The outcome of this committee's work was a document endorsing: (a) some form of monitoring school district practices relative to the testing of Hispanic children for special education considerations, (b) *a new emphasis on the competencies of the testers rather than just the properties of the test,* and (c) the use of specific and special procedures to be used with Hispanic children (e.g., measuring language proficiency).

Throughout 1979, negotiations between the SDE and *Diana's* lawyers (California Rural Legal Assistance) produced several drafts of the *Diana* Remedy Memorandum. The last of these provided for several major new directions. The emphasis was not on the elimination of tests such as the WISC, WISC-R, and Stanford Binet, but rather, the primary focus was on the *use* and *users* of these tests.

The tests were to be: (a) monitored in their ethnic impact, (b) used in the context of an extended child study, (c) accompanied by measures of linguistic proficiency, and (d) made culturally appropriate. The first and last of these provisions are notable.

During the 1979 negotiations, the SDE did not want to continue using the "E Formula" to identify overrepresented districts. This was due to a persistent view of such a formula as a quota system. More critically, however, the "E Formula" threatened to come up in the *Larry P.* case. It was mutually agreed to drop the "E Formula." Instead, the *Diana* Remedy Memorandum stipulated that annually the 30 school districts in California that had the greatest Chicano EMR overrepresentation above their Chicano school population percentage were to be audited. This index, it was felt, avoided a practice that supposedly occurred in some school districts (i.e., the denial of assessment and services to Hispanic children possibly eligible for EMR placements because the districts' "E" maximum had been reached).

The SDE also committed itself to funding the development of tests for measuring Hispanic children's intelligence. This was a major concession, particularly given the Hispanic school population (30%) in the state. It also, nominally at least, endorsed a more culturally pluralistic approach to testing. Also, unique to the *Diana* Remedy Memorandum was the refocus from the tests (exclusively) to the users of the tests. The California State Department of Education committed itself to supporting a special credentialing requirement for school-based assessment personnel who test Hispanic LEP children.

On November 29, 1979, the decision on the *Larry P.* case became public. Larry P. won. Since that time, the *Diana* Remedy Memorandum and the *Diana* case have remained in limbo.

It remains to be seen whether *Diana* will return to Judge Peckham's court. One area is particularly noteworthy in this regard, the requirement that districts, on an annual basis, report the representation of Hispanic EMR pupils using the "E Formula" to check for overrepresentation.

From 1973 to 1978, the California SDE reported district data on overrepresentation for 1974-74, 1976-77, 1977-78, and 1978-79. Figure 5.2

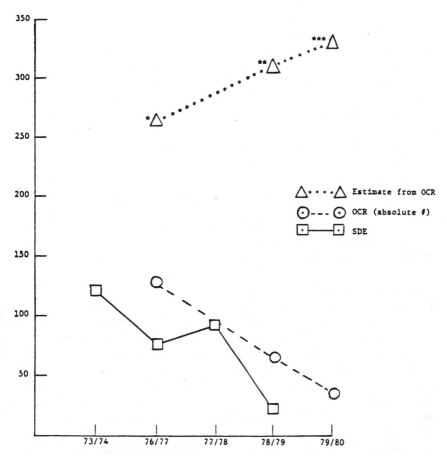

Figure 5.2.   Number of overrepresented school districts in California from three data
sources.
*Estimate taken from 127/493 × 1024
**Estimate taken from 66/217 × 1024
***Estimate taken from 37/114 × 1024

depicts the number of California school districts that, according to SDE,
were overrepresented in their EMR Hispanic disparities.

Paradoxically, the OCR data collected from all 1024 California school
districts in 1976–77 (U.S. Dept. of Health, Education, & Welfare/Office for
Civil Rights, 1978) as well as from a random sample (325) in 1978–79 (U.S.
Department of Education/Office for Civil Rights, 1980) and a nonrandom
sample (158) in 1979–80 (Braff, 1981) contradict the SDE data.

The middle, broken line in Figure 5.2 shows the *absolute* number of
districts with EMR Hispanic overrepresentation as reported by OCR. The
data are substantially different from that presented by SDE (continuous

line), but not dramatically so. The data is deceptive, however. In 1976–77, 531 California school districts either did not have EMR programs[2] or did not report their EMR data. The 127 districts, in effect, comprise 25.76% of the reporting districts. This percentage, 25.76, when applied to all California school districts, would total 264 overrepresented districts. The same procedure is applied to 1978–79 (66/217) and 1979–80 (37/114) OCR data and the results are depicted in the top profile in Figure 5.2. The assumption here is, of course, that the districts without EMR programs were not doing anything significantly different in their assessments to change Hispanic overrepresentation in any new, even if more mainstreamed, special education programs.

The question arises as to why there is such a discrepancy between what the California SDE publicly reported and what the U.S. Office of Civil Rights reports. At present, the *Diana* case appears to be inert. Neither the plaintiffs' lawyers nor the defendants' seem interested in determining its present status before the court.

***Larry P. v. Riles* (1979).** The *Larry P.* case went to Judge Robert Peckham's court in San Francisco in 1970. The facts of the case were very similar to those in *Diana*. A small group of black children who had been in EMR classes brought a class action suit against the San Francisco Unified School District and the State of California because they were misplaced in those classes on the basis of biased, invalid IQ tests. In 1972, Judge Peckham imposed a temporary injunction on California forbidding the use of IQ tests that did not properly account for black children's cultural background and experience. In 1979, he banned the use of IQ tests with black children referred for EMR placement in California. During the decade, the plaintiffs' case got stronger as other courts litigated similar cases and as federal laws and regulations emerged (especially Public Law 94–142).

The lengthy *Larry P.* decision (130 pages), handed down in 1979, outlines how IQ tests are historically linked to genetic notions of racial differences in intelligence. It also traces the history of EMR programs in California and how from their beginning they were not considered "remedial" or temporary. The judge underscores the California State Department of Education's nonresponsiveness to legislative and public concerns about the overrepresentation of black and Hispanic children in these classes during the 1960s.

For the judge, the SDE's desire to bring back IQ tests (banned in a 1974 injunction) seemed inconsistent. Though the tests had not been in use for three years, educators from San Francisco, Bakersfield, and Los Angeles testified that the quality of assessment had not changed during that time.

Inquiries about the 15 IQ-point difference between black and white

---

[2]California was mainstreaming EMR children into other special education programs.

children were not explained in terms of genetic differences by any witness for the plaintiff, and by only two witnesses (Robert Gordon and Lloyd Humphreys) for the defense. Though some witnesses explained the IQ differences in terms of environmental deprivation, the judge notes how data were presented showing how even when socioeconomic status was controlled, black children still scored 15 points lower. Invariably then, because neither environment nor genetics served to explain this difference, the question of bias became critical. David Wechsler, Wilson Riles, Asa Hilliard, and others led Judge Peckham to conclude that "there was general agreement by all sides on the inevitable effect of cultural differences on IQ scores" (p. 48). The question of bias, according to the decision, was hardly disputed by most of the witnesses (p. 49).

Given these basic facts, as Judge Peckham's opinion outlines, the plaintiffs' suit finds relevance in an extensive set of legal precedents going back to *Brown v. Board of Education* (1954), *Hobson v. Hansen* (1967), and *Lau v. Nichols* (1974), and even more extensive legislative background going back to the United States Constitution, Title VI, the Emergency School Act, the Rehabilitation Act of 1973, and P.L. 94-142. The entire matter becomes one of racial discrimination, denial of equal protection, and a denial of a meaningful education.

The case, according to Judge Peckham, would have been decided differently if the black–white EMR disparities reflected the true EMR incidence in the black population, or if the tests had been validated for EMR placements. But, he notes, these tests are acknowledged to be biased for blacks by experts like David Weschler. Also, other experts (i.e., Robert Thorndike, Lloyd Humphreys, and Jerome Sattler) are unwilling or unable "to reach conclusions about (the tests') validation for EMR placement" (p. 69). Further, these tests' predictive validity for black pupils was not clearly established (reference to Jerome Sattler, p. 71) and, in fact, there is evidence of differential validity (references to Jerome Sattler and Robert Thorndike, pp. 71–72). But even if these tests were predictive, for Judge Peckham this fact would not have prevailed. Judge Peckham points out that alternative procedures for diagnosis were available and had been in use for three years and had produced less of an overrepresentation of blacks in EMR classes.

Judge Peckham banned the use of IQ tests for assessing black children considered eligible for EMR classes. Instead of IQ tests, he proposed a remedy. That is, that prior to using an IQ test, the California State Board of Education had to get approval from the court. The approval would be granted if: (a) the tests were not racially or culturally discriminatory, (b) would not lead to overrepresentation of black pupils, and (c) were validated for EMR placement. Further, statistical data had to support these points, and public hearings had to be called concerning the state's intent to use these tests. The state also had to monitor district overrepresentation using a procedure which seems essentially identical to the *Diana* "E Formula," and require district plans to eliminate such imbalances. This,again, is essentially identical to the *Diana* Order and Stipulation. All black children in EMR classes had to be reevaluated without using unapproved IQ or ability tests. This reevaluation would include: (a) diagnostic tests designed to reveal specific learning needs and to prescribe specific pedagogical approaches, (b) adaptive behavior observation, and (c) developmental and health histories.

The California State Board of Education, in executive session, voted to accept the remedy. Dr. Riles did not. As a constitutionally elected official, he appealed the case. In March 1984, the Ninth Circuit Court of Appeals ruled on behalf of *Larry P.* By 1986, the adversarial climate between plaintiffs and defendants in this case had significantly changed. In September 1986, Armando Menocal, the principal attorney from Public Advocates Inc., the lawyers representing *Larry P.*, and the California Department of Education met in Judge Peckham's chambers to iron out: ongoing problems in the assessment of African-American children in California's public schools, the need for collecting data on the overrepresentation of African-American children in mentally retarded classes, and the possible wording for a directive to all school districts in California on the use of IQ tests for identifying, or placing, African-American pupils in special education. The heart of this agreement (*Larry P. v. Riles*, Order Modifying Judgment, 1986) entailed the following:

> The purpose of this notice is to clarify the proper use of I.Q. tests in the assessment of Black pupils for special education services.

> School districts are not to use intelligence tests in the assessment of Black pupils who have been referred for special education services.

> In lieu of I.Q. tests, districts should use alternative means of assessment to determine identification and placement. Such techniques should include, and would not be limited to, assessment of the pupil's personal history and development, adaptive behavior, classroom performance, academic achievement, and evaluative instruments designed to point out specific information relative to a pupil's abilities and inabilities in specific skill areas.

> The complete prohibition against using I.Q. tests for identifying or placing Black pupils in special education means that parents of Black pupils shall not be asked if they want to consent to the use of such tests. An I.Q. test may not be given to a Black pupil even with parental consent. Moreover, when a school district receives records containing test protocols from other agencies such as regional centers, out-of-state school districts, military facilities, or independent assessors, these records shall be forwarded to the parent. I.Q. scores contained in the records shall not become a part of the pupil's current school record.

There are no special education related purposes for which I.Q. tests shall be administered to Black pupils. The following reasons are *not* permissible justifications for the administration of an I.Q. test to a Black pupil:

1. As part of a comprehensive educational plan to which a parent has consent[ed];
2. To gain diagnostic information;
3. To develop goals and objectives;
4. To determine a special education pupil's educational needs; or
5. To develop a pupil's strengths and weaknesses as elicited by the I.Q. test.

Further, an I.Q. test has been determined to be invalid with regard to Black pupils in assessments for specific learning disabilities. Thus, an I.Q. test may not be utilized for specific learning disabilities assessment purposes.

The Department is aware that districts do not place or identify pupils on the basis of only I.Q. scores. However, the prohibition on I.Q. tests goes further and prohibits *any* use of an I.Q. test as part of an assessment which could lead to special education placement or services, even if the test is only part of a comprehensive assessment plan.

The prohibition on I.Q. testing applies even though pupils are no longer placed in special day classes designated as 'E.M.R.'. (pp. 4-5)

This new 1986 Order met with opposition from the California Association of School Psychologists (CASP):

It is the position of the California Association of School Psychologists that individually administered tests of cognitive ability and intelligence, when administered and interpreted by personnel properly trained and credentialled, can yield valuable information on the capabilities and learning processes of children. This information provides an understanding of unique abilities, communication difficulties, and learning and emotional disabilities which can effect (sic) school performance. We believe that intelligence tests, when used as part of a comprehensive evaluation, are appropriate for use with all children. (CASP, 1991, p. 1)

This position statement was buttressed by "facts" about IQ tests: They are valid when given in the student's primary language, they predict as well for minority and majority children, they are reliable, their results are defensible, they meet state and federal laws in terms of validity and reliability, they contribute to instruction, and the alternatives are more problematic.

In an accompanying piece by Lopez, Braden, and Sneed (1991), the CASP position is further buttressed along the same lines and also in terms of IQ's superiority to clinical judgment, its validity for minority pupils, improvements in reducing black–white differences in mean scores, improvements in the theoretical underpinings of the tests, their value to differential instruction (e.g., determining which pupils would profit from "survival skills" [p. 4]), and their superior scientific standing compared to "alternatives" (p. 4). At its core, one of the main messages of this apologia is that "intelligence tests are not culprits" (p. 5). What is missing in Lopez, Braden, and Sneed's (1991) work is reflected in their list of references: less than 20% of them focus directly on the issues surrounding the court cases, the overrepresentation, the misdiagnosis, the misplacement, the dead-end programs, the impact of culture on tests, and the effect of bilingualism on tests.

***Lau v. Nichols* (1974).** On January 2, 1974, the United States Supreme Court decided that 1, 800 Chinese-speaking students in the San Francisco Unified School District who were sitting in the same classes with their English-speaking peers, receiving the same instruction and using the same textbooks, were not receiving an equal educational opportunity "for students who do not understand English are effectively foreclosed from any meaningful education." This opinion is a significant change from "the same for all" philosophy espoused under *Brown v. Board of Education* (1954). In fact, it changes the entire meaning of equal educational opportunity where language differences are involved. Justice Blackmum, with Justice Burger, filed a small separate opinion so as not to interpret *Lau* "too broadly." As they state, "Numbers are at the heart of this case" (p. 2). The *Lau* requirement that some special instruction be given to non-English speakers, seems to apply in the case of many from one language group.

Lau has been broadly conceived as the foundation for bilingual instruction, the authorization for providing a special, linguistically different program. It has not been viewed as having relevance for assessment or special education, in spite of the fact that it does. Would a handicapped non-English-speaking child have any rights under *Lau* relative to testing? For the Hispanic population of limited-English-proficient (LEP) pupils, who are in the hundreds of thousands, *Lau* bears directly on the language used in assessment and on the Individualized Education Program (IEP).

Many assessment personnel throughout the United States have come to appreciate the need for doing assessments in the primary language of the child. Even university programs have recently appeared that directly attempt to do linguistically appropriate preservice training. Some movement toward state certification has also begun.

***Parents in Action for Special Education (PASE) v. Hannon* (1980).** In this case, Judge John Grady looks at the same questions of overrepresentation, at the role of IQ tests in this, and at the question of test bias as in *Larry P.* However, he never goes beyond examining whether IQ tests are culturally biased against black pupils. All other matters, issues, and law wait on the question of bias, even though evidence of overrepresentation is there, together with evidence of differences between EMR and regular programs, and together with acknowledgement that "an erroneous assessment of mental retardation, leading to an inappropriate placement . . . in an EMR class, is clearly an educational tragedy" (p. 4). The trial lasted two weeks. The United States Government, as in *Larry P.*, sided with the plaintiffs.

In his lengthy opinion, Judge Grady examines every item and its correct answer in the WISC, WISC-R, and the Stanford-Binet IQ tests. Aside from the fact that this may substantially invalidate the use of IQ tests for children whose parents are either lawyers or judges, Judge Grady's opinion essentially does battle with the testimony of Dr. Robert Williams (an influential black psychologist) outmatching him in the number of opinions expressed as to which items are biased. The judge decided that eight items on the WISC and WISC-R combined, and one item on the Binet, are biased.

For Judge Grady, experts for the plaintiffs failed to address or prove the question of bias in IQ tests. Dr. Williams comes closest to addressing this topic, although as mentioned, his analysis is hardly comparable to Judge Grady's lengthy item analysis, or the judge's observations about how many inconsistencies Dr. Williams failed to explain. The judge also determined that in Chicago IQ was not the primary determinant in placement, that the placement process was long and not hastily carried out, that the psychologists had extensive professional training, and that there were sufficient numbers of black psychologists in Chicago (22%) to control for unfair placements. As to why the black–white differences on IQ exist, Judge Grady sided with the evidence that points to the effects of poverty: "The IQ difference . . . is caused by socioeconomic factors which interfere with the development of intellectual skills . . . what is involved is not simply race but something associated with poverty" (p. 105). For him, the fact that 15–20% of black children score above the mean for white children contradicts the arguments of bias.

As for P.L. 94–142's requirements that testing materials and procedures be nondiscriminatory, Judge Grady noted that IQ is not singled out and inferred that P.L. 94–142 does not speak to a test or a procedure in terms of nondiscriminatory assessment, but to the entire process of assessment.

Also, the EMR program in Chicago allows for movement out of it: "Some of these transfers are due to the fact that the child has progressed in the EMR class and is ready for a greater challenge."

As for the *Larry P.* case, Judge Grady not only acknowledged that the issue of test bias was not in dispute there, but he also finds that the issues in that case "cannot properly be analyzed without a detailed examination of the items on the test" (p. 115).

***Crawford v. Honig* (1988).** On May 10, 1988, *Crawford v. Honig* was filed in southern California. The parents of an African-American youth sued the state in federal court because their child had been denied his right to take an IQ test, a right that could be exercised by parents and children of all other ethnic groups. This was a direct challenge to the 1986 Order in *Larry P.*

The 1988 *Crawford* complaint challenged the 1986 Order on the grounds that it denied children such as Crawford their 14th Ammendment rights to equal protection, due process, privileges, and immunities. It was alleged that the 1986 Order was racially discriminatory because it singled out only African-American children. Further, it exceeded the 1979 *Larry P.* ruling, it was imposed without a fairness hearing in which children such as Crawford could be represented, it precluded black pupils from receiving the benefits of special education, and it violated the provisions in P.L. 94–142 for nondiscriminatory testing materials and procedures (20 U.S.C. Sect.1412(5)(c)).

In April 1991, Judge Peckham held a public hearing in the Ninth Circuit Court to address Crawford's complaints. Interestingly, the judge kept on raising the issue of *Diana v. California*, continually asking how Hispanic children were faring under California's special education system.

The *Crawford* lawyers were relentless in pointing out the procedural error in the 1986 Order, that is, the failure to hold a fairness hearing concerning the text of an expanded *Larry P.* decision. Repeatedly, they also pointed out that since 1979 the "EMR" programs in California had virtually disappeared, ostensively making *Larry P.* moot and the 1986 Order unwarrented and excessive. Concurrently, Judge Peckham continued wondering whether newer "dead-end" programs that were overrepresented by minority pupils had come to take the place of the old "EMR" classrooms.

In December 1991, Judge Peckham held a second public hearing on *Crawford*. Again, the issue of "dead-end" programs surfaced. So did the question of how to protect African-American children and whether banning IQ, even if against parents' wishes, was the best safeguard. But, the overriding concern continued to be whether the 1986 Order violated equal protection guarantees and due process rights.

Some of the most surprising elements during 1991, however, were the positions taken by the California Department of Education. At both hearings in 1991, the department, through its attorney, Mr. Barry Zolotar, continually forged new ground in arguing before the court that IQ was not a necessary precondition for receiving special education services and that it was the state's intention to remove IQ for all pupils referred for special education (making *Crawford* moot). This position was crystallized and even broadened in 1992 by State Superintendent Bill Honig. His deposition to the Court (Honig, 1992) stated that IQ was not the only element being considered for elimination. The entire medical model and the role of testing were also being reconsidered, so was the criterion for determining test effectiveness, from prediction to instructional validity:

> I believe that special education assessment for all children can and should be done without the use of IQ tests or the medical model which undergirds current special education assessment. These tests have proven expensive, and ineffective in providing teachers with information on how students actually learn. I am committed to implementing an appropriate nondiscriminatory assessment method for determining special education eligibility that does not utilize I.Q. tests or the medical model for any child. This is in line with a growing body of books and articles in the educational literature (e.g., *The Harvard Educational Review, Phi Delta Kappan*), and the National Association of School Psychologists which are redefining the role and functions of testing in special education. (Honig, 1992, pp. 2-3)

On August 31, 1992, Judge Peckham ruled on the side of *Crawford* (Memorandum and Order No. C-89-0014 RFP, No. C-71-2270, RFP, August 31, 1992). IQ tests were reinstated for use with African-American pupils in all special education categories and programs, except the original "EMR" program. This essentially left the original *Larry P.* decision in place. He dismissed the 1986 Order because it denied the *Crawford* students their due process rights insofar as they were not represented when the 1986 Order was drafted.

The ruling was widely hailed as a victory for CASP and for school districts anxious to return to IQ. Lost in the win–lose aspects of the ruling, however, was one key feature of that ruling that breaks new ground in testing, assessment, and diagnosis in special education. Judge Peckham's worries about the possible existence of "dead-end" classrooms were operationalized. He defined such contemporary "dead-end," or "substantially equivalent" classrooms. These were special education classrooms in which ethnic children were overrepresented, in which movement out of such classes was minimal, and in which academic achievement was low. The judge virtually invited a new *Larry P.* hearing, possibly in conjunction with the *Diana* plaintiffs. The intriguing aspect to this part of the 1992 ruling is the shift in focus from testing to instruction, from IQ to "dead-end" programs that harm students.

On September 10, 1992, Mr. Zolotar issued a Legal Advisory (Office of The General Counsel, 1992) for the California State Department of Education to all school districts. In it he clarified the meaning of the *Crawford* ruling. First, he noted that the original *Larry P.* ruling was left standing. Second, he underscored that the *Crawford* decision by Judge Peckham was based on procedural grounds (not being represented when the 1986

Order was drafted) not "as to whether the prohibition of IQ testing of some African-American students is a violation of their constitutional right to equal protection of the law" (p. 1). Third, he reiterated the original *Larry P.* ruling that IQ tests were racially and culturally biased and were responsible for the overrepresentation of black pupils in "dead-end" classes. Fourth, he emphasized that because of their bias and adverse impact on black children, the original *Larry P.* decision had "prohibited their [IQ] use for placement in E.M.R. classes *or* their 'substantial equivalent' " [emphasis added]. Fifth, he asserted that in spite of the ambiguity surrounding the existence or nonexistence of "substantial equivalent" dead-end classrooms, the California Department of Education and school districts in California "are still legally obligated to comply with the 1979 decision banning the use of I.Q. tests" (p. 2) with black children in E.M.R or "substantial equivalent" placements. Sixth, he directed school districts to use alternative, non-IQ assessments with African-American pupils if, "as the result of the [IQ-based] assessment, the pupil could be enrolled" in a classroom that was overrepresented, with little possibility of exiting out of it, and with poor prospects for academic achievement. Seventh, he opined that, on the basis of internal studies in the California Department of Education there was sufficient evidence indicating that "substantially equivalent" classrooms existed in California programs for the mildly handicapped and that as per *Larry P.* they were "educationally unsound and unconstitutional" (p. 3).

Zolotar (1992) recommended that school districts evaluate their programs to see if they met the criteria for "substantially equivalent" programs and cautioned not to assume that the *Larry P.* decision did not apply to them simply because the EMR program no longer existed. He noted that the California Department of Education, as part of its educational reform efforts, intended to change "the entire special education assessment process" (p. 3). He specifically mentioned that the new alternative assessment procedures

> will focus on many, if not all, aspects of how each child learns, their unique approach to reading, writing, listening and speaking; their home and school-based achievements, abilities, developmental background, areas in which they do poorly and in which they do well; and, most critically, the educational contexts which are likely to help them overcome their learning problems. (p. 4)

Finally, he recommended that IQ not be administered to any child referred for special education or for the gifted and talented programs.

On October 18, 1992, the California Association of School Psychologists (CASP) distributed a position paper on "The Use of Intelligence Tests with

African-American Students." The principal message of this position paper was that, contrary to California's legal advisory, an IQ test could be given to African-American children under the following circumstances: (a) when professional judgment indicated that an IQ test could yield "valid and important information to the referral/assessment question" (p. 1), (b) when EMR diagnosis or placement in substantially equivalent classrooms was precluded, (c) when there was parental consent for the IQ test, and (d) when there was "administrative support" for the the school psychologist's decision to give an IQ test.

Though concerns about overrepresentation, "substantially equivalent" classrooms, and making careful decisions in placing pupils in special education were voiced in the position paper, the message was that IQ tests can be useful for African-American students, and that parents should have a right to decide the matter. The position paper also included a sample parent-permission form that could be used by school psychologists and their school districts.

On November 23, 1992, Laura Schulkind, writing on behalf of *Larry P.'s* attorneys, Public Advocates, Inc., issued a friendly warning to the California Association of School Psychologists about their position regarding the 1992 *Crawford* ruling. The text of this letter is presented below. Its importance in the history of testing litigation rests on the possible, future involvement of testers and their use of tests judged to be biased and harmful to children's lives. Certainly, if one considers the misuse and misapplication of tests given in English to non- or limited-English speakers, the issue of tester liability is neither far-fetched nor rare.

LETTER FROM LAURA SCHULKIND, ATTORNEY FOR *LARRY P.*, TO BETTY HENRY, PRESIDENT OF CASP, NOVEMBER 23, 1992

I am equally convinced that the current course of action that CASP has charted—i.e., interpreting the court's recent decision as permitting I.Q. testing of African American school children with parental consent—is misguided for three reasons:

First, the CASP position advises psychologists to take potentially illegal action. At a minimum, any African American child who is tested and scores in the MR range will have been tested illegally; the impact of the test cannot legally be undone. Moreover, the "informed" parental consent form drafted and disseminated by CASP is anything but informing. It makes only an oblique reference to the "controversy" over IQ testing while overstating the impact of the court's recent ruling. The court's ruling was procedural and nothing in it can be read to have found that a substantive, constitutional right to IQ testing exists, ever existed or has now been restored. In fact, the CDE [California Department of Education] has already received at least one formal complaint from parents in a school district where the form was provided to African American parents.

Second, as the first point demonstrates, the CASP position puts individual psychologists in an impossible situation. It puts the burden on each individual psychologist to the define "substantial equivalent" in his or her own way, decide whether parental consent legally protects them, analyze the CASP interpretation of the recent ruling and evaluate the legal sufficiency of the CASP parental consent form. In short, this approach inappropriately forces psychologists to play the role of lawyers–putting them at risk of acting illegally should their individual legal interpretations ultimately differ from the court's. Moreover, the CASP decision to focus on the legal meaning of the current ban, rather than the educational basis of alternative assessment, unfairly puts psychologists in the middle of a legal and political tug of war between CASP and the CDE.

Finally, as I indicated in my remarks last Friday, the CASP approach guarantees that it will be marginalized in the emerging dialogue over the nature of assessment in California's public schools. A revolution in assessment is underway in California and nationally–the move toward alternatives to IQ testing is not going to go away. The question is whether CASP is going to influence the outcome of this revolution. To date, CASP has chosen to try to "outlawyer the lawyers," attacking the CDE Legal Advisory, issuing its own legal opinion on what psychologists may do under the new ruling and disseminating a parental consent form that within days of its issuance has already started to produce complaints from African American parents. If CASP continues to engage the CDE in legal debates, it is not going to be in a position to shape CDE educational policy.

At the very least, I would suggest that CASP endorse the CDE position that while we await further clarification from the court, a broad reading of the potential "substantial equivalents" of EMR classification and placement is appropriate.

From its inception, the *Crawford* challenge involved CASP in a fairly direct manner. CASP and the legal team handling the *Crawford* case, the Landmark Legal Foundation, conferred regularly. The head attorney for *Crawford* published in the organization's newsletter (Bredemeier, 1991). Throughout the two public hearings held in Judge Peckham's court in 1991, one of the CASP's officers sat with the *Crawford* team and in one instance informed the court that he was ready to testify for the plaintiffs as an expert witness (the offer was not taken up by the court). The teaming of CASP with the Landmark Legal Foundation is unique in several respects. It not only placed this professional organization squarely on one side of the legal issues raised in *Larry P.*, it also linked it to a legal group with an impressive record of overturning civil rights cases during the 1980s.

In recent CASP publications, there is considerable debate and speculation about such issues as the future of special education (*CASP TODAY*, September/October, 1992) the role of school psychologists and the emerging CDE policy regarding assessment of children. One particular observation is often made in CASP publications. They point out that from 1986, when the Order banning IQ for all children for all special education programs was enacted, to 1992 when it was withdrawn under the *Crawford* challenge, the overrepresentation of African-American children in special education did not disappear. This, to CASP and others, indicates that IQ is not the causal factor in overrepresentation.

What is often overlooked, however, is that IQ tests and the "alternative" assessment procedures tried during this period were not that different in many school districts. Often, other psychometric tests were substituted. Many of these have high correlations with IQ, so high that they often constitute alternate forms of IQ tests (e.g., the Woodcock Johnson Psychoeducational Battery's "cognitive tests"). Also, many of the "alternative" assessment procedures" use IQ-like test items albeit in a different format (e.g., the Learning Assessment Potential Device). Similarly, all "alternative assessment" procedures function under the medical model: the belief that the problem resides in the child's brain, the belief that the "tests" access mental ability in the decontextualized, unnatural situations known as individualized testing, and the belief that it is possible to "diagnose" mild mental handicaps such as "learning disabilities" with a 1- or 2-hour examination. In instances in which the "alternative assessment" procedures are different from IQ sort of questions and procedures, the medical model and its attendant unvalidated set of eligibility criteria for mild mental handicaps (Skrtic, 1991a) virtually guarantees that a handicap will be found (Mehan, Hertweck, & Meihls, 1986; Skrtic, 1991b, Taylor, 1991), even when the children are not in special education, have not been referred for special education, are in good standing in regular education classrooms, and are simply part of an experimental group given a battery of tests in their primary language to see how the tests function (Rueda, Figueroa, Mercado, & Cardoza, 1984).

It is interesting to speculate what would have happened if Judge Peckham had continued his long, distinguished legal journey in the area of testing minority group children related to *Diana, Larry P.*, and *Crawford*. Tragically, this outstanding jurist died on February 16, 1993. The Ninth Circuit will undoubtedly carry on the inquiries, but it may never again show the care and sensitivity towards minority children that Robert F. Peckham continually demonstrated from the bench.

All of the court cases in the 1970s, 1980s, and 1990s concerned with minority children and special education testing have had and will continue to have a considerable impact on intelligence testing and all standardized testing. The cases' application to bilingual populations remains unclear. In most school districts throughout the United States, IQ continues to affect the lives of bilingual students who have problems with traditional forms of school-related learning. This has been uniquely documented by the Handicapped Minority Research Institutes in California and in Texas.

The Handicapped Minority Research Institutes

The Texas Institute has studied various subgroupings of Hispanic pupils as these were found in special education programs. A great amount of the data come *ex post facto*. The conclusions reported on the assessment of these pupils are:

1. On language proficiency dominance: Home data and school data identifying the language predominantly spoken by the student were quite contradictory; special education files kept outdated language proficiency scores; and the traditional assessment of language proficiency failed to capture the pragmatic, contextual, and spontaneous uses of language of bilingual pupils. A language handicap should be manifest in L1 and L2 (Garcia, 1985; Ortiz, 1986; Ortiz & Maldonado-Colon, 1986; Ortiz & Polyzoi, 1986, 1987; Ortiz & Yates, 1987; Swedo, 1987; Wilkinson & Holtzman, n.d.; Wilkinson & Ortiz, 1986; Willig & Swedo, 1987). The language description of a CH- and LD-referred child includes poor comprehension, limited vocabulary, grammar errors, syntax errors; this is also the profile of a second language learner.
2. The psychometric tests most often given were IQ, achievement, and visual motor. The least given tests were adaptive behavior and school readiness.
3. Most tests are administered in English, few in Spanish. In these, the test reports usually failed to describe what special adaptations were made. Also, testing in English produced a greater likelihood of an achievement/intelligence discrepancy.
4. The WISC-R Hispanic profile typically depicts a low verbal IQ and a higher (+ 15) performance IQ.
5. The initial "assessment" made by the classroom teacher usually referred pupils to LD placement and CH placement. However, an analysis of the behaviors triggering referrals showed that language-related problems in English accounted for the majority of the referrals.
6. The higher cognitive scores on the K-ABC made it easier to certify Hispanic pupils as LD on this test than on others.

7. EMR-placed pupils had low scores on tests given in Spanish, English, and adaptive behavior.
8. In Texas, Hispanic children are overrepresented in classes for LD and underrepresented on virtually every other category.
9. On the reevaluation of Hispanic LD students: (a) fewer IQ tests were given, (b) there were fewer teacher language ratings, (c) more of the testing was done in English, (d) the PIQ and FSIQ (WISC-R) of all the LD pupils *decreased*, and (e) more limited-English-proficient (LEP) Hispanic LD students changed the category of their handicapping condition than non-LEP students.

The California Handicapped Minority Research Institute conducted two principal studies: (a) on the impact on eligibility rates in LD, EMR, and non-handicapped Hispanic students when Spanish-language psychometric tests and socioculturally adjusted scores (SOMPA Estimated Learning Potential) are used (Rueda, Figueroa, Mercado, & Cardoza, 1984); and (b) on the decision-making process in special education as inferred, *ex post facto*, from data in the cum folders of 1319 (K–12) Hispanic pupils (Rueda, Cardoza, Mercer, & Carpenter, 1984). This last study is actually disappointing because the main findings are that LD and CH are the two principal decision tracks for these pupils, a conclusion more directly reached by the Texas Institute. In actual fact, the most interesting results from the second study are in the specifics on what was in the folders.

On assessment, outcomes 1–3 were reported in Rueda, Figueroa, Mercado, and Cardoza (1984); outcomes 4–12 were reported in Rueda, Cardoza, Mercer, and Carpenter (1984).

1. Spanish verbal measures (IQ or achievement) were problematic for the Hispanic pupils studied.
2. The tests used all had good measures of internal consistency (reliability, standard error of measurement).
3. The diagnostic validity of these tests, however, was unacceptable. (Note: This is not the conclusion reached by the study; it is, rather, the conclusion reached upon examining Table 4.) For example, an average of 53% of the non-handicapped students were found eligible for the LD program by these tests; 43% of the EMR students were also found eligible for the LD placement; if one wants to increase the likelihood of finding virtually any student eligible for LD, use ELP IQs; if one wants to increase the likelihood of keeping children *out* of LD, use WISC-RM Verbal IQs or Full-Scale IQs, or the Mexican K-ABC Sequential Processing Score; if one wants to eliminate the EMR category, virtually

precluding anyone's admittance into the program, use the Spanish version of the adaptive behavior scales from SOMPA.

4. Children were predominantly assessed in English.
5. Two categories of exceptionalities made up 83% of the pupil files studied ($N = 1193$).
6. The $\overline{X}$ age of the children was 8.3 years and 11% had siblings in special education.
7. 79% of the parents were born abroad, 69% of the children were born in the United States, suggesting that having parents born in Mexico or Latin America increases your likelihood of special education.
8. There were few explicit behavioral reasons given for referral to assessment.
9. 6% of the pupils had their assessment in Spanish only and 23% had it in Spanish and English.
10. .01% had home visits made by assessment personnel.
11. In bilingual testing, the principal instruments were the Leiter, DAP, Bender, WISC-R, and WRAT.
12. A high percentage of the pupils went to CH programs.

More recently, Figueroa (1989) has suggested that the capricious character of IQ tests when used with bilingual populations can actually be manipulated to yield whatever diagnostic outcomes one desires. For example, to diagnose a bilingual child as learning disabled, a tester need only administer a nonverbal IQ test and an English test of reading achievement. More often than not, the discrepancy between the two will be substantial enough to "fit" the eligibility criteria for a learning disability. If a processing problem is also required, a digit span test will nicely provide this additional diagnostic index, because bilingual pupils, in L2, often perform poorly on such speed-of-processing tasks.

The data from the Handicapped Minority Research Institutes are of critical importance in underscoring the following conclusion: The laws and court cases proscribing malpractice with bilingual children have not affected diagnostic testing practices. The following section empirically demonstrates how diagnostic decisions based on test outcomes result in capricious outcomes.

DIAGNOSIS AND PSYCHOMETRICS IN SPECIAL EDUCATION: A STUDY OF DECISION-MAKING ACCURACY

The prevalent paradigm in the study of test bias usually involves examining the predictive power of a test across racial/ethnic and socioeconomic groups (Cleary et al., 1975; Jensen, 1982; Reynolds, 1982). Correlation and regression analyses are the principal procedures used in this paradigm. To date, most studies on test bias using these procedures have failed to find racial/ethnic bias in psychometric tests (e.g., Reschly, 1982; Reynolds & Kaiser, 1990; Sattler, 1982). The common assertion among psychometricians is that well-normed and standardized tests, such as the WISC-R and the Binet, predict as well, if not better, for ethnic students as for Anglo students. Typically, however, predictive validity is established by using large N s that encompass a wide range of ability and achievement. The resultant scatter plot on such a bivariate distribution is summarized by a least-squares, running mean (the regression line). As with any other "averaging," anomalous or important data can be lost. This is particularly true in cases where tests are used to make selection or placement decisions. In these situations, a validity coefficient fails to inform the test user as to the expected "correct" and "incorrect" decisions that will obtain given the use of a particular test for making placement decisions. As Brown (1984) has noted:

> In many situations, tests are used as aids in making practical decisions. In selection, the decision is which applicants to select and which to reject. In placement, the decision is which alternative treatment or program to assign each individual. In diagnosis, the decision is which diagnostic category to assign. In each of these situations, the goal is to maximize the number of correct decisions. Thus an obvious index of the effectiveness of the decision-making process is the proportion of correct decisions made. When decisions are made on the basis of test scores, the most valid test will be the one that results in the higher proportion of correct decisions. (p. 107)

Special education testing involves precisely this type of decision making. Further, IQ tests have had and continue to have the greatest impact on special education placement decisions (Rueda, Figueroa, Mercado, & Cardoza, 1984). Given the fact that so much of the controversy surrounding test bias has emanated from the overplacement of minority pupils in special education, it is difficult to understand why there is virtually no research on the decision-making paradigm suggested by Brown (1984).

In an attempt to address this knowledge gap, an empirical study is presented in this section. The study provides evidence on whether tests are or are not flawed with children from different linguistic backgrounds.

The 2,100 pupils (5–11 years old) in the triethnic sample of the norming study of the System of Multicultural Pluralistic Assessment (SOMPA) (Mercer, 1979) produced WISC-R IQ scores in 1972. The Validation Study of SOMPA (Figueroa & Sassenrath, 1989), in 1982, produced academic achievement scores for approximately 60% of the 1972 SOMPA sample. These data banks present a unique opportunity for studying the decision-making paradigm described by Brown (1984) to see whether decisions based on IQ yield similar predictive outcomes for Anglo children and for Hispanic children who in 1972 were judged to by English proficient at school though their home language backgrounds were really very different (English only, English-Spanish, Spanish only). As noted elsewhere (Figueroa, 1990), the scientific test literature on test bias has seldom controlled for language proficiency or language background.

The Full-Scale IQ from the 1972 WISC-R scores (Mercer, 1979) is used as the predictor. Academic GPA, total GPA, standardized reading scores, and standardized mathematics scores are used as the criteria for 1982 school achievement (Figueroa & Sassenrath, 1984).

This study sets out to investigate the number of *incorrect* decisions made for Anglo, Hispanic Spanish-speakers, Hispanic Spanish/English speakers, and Hispanic English-speakers when the WISC-R Full Scale IQ is used for making decisions (predicting) about school achievement. As Figure 5.3 shows, there are two types of "incorrect" decisions that can be made. Quadrant II is where "overachievers" fall (i.e., those students whose school achievement was higher than what IQ predicted); and Quadrant IV is where "underachievers" fall. In the parlance of special education diagnosis, Quadrant II is for "false positives" and Quadrant IV is for "false negatives." The litigation surrounding special education, of course, has been concerned with Quadrant II, where the disproportionate rates of ethnic misdiagnosis occur.

Two analyses were done. First, the outcome rates for Anglo, Hispanic, and Hispanic language groups in each of the four possible quadrants were calculated. Five sets of quadrants were generated: -2 SD, -1 SD, $\bar{x}$, $+1$ SD, and $+2$ SDs for both the predictor and each of the four criterion measures. A similar set of outcome rates were calculated using Mercer's Estimated Learning Potential (ELP) (Mercer, 1979) as the predictor. ELP supposedly corrects for the sociocultural and ethnic bias in IQ and yields fairly identical distributions around a mean of 100 for each ethnic group. The intent here is to see if ELP offers a different set of decision-making outcomes and also to statistically correct for any artificially inflated rates of ethnic overrepresentations in Q II and Q IV (artificial in that the 1972 FSIQs have proportionally more Hispanic pupils below the mean of 100, thereby providing an increased likelihood of greater numbers of "false negatives"). Figure 5.4 depicts the five sets of quadrants.

Second, conditional probability (CP) values were calculated for Quadrants II and IV for each ethnic and language group when the quadrant boundaries were set at the -2 SD to $+2$ SD boundaries. The conditional probabilities for Q II and Q IV are defined as:

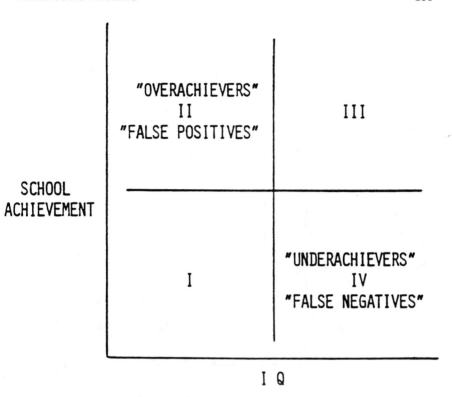

Figure 5.3. Possible Outcomes from Using IQ to Predict School Achievement

$$CP_{QII} = \frac{Q\,II}{Q\,I + Q\,II}$$

$$CP_{QIV} = \frac{Q\,IV}{Q\,III + Q\,IV}$$

The CP value of Q I is: CP Q II + CP Q I = 1.00; and for Q III: CP Q IV + CP Q III = 1.00.

CPs yield the probabilities of having either high school achievement given low IQ or low school achievement given high IQ within each group. Like ELP, CPs correct for possibly artificially inflated rates of representation in Quadrants II (i.e., more Hispanics because IQs are negatively skewed) and IV (i.e., fewer Hispanics because their IQ's are negatively skewed). Unlike ELP, they do not have to rely on the sociocultural and statistical assumptions inherent in ELP. CPs, however, inherently assume that IQ is a legitimate and effective predictor. For Quadrant II, for example, they begin with the proposition that "Given a low IQ, what is the probability of getting a higher than expected achievement score." Ques-

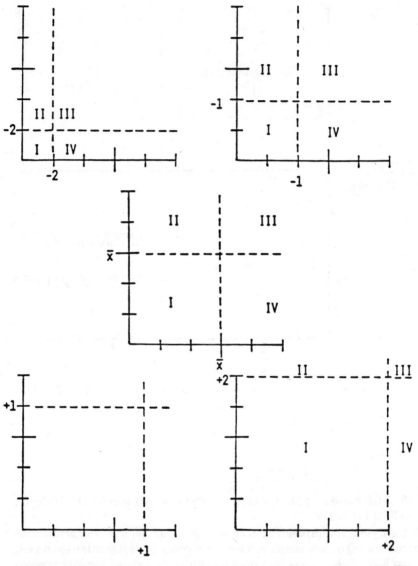

Figure 5.4. Quadrant Areas as Defined by Boundaries Set at −2SD, −1SD, x̄, +1SD, +2SD's

tions about one group's overrepresentation in the "low IQ" category are never considered. CPs, accordingly, are the most "conservative" indices of decision-making accuracy based on IQ. Substantial and persistent fluctuations in CPs across ethnic or language-background groups provide evidence of special education decision-making bias stemming from the use of IQ.

Figure 5.5 presents the rates of ethnic representation in each of the four quadrants with boundaries set at -2 SD, -1 SD, $\bar{x}$, $+1$ SD, and $+2$ SDs for each school achievement criterion (academic GPA, and standardized reading and math scores) using FSIQ as the predictor.

Two broad sets of results emanate from the data in Figure 5.5. The first involves the rates (percentages) or representation in each quadrant as the boundaries (see Figure 5.4) move from -2 SDs to $+2$ SDs irrespective of ethnic group. For grades (GPA's) the pattern is consistent: going from -2 SDs to $+2$ SDs in Quadrant I, rates increase; in Quadrant III, rates decrease. For reading and math, the same pattern emerges. Quadrants II and IV, for all achievement measures, are characterized by somewhat symmetrical distributions of representations around $\bar{x}$.

The second set of results that emanate from Figure 5.5 involves the ethnic differences in the rates of representation in each quadrant as the boundaries move from -2 SDs to $+2$ SDs.

For grades (GPA's), Quadrants I and III show a greater overall Hispanic representation in Quadrant I and a lower Hispanic representation in Quadrant III. In effect, throughout the entire range of boundaries, more Hispanic pupils score low on IQ and school achievement (Q I), and more Anglo pupils score high on IQ and school achievement (Q III). But in Quadrant II, an interaction appears. Whereas proportionally *more* Hispanics are represented in Quadrant II when the boundaries are at -2 SDs, -1 SD, and $\bar{x}$, the opposite is true at $+1$ SD, and $+2$ SDs. In real-life terms, this means that Hispanic pupils who in 1972 scored at or below the mean on IQ are more likely than their Anglo counterparts to show above-expected school grades in 1982. Above an IQ of 100, Anglo students are more likely to receive grades higher than their IQ would predict.

For reading and math scores, Hispanic students are overrepresented in Quadrant I and underrepresented in Quadrant II and IV, the interaction again appears, albeit most clearly defined when the boundaries are ≤ -1 SD and $\geq +1$ SD. At these boundaries, Hispanic pupils are overrepresented below the mean and underrepresented above the mean. In real-life terms, this means that when IQ is used to predict to standardized reading and math scores, Hispanic pupils with IQs below 85 (-1 SD) will receive achievement scores above -1 SD achievement values in greater proportions than their Anglo peers in Quadrants II (overachievers) and Quadrant IV (underachievers).

Figure 5.6 presents the rates of ethnic representation in each of the four quadrants with boundaries set at -2 SD to $+2$ SDs for each school achievement criterion (academic GPA, total GPA, and standardized reading and math scores) using Mercer's (1979) Estimated Learning Potential Full-Scale IQ (ELPIQ) as the predictor.

Looking first at the rates of representation in each quadrant as the

Academic GPA/FSIQ

	Q2 −2	−1	$\bar{x}$	+1	+2	Q3 −2	−1	$\bar{x}$	+1	+2	n
Anglo	1	3	19	21	7	98	90	52	12	1	411
Hispanic	4	22	28	16	1	93	63	19	3	0	334

	Q1 −2	−1	$\bar{x}$	+1	+2	Q4 −2	−1	$\bar{x}$	+1	+2
Anglo	0	2	16	58	90	1	5	13	9	2
Hispanic	0	3	40	80	98	3	13	13	2	0

Total GPA/FSIQ

	Q2 −2	−1	$\bar{x}$	+1	+2	Q3 −2	−1	$\bar{x}$	+1	+2	n
Anglo	1	4	20	21	3	98	90	55	12	0	411
Hispanic	4	22	30	14	1	92	64	20	3	0	335

	Q1 −2	−1	$\bar{x}$	+1	+2	Q4 −2	−1	$\bar{x}$	+1	+2
Anglo	0	1	14	58	93	1	4	11	9	3
Hispanic	0	3	38	81	99	4	11	12	2	0

Reading/FSIQ

	Q2 −2	−1	$\bar{x}$	+1	+2	Q3 −2	−1	$\bar{x}$	+1	+2	n
Anglo	1	2	16	20	0	98	89	55	13	0	415
Hispanic	4	10	17	8	0	92	63	22	2	0	343

	Q1 −2	−1	$\bar{x}$	+1	+2	Q4 −2	−1	$\bar{x}$	+1	+2
Anglo	0	2	18	59	97	1	6	11	7	3
Hispanic	1	15	50	87	100	3	11	10	3	0

Math/FSIQ

	Q2 −2	−1	$\bar{x}$	+1	+2	Q3 −2	−1	$\bar{x}$	+1	+2	n
Anglo	1	3	17	29	6	99	92	57	16	1	414
Hispanic	5	19	22	15	1	95	68	25	4	0	344

	Q1 −2	−1	$\bar{x}$	+1	+2	Q4 −2	−1	$\bar{x}$	+1	+2
Anglo	0	2	17	50	90	0	4	9	5	2
Hispanic	0	7	46	80	99	0	6	7	1	0

Figure 5.5. Rates (Percentages) of ethnic representation in each possible outcome-quadrant set at −2, −1, $\bar{x}$, +1, and +2 standard deviation boundaries for each measure of school achievement (1982) using Full Scale IQ as the predictor

Academic GPA/ELPIQ

		-2	-1	x̄	+1	+2	n
Anglo	Q2	1	4	18	21	7	
	Q3	98	90	54	12	1	381
	Q1	0	1	14	56	89	
	Q4	1	6	14	10	3	
Hispanic	Q2	3	10	20	13	1	
	Q3	95	75	27	5	1	294
	Q1	0	1	28	70	98	
	Q4	2	14	25	12	1	

Total GPA/ELPIQ

		-2	-1	x̄	+1	+2	n
Anglo	Q2	1	4	19	21	3	
	Q3	98	91	57	12	0	380
	Q1	0	1	13	56	98	
	Q4	1	4	11	11	3	
Hispanic	Q2	3	10	19	12	2	
	Q3	93	75	30	5	0	295
	Q1	0	1	29	71	98	
	Q4	4	14	22	12	1	

Reading/ELPIQ

		-2	-1	x̄	+1	+2	n
Anglo	Q2	1	2	16	20	0	
	Q3	98	90	57	14	0	382
	Q1	0	2	16	58	96	
	Q4	1	6	11	9	4	
Hispanic	Q2	2	5	11	8	0	
	Q3	94	70	30	4	0	298
	Q1	1	7	37	76	99	
	Q4	3	19	22	13	1	

Math/ELPIQ

		-2	-1	x̄	+1	+2	n
Anglo	Q2	1	3	16	29	6	
	Q3	99	92	59	16	2	382
	Q1	0	2	16	48	90	
	Q4	0	4	9	7	2	
Hispanic	Q2	3	10	15	13	1	
	Q3	97	78	33	7	0	299
	Q1	0	2	33	71	98	
	Q4	0	11	19	9	1	

Figure 5.6. Rates of ethnic representation in each possible outcome-quadrant set at -2, -1, $\bar{x}$, $+1$, and $+2$ standard deviation boundaries for each measure of school achievement (1982) using Estimated Learning Potential Full Scale IQ (ELP-IQ (1972) as the predictor.

159

boundaries (cf. Figure 5.4) move from −2 SDs to +2 SDs (irrespective of ethnic group), the ELPIQ results are fairly identical to those for FSIQ (cf. Figure 5.5).

Concerning the ethnic differences in the rates of representation in each quadrant and boundary for each school achievement outcome, the ELPIQ results are also virtually identical to those for FSIQ. The only difference noted is in Quadrant IV for reading and math. Here, ELPIQ results indicate that Hispanic pupils are more represented throughout most of the boundaries, unlike the pattern noted in the FSIQ results where they tended to be more represented than Anglos below the mean and more represented than Anglos above the mean.

There is, however, one very pronounced difference between FSIQ and ELPIQ results. Though the rates of representation for every quadrant and across all boundaries remains virtually unchanged for Anglo pupils, these change substantially for Hispanic pupils when ELPIQ is used. In Quadrants I and II, ELPIQ "produces" smaller rates of Hispanic representation than does IQ. In Quadrants II and IV, it produces higher rates. In retrospect, this is actually quite predictable, because as one shifts from IQ scores to ELP scores for Hispanics (and also for Black pupils), the entire Hispanic scatter plot shifts horizontally to the right. Figure 5.7 depicts this.

Figure 5.8 presents the actual shifts in Hispanic representation rates for each quadrant, boundary, and school achievement measure when ELPIQ rates are subtracted from FSIQ rates.

Some of these outcomes merit being underscored. First, the greatest left-to-right shift occurs for reading. Second, except for reading, the left-to-right shift is quite symmetrical, that is, what is lost in Quadrant II goes to Quadrant III and what is lost in Quadrant I goes to Quadrant IV.[3]

Figure 5.8 also shows that ELPIQ's have the salutary effect of enhancing the percentages of "hits" for Hispanic pupils in Quadrant III and concomitantly of lowering the rates of false positives (overachievers) (Q II). However, the downside of ELPIQs is that they increase the rates of "misses" in Quadrant IV, "producing" more false negatives (underachievers).

Figure 5.9 presents changes in the Hispanic language-background groups' rates of representation as the boundaries move from −2 SD to +2 SDs when FSIQ is used as the predictor.

Several interesting patterns emerge. In Quadrants I and II, and for each achievement measure, the more Spanish in the home, the more that representation rates tend to increase. *This is particularly manifest in*

---

[3]Loss of percentage points in shifting from left to right is due to ELPIQ values that fall at the mean. These are randomly distributed left and right by the computer program.

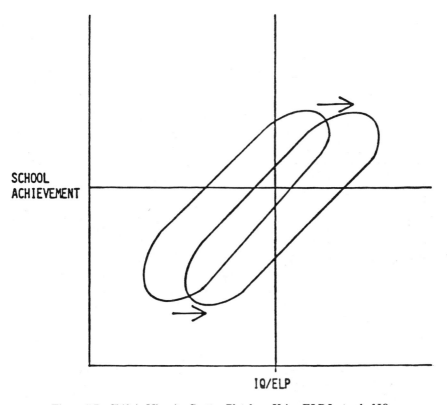

Figure 5.7.   Shift in Minority Scatter Plot from Using ELP Instead of IQ

Quadrant II at the −1 *SD boundary.* Also, in Quadrants III and IV (and for each achievement measure), the more Spanish in the home, the smaller that the rates of representation tend to be. This is particularly manifest in Quadrant IV, particularly at the +1 SD and +2 SD boundaries. In effect, "underachievers" barely exist in the Spanish-only home language-background group.

Quadrants II and IV in every school achievement area also show a generally negatively skewed distribution of representation rates, particularly for the "Spanish" home language group in Quadrant II. "Overachievers" from Spanish-only homes disproportionately appear.

Quadrant II for reading and math shows an interaction similar to the one noted in Figures 5.5 and 5.6. Below the x̄ boundary, the more Spanish in the home, the greater the representation of overachievers. Above the x̄, the opposite appears.

Finally, Figure 5.9 shows a somewhat unexpected, if perhaps not anomalous, trend in Quadrant IV for the "English/Spanish" group. More of them tend to appear in this quadrant ("underachievers") at boundaries

Academic GPA

	Q2 -2	-1	$\bar{x}$	+1	+2		Q3 -2	-1	$\bar{x}$	+1	+2	n
Anglo	0	1	-1	0	0		0	0	2	2	0	0
Hispanic	1	-12	-8	-3	0		2	12	8	2	1	1

	Q1 -2	-1	$\bar{x}$	+1	+2		Q4 -2	-1	$\bar{x}$	+1	+2	n
Anglo	0	1	-2	-2	-1		0	1	1	1	1	1
Hispanic	0	-2	-12	-10	0		-1	1	12	10	1	1

Total GPA

	Q2 -2	-1	$\bar{x}$	+1	+2		Q3 -2	-1	$\bar{x}$	+1	+2	n
Anglo	0	0	-1	0	0		0	1	2	0	0	0
Hispanic	-1	-12	-11	-2	-1		1	11	10	2	0	0

	Q1 -2	-1	$\bar{x}$	+1	+2		Q4 -2	-1	$\bar{x}$	+1	+2	n
Anglo	0	0	-1	-2	0		0	0	0	2	0	0
Hispanic	0	-2	-9	-10	-1		0	3	10	10	0	0

Reading

	Q2 -2	-1	$\bar{x}$	+1	+2		Q3 -2	-1	$\bar{x}$	+1	+2	n
Anglo	0	0	0	0	0		0	1	2	1	0	0
Hispanic	-2	-5	-6	0	0		2	7	8	2	0	0

	Q1 -2	-1	$\bar{x}$	+1	+2		Q4 -2	-1	$\bar{x}$	+1	+2	n
Anglo	0	0	-2	-1	-1		0	0	0	2	1	1
Hispanic	0	-8	-23	-11	-1		0	8	12	10	1	1

Math

	Q2 -2	-1	$\bar{x}$	+1	+2		Q3 -2	-1	$\bar{x}$	+1	+2	n
Anglo	0	0	-1	0	0		0	0	2	0	1	1
Hispanic	-2	-9	-7	-2	0		2	10	8	3	0	0

	Q1 -2	-1	$\bar{x}$	+1	+2		Q4 -2	-1	$\bar{x}$	+1	+2	n
Anglo	0	0	-1	-2	0		0	0	0	2	0	0
Hispanic	0	-5	-13	-9	-1		0	5	12	8	1	1

Figure 5.8. Shifts in Hispanic and Anglo representation rates for each quadrant, boundary, and school achievement measure when FSIQ rates are subtracted from ELP FSIQ rates.

Academic GPA/FSIQ

	Q2					Q3					
	-2	-1	x̄	+1	+2	-2	-1	x̄	+1	+2	n
English	3	16	24	14	2	95	72	24	5	1	152
English/Spanish	5	20	25	20	1	88	58	20	1	0	91
Spanish	4	33	36	13	1	96	53	11	0	0	91

	Q1					Q4				
	-2	-1	x̄	+1	+2	-2	-1	x̄	+1	+2
English	0	2	36	77	97	2	11	16	3	0
English/Spanish	0	4	44	77	99	7	18	11	2	0
Spanish	0	3	45	87	99	0	11	8	0	0

Total GPA/FSIQ

	Q2					Q3					
	-2	-1	x̄	+1	+2	-2	-1	x̄	+1	+2	n
English	3	16	24	15	1	95	71	26	5	1	152
English/Spanish	5	20	27	16	0	86	60	19	1	0	91
Spanish	4	33	43	11	1	93	55	12	0	0	92

	Q1					Q4				
	-2	-1	x̄	+1	+2	-2	-1	x̄	+1	+2
English	0	1	35	76	99	3	11	14	3	0
English/Spanish	0	4	42	80	100	9	15	12	2	0
Spanish	0	4	38	89	99	2	8	7	0	0

Reading/FSIQ

	Q2					Q3					
	-2	-1	x̄	+1	+2	-2	-1	x̄	+1	+2	n
English	3	7	21	11	0	93	75	32	5	0	151
English/Spanish	4	9	11	5	0	93	61	19	0	0	94
Spanish	4	18	17	6	0	91	48	9	0	0	98

	Q1					Q4				
	-2	-1	x̄	+1	+2	-2	-1	x̄	+1	+2
English	0	10	35	79	99	4	9	11	4	1
English/Spanish	1	16	59	90	100	2	15	12	4	0
Spanish	2	21	66	94	100	3	12	7	0	0

Math/FSIQ

	Q2					Q3					
	-2	-1	x̄	+1	+2	-2	-1	x̄	+1	+2	n
English	3	11	20	18	1	97	77	35	7	0	152
English/Spanish	5	16	17	13	1	95	68	22	3	0	94
Spanish	6	33	30	13	1	94	55	13	0	0	98

	Q1					Q4				
	-2	-1	x̄	+1	+2	-2	-1	x̄	+1	+2
English	0	5	36	73	98	0	7	9	3	1
English/Spanish	0	9	52	83	99	0	7	9	1	0
Spanish	0	7	54	87	99	0	5	3	0	0

Figure 5.9. Rates (Percentages) of language-background group representation in each possible outcome-quadrant set at −2, −1, x̄, and +2 standard deviation boundaries for each measure of school achievement (1982) using Full Scale IQ as the predictor.

below the mean. This group, in effect, achieves *below* its predicted level when its members score around the 85 IQ range. This isolated finding would be strictly anomalous were it not for the fact that data exist suggesting that this group may be particularly vulnerable to slow cognitive processing speed in English (Figueroa, 1987).

Figure 5.10 presents the representation rates in each quadrant for each Hispanic language-background group using ELPIQ's as the predictor. By and large, ELPIQs tend to reverse the patterns observed in Figure 5.9. Where IQ increased the rates in Quadrant I and Quadrant II in direct proportion to the degree of Spanish in the home, ELPIQ *generally* reverses this trend. "Spanish" homes generally have the lowest rates. Also, whereas FSIQs in Figure 5.9 tended to increase the representation rates in Quadrant III and Quadrant IV in direct proportion to the amount of English in the home, ELPIQ tends to do the opposite.

Perhaps the most striking aspect of Figure 5.10 is the "trend-breaking" rates exhibited by the English/Spanish group. Rather than being in the middle of a trend, this group, more often than not, is at the extreme. In every Quadrant I, for example, it turns up with the highest representation rates in most of the boundaries. They are consistently low on ELPIQ and each school achievement measure. For them, ELPIQ predicts well in Quadrant I. Yet in Quadrant II for GPAs, the English/Spanish group is the most overrepresented.

These results notwithstanding, however, Figure 5.10 is best examined in contrast to Figure 5.9, or the degree of shifts in representation rates as we move from FSIQ to ELPIQ. Figure 5.11 presents the shifts in rates as FSIQ rates are subtracted from ELPIQ rates.

As Figure 5.11 shows, ELP most dramatically affects the rates of the "Spanish" home-language group: at the $\bar{x}$ and -1 SD boundaries for academic GPA, math and reading in Quadrants II and III (in shifting from the former to the latter), and at the $\bar{x}$, and $+1$ SD boundaries for academic GPA, total GPA, and math in Quadrants I and IV (for reading, the shifts from Quadrant I and Quadrant IV are quite pronounced at -1 SD, $\bar{x}$, and $+1$ SD).

ELP for the "Spanish" group very substantially lowers the IQ error of "overachievers," but also creates the problem of too many "underachievers" (Quadrant IV).

Figure 5.12 presents the results of the "Conditional Probabilities" analyses. Only results for Quadrants II and IV are presented because these are the critical outcome areas in making decisions based on special education testing (where IQ predominates). In these quadrants, the most useful values in terms of interpretation are at -1 SD, $\bar{x}$, and $+1$ SD. Values at -2 SD and $+2$ SD are based on very small N s and all too often present all-or-nothing probabilities (0 or 1.0). As in previous results, the outcomes

Academic GPA/ELPIQ

	Q2					Q3					n
	-2	-1	x̄	+1	+2	-2	-1	x̄	+1	+2	
	3	12	20	12	1	96	75	30	8	1	138
	4	12	25	16	1	90	66	18	4	0	77
	1	5	15	11	0	99	82	30	3	0	79
	Q1					Q4					
English	0	1	29	68	96	1	12	21	12	1	
English/Spanish	0	3	34	75	97	6	19	23	5	1	
Spanish	0	1	22	67	100	0	11	33	19	0	

Total GPA/ELPIQ

	Q2					Q3					n
	-2	-1	x̄	+1	+2	-2	-1	x̄	+1	+2	
	3	12	20	14	1	95	76	31	7	1	138
	4	12	22	12	0	87	66	19	4	0	77
	1	6	16	6	0	96	81	38	4	0	80
	Q1					Q4					
English	0	1	30	66	97	2	12	20	13	1	
English/Spanish	0	3	36	79	99	9	19	22	5	1	
Spanish	0	1	21	73	100	3	11	25	18	0	

Reading/ELPIQ

	Q2					Q3					n
	-2	-1	x̄	+1	+2	-2	-1	x̄	+1	+2	
	3	6	18	10	0	94	76	36	7	0	140
	3	4	7	5	0	93	66	26	0	0	73
	1	2	5	6	0	94	64	22	1	0	85
	Q1					Q4					
English	0	6	29	70	99	4	12	16	13	1	
English/Spanish	1	8	51	85	97	3	22	16	10	3	
Spanish	2	7	36	78	100	2	27	36	15	0	

Math/ELPIQ

	Q2					Q3					n
	-2	-1	x̄	+1	+2	-2	-1	x̄	+1	+2	
	3	9	16	15	1	97	80	41	11	1	141
	4	12	14	12	1	96	73	23	4	0	73
	4	8	14	9	0	96	78	27	5	0	85
	Q1					Q4					
English	0	3	31	65	98	0	8	12	9	1	
English/Spanish	0	0	44	78	96	0	15	19	5	3	
Spanish	0	1	27	74	100	0	13	32	12	0	

Figure 5.10. Rates (Percentages) of language-background group representation in each possible outcome-quadrant set at −2, −1, x, and +2 standard deviation boundaries for each measure of school achievement (1982) using Full Scale ELPIQ as the predictor.

Academic GPA

	Q2 -2	-1	x̄	+1	+2		Q3 -2	-1	x̄	+1	+2	n
	0	-4	-4	-2	-1		1	3	6	3	0	0
	-1	-8	0	-4	0		2	8	-2	3	0	0
	-3	-28	-21	-2	-1		3	29	19	3	0	0
	Q1						Q4					
English	0	-1	-7	-9	-1		-1	1	5	9	1	1
English/Spanish	0	-1	-10	-2	-2		-1	1	12	3	1	1
Spanish	0	-2	-23	-20	-1		0	0	25	19	0	0

Reading

	Q2 -2	-1	x̄	+1	+2		Q3 -2	-1	x̄	+1	+2	n
	0	-1	-3	-1	0		1	1	4	2	0	0
	-1	-5	-4	0	0		0	5	7	0	0	0
	-3	-16	-12	0	0		3	16	13	1	0	0
	Q1						Q4					
English	0	-4	-6	-9	0		0	3	5	9	0	0
English/Spanish	0	-8	-8	-5	-3		1	7	4	6	3	3
Spanish	0	-14	-30	-16	0		-1	15	29	15	0	0

Total GPA

	Q2 -2	-1	x̄	+1	+2		Q3 -2	-1	x̄	+1	+2	n
	0	-4	-4	-1	0		0	5	5	2	0	0
	-1	-8	-5	-4	0		1	6	0	3	0	0
	-3	-27	-27	-5	0		3	26	26	4	0	0
	Q1						Q4					
English	0	0	-5	-10	-2		-1	1	6	10	1	1
English/Spanish	0	-1	-6	-1	-1		0	4	10	3	1	1
Spanish	0	-3	-17	-16	1		1	3	18	18	0	0

Math

	Q2 -2	-1	x̄	+1	+2		Q3 -2	-1	x̄	+1	+2	n
	0	-2	-4	-3	0		0	3	6	4	1	1
	-1	-4	-3	-1	0		1	5	1	1	0	0
	-2	-25	-16	-4	-1		2	23	14	5	0	0
	Q1						Q4					
English	0	-2	-5	-8	0		0	1	3	6	0	0
English/Spanish	0	-9	-8	-5	-3		0	8	10	4	3	3
Spanish	0	-6	-27	-13	1		0	8	29	12	0	0

Figure 5.11. Shifts in representation rates of language-background groups for each quadrant, boundary and school achievement measure when FSIQ rates are subtracted from ELP FSIQ rates.

Academic GPA/FSIQ

	Q2						Q3				
	-2	-1	x̄	+1	+2		-2	-1	x̄	+1	+2
Anglo	1.0	.64	.55	.26	.07						
Hispanic	1.0	.88	.41	.16	.02						
	Q1						Q4				
							.01	.05	.20	.42	.69
							.03	.17	.39	.44	0

Total GPA/FSIQ

	Q2						Q3				
	-2	-1	x̄	+1	+2		-2	-1	x̄	+1	+2
Anglo	1.0	.82	.59	.26	.04						
Hispanic	1.0	.88	.45	.15	.01						
	Q1						Q4				
							.01	.05	.17	.44	.92
							.04	.15	.36	.44	0

Reading/FSIQ

	Q2						Q3				
	-2	-1	x̄	+1	+2		-2	-1	x̄	+1	+2
Anglo	.80	.50	.48	.25	0						
Hispanic	.81	.41	.24	.09	0						
	Q1						Q4				
							.01	.06	.16	.36	1.0
							.03	.15	.32	.56	1.0

Math/FSIQ

	Q2						Q3				
	-2	-1	x̄	+1	+2		-2	-1	x̄	+1	+2
Anglo	.80	.60	.51	.36	.07						
Hispanic	1.0	.74	.33	.16	.01						
	Q1						Q4				
							0	.04	.13	.25	.57
							0	.09	.22	.28	.10

Figure 5.12. Conditional probabilities (CP's) for quadrants II and IV for Anglo and Hispanic pupils at −2SD, −1SD, ×, +1SD and +2SD boundaries.

167

presented here focus primarily on discrepancies in Hispanic pupils' outcomes *from* those of Anglo pupils'. The assumption here is that fairness is manifest when conditional probabilities are generally similar, or that when given a high or a low IQ, the probabilities for getting a high achievement score (Quadrant II) or a low achievement score (Quadrant IV) are fairly similar across ethnic and language-background groups. Figure 5.12 presents the conditional probabilities for Quadrant II and Quadrant IV for Anglo and Hispanic pupils.

For academic GPA in Quadrant II, Hispanic students who score at -1 SD on IQ have a much higher likelihood of doing better than predicted academically than their Anglo peers. Interestingly, in Quadrant IV, Hispanic students who score above any one of the five IQ boundaries have a greater likelihood than their Anglo peers of achieving below these same boundaries on their subsequent grades of academic achievement.

Virtually the same pattern appears for Quadrant II and Quadrant IV for total GPA.

For reading, Hispanic pupils are less likely than their Anglo peers to achieve above their predicted levels (Quadrant II) for virtually all boundaries but especially at and above $\bar{x}$. Yet, in Quadrant IV Hispanic pupils are more likely than their Anglo peers to do better than their IQ's would predict at virtually every boundary.

For math, Hispanic pupils at -1 SD are more likely to do better than their IQ would predict (Quadrant II), whereas, at and above $\bar{x}$, Anglo pupils are more likely to appear in Quadrant II. Again, however, in Quadrant IV Hispanic pupils are more likely than Anglos to fare less well than their IQ's would predict at virtually every boundary.

Figure 5.13 presents the conditional probabilities for each of the Hispanic language background groups for Quadrant II and Quadrant IV. By far the most striking results for GPA's involve the "English/Spanish" group. This group generally has the lowest probabilities in Quadrant II at and below the mean, but the highest probabilities in every boundary in Quadrant IV. Hispanic pupils from English/Spanish-speaking homes achieve (in terms of GPAs) below what their IQ's would predict.

For reading achievement, the "Spanish" group has the highest conditional probability at -1 SD, although at the $\bar{x}$ and $+1$ SD it is the "English" group that has the highest probabilities. In Quadrant IV, a much clearer pattern emerges with the "Spanish" and "English/Spanish" groups having the highest conditional probabilities at and below the mean, and the "English" group having the highest values above the mean.

For math, the pattern is similar to that for GPAs. The "Spanish" home-language group has the highest likelihood of doing better in math than their IQ would predict (Quadrant II) at -1 SD, whereas the "English/Spanish" group gets the highest probabilities in Quadrant IV — the "underachievers."

Academic GPA/FSIQ

Q2

	-2	-1	x̄	+1	+2
English	1.0	.89	.40	.16	.02
English/Spanish	1.0	.82	.37	.20	.01
Spanish	1.0	.91	.45	.13	.01

Q1 / Q4

	-2	-1	x̄	+1	+2
English	.02	.13	.40	.38	0
English/Spanish	.07	.23	.36	.67	0
Spanish	0	.17	.41	0	0

Total GPA/FSIQ

Q2

	-2	-1	x̄	+1	+2
English	1.0	.93	.41	.17	.02
English/Spanish	1.0	.82	.40	.17	0
Spanish	1.0	.88	.53	.11	.01

Q3 / Q4

	-2	-1	x̄	+1	+2
English	.03	.14	.35	.38	0
English/Spanish	.09	.20	.39	.67	0
Spanish	.02	.12	.35	0	0

Reading/FSIQ

Q2

	-2	-1	x̄	+1	+2
English	1.0	.40	.38	.12	0
English/Spanish	.80	.35	.15	.06	0
Spanish	.67	.46	.21	.06	0

Q1 / Q4

	-2	-1	x̄	+1	+2
English	.04	.10	.26	.43	1.0
English/Spanish	.02	.20	.38	1.0	0
Spanish	.03	.20	.44	0	0

Math/FSIQ

Q2

	-2	-1	x̄	+1	+2
English	1.0	.92	.80	.71	0
English/Spanish	1.0	.90	.72	.75	0
Spanish	1.0	.92	.81	0	0

Q3 / Q4

	-2	-1	x̄	+1	+2
English	0	.08	.20	.29	1.0
English/Spanish	0	.10	.28	.25	0
Spanish	0	.08	.19	0	0

Figure 5.13. Conditional probabilities (CP's) for quadrants II and IV for the three Hispanic home-language background groups at −2SD, −1SD, ×, +1SD and +2 SD boundaries.

Proceeding from the assumption that IQ has been (Mercer, 1979) and continues to be (Rueda et al., 1984; Twomey et al., 1980) the most frequently used type of test in special education assessment and in all likelihood the most influential in special education diagnosis and placement (Figueroa, 1990), the data presented in this study strongly suggest that decisions based on IQ can lead to inaccuracies in decision making for English-proficient Hispanic pupils, particularly for those who come from homes where some degree of Spanish is spoken.

Three types of analyses were done in this study. First, 1972 IQs and 1982 school achievement outcomes were examined to see whether disparate ethnic and language-group representation rates appeared within the four possible quadrants of the IQ/achievement bivariate scatter plot (using several boundaries to define the quadrants). The first analysis looked at the representation rates *as they occurred.* The fact that Hispanic children may disproportionally scored low on IQ and hence may be overly concentrated in Quadrants I and II is not controlled for. In this analysis the data show that Hispanic pupils who in 1972 scored at or below the mean on the WISC-R FSIQ are more likely than their Anglo counterparts to show above-expected school grades (GPAs, reading, math scores) in 1982. Above an IQ of 100, Anglo students are more likely to receive grades higher than their IQ would predict. Hispanics, in effect, tend to "overachieve" in relation to their 1972 "85" IQ, whereas Anglos "overachieve" in relation to their 1972 > 100 IQs. On the other hand, more Hispanics than Anglos fail to actualize their "potential." Many more of them show up as "underachievers" (particularly those with IQ's around 85) in 1982 than their 1972 IQs would predict.

Among the Hispanic language background groups, the more Spanish in the home the more that "overachievers" appear in Quadrant II in every school achievement measure and especially at the −1 SD boundaries (i.e., pupils with 1972 IQs of 85 or below tend to do better than that in 1982, especially "Spanish" home-language Hispanic students). Unexpectedly, the students from "English/Spanish" homes tend to be overrepresented in the "underachievement" quadrant (Q IV), particularly at the −1 SD boundary. For them, their educational level falls below what IQ would predict.

The second set of analyses uses Mercer's controversial, adjusted IQ, the Estimated Learning Potential (ELP), to correct for the uneven distribution of IQs between ethnic groups. Examining the representation rates in the four quadrants when 1972 ELP is used in the x-axis and school achievement is used in the y-axis, several unexpected outcomes (representation rates) emerge. ELP reduces the percentages of Hispanics in the "overachievement" quadrant (Q II) and increases it in the "underachievement" quadrant (Q IV) for virtually every school achievement measure but especially for reading.

For the language groups, ELP is particularly important in reducing the "Spanish" group's overrepresentation in Quadrant I and Quadrant II (particularly at the $\bar{x}$ and -1 SD boundaries) and shifting these to Quadrant III and Quadrant IV. Interestingly, when ELPIQs are used, the "English/Spanish" home language group shows up with the highest representation in Quadrant I, the low IQ/low achievement quadrant. Also this group tends to overpopulate Quadrant II (overachievers) for 1982 GPA measures when ELP is used.

The final set of analyses used "conditional probabilities" (CPs) to examine the representation rates across ethnic and language groups. CPs are another way of controlling for the initial (1972) negatively skewed IQ distribution in the Hispanic groups. They (CPs) are very conservative indices in that they work from the proposition that "given a low, or high IQ . . ." without any debate as to why in using IQ one group may be significantly below the mean of the other group.

The results from the CP analyses corroborate what has already been presented. Hispanics tend to have a higher probability of being "overachievers" (Q II) (especially at -1 SD) and "underachievers" (Q IV) than their Anglo peers on most school achievement measures. Examining the CPs of the language groups, it is surprising to find that the "English/ Spanish" group is the one most at risk in the sense of winding up in either Quadrant II (overachievers) or Quadrant IV (underachievers).

These data strongly suggest that IQ and school achievement may not have the same rank-order relationship for Hispanic pupils (particularly at the critical ≤ 85 IQ range) that they have for Anglo pupils. Together with all the other material presented up to now, this empirical study supports one inescapable conclusion: Testing circumstantial bilingual individuals entails an inequitable and unknown degree of error. What follows are the research and policy implications from this conclusion.

CHAPTER 6

Testing Bilinguals: From Issue Examination to Issue Implications

When a bilingual individual confronts a monolingual test, developed by monolingual individuals, and standardized and normed on a monolingual population, both the test taker and the test are asked to do something that they cannot. The bilingual test taker cannot perform like a monolingual. The monolingual test can't "measure" in the other language.

In the light of the issues that we have raised in the previous five chapters, and in the light of the fact that the use of standardized tests with bilingual individuals is both frequent and common, the question to be answered by this book now becomes: What are the implications of these findings for both policy and practice? Given the difficulties involved in measuring bilingual individuals and given a growing body of empirical evidence that such individuals are not being measured validly by existing methods and instruments, what are test users to do?

From our perspective, there are three different options available to both the testing and policy communities. These are:

Option 1 attempt to minimize the potential harm of using existing tests,
Option 2 temporarily ban all testing of circumstantial bilinguals until psychometrically valid tests can be developed for this population, or
Option 3 develop alternative approaches to testing and assessment.

The first option involves attempting to minimize potential harm to bilingual individuals as a result of mismeasurement. Such attempts would most likely depend on the "careful" and "responsible" use of standardized tests by test users.

A second option, and one which in our opinion is the most radical, is to suspend all testing of bilingual students until research on the questions raised here has been carried out and a theory advanced that can support the development of valid tests or assessment procedures for circumstantial bilinguals. This alternative requires the careful construction of a research agenda designed to contribute to the development of a theory of bilingual testing. It also requires both federal and private funding and a well-publicized set of policies for dealing with *no psychometric information* about bilingual students as opposed to *faulty* and *uninterpretable* psychometric information for these same individuals.

Finally, a third option that can be followed involves a new conceptualization of the nature and function of assessment and the rejection of traditional psychometric approaches to measurement and assessment. New conceptualizations, such as those that are based on a cognitive-science perspective, are already in existence and offer some promise to those concerned about finding ways in which individuals can be helped to reach their true potential.

In this chapter then, the issues to be faced in following each of the above three alternate options will be discussed at some length. In the first section, we examine the possibility of minimizing the potential harm of using standardized tests with circumstantial bilinguals. We examine contemporary policy statements on testing that apply to bilingual individuals and we discuss and critique existing efforts in this direction. Essentially, we call into question recommendations for the careful and responsible use of standardized tests with linguistic minority populations.

In the second section, we explore the effects of abolishing the use of standardized tests with circumstantial bilinguals during a specified period of time within which focused work on producing a sound and coherent theory of testing bilingual individuals *within the psychometric perspective* would be studied. We discuss the implications of such a policy and we refer the reader to a multifaceted research agenda (included as an appendix to this volume) which we believe can be used as a point of departure by researchers, policymakers, and funding agencies.

Finally, in the third section, we discuss *alternative* (nonpsychometric) *approaches* to testing and measurement. The work carried out by leading scholars in the area of cognitive science for the National Commission on Testing and Public Policy[1] is highlighted. Their work provides some

---

[1]The National Commission on Testing and Public Policy was formed in 1987 and supported by the Human Rights and Governance Program and the Education and Culture Program of the Ford Foundation. The Commission was composed of individuals with expertise in a variety of areas, including education, law, business, labor, assessment and measurement, and manpower development. Its mandate was: (a) to investigate trends, practices, and impacts of the use of standardized testing instruments and other forms of assessment in schools, the

guidelines on how assessment issues might be approached and studied with bilingual populations.

OPTION 1: MINIMIZING THE POTENTIAL HARM OF USING EXISTING STANDARDIZED TESTS WITH CIRCUMSTANTIAL BILINGUALS

In spite of the serious difficulties that circumstantial bilinguals encounter on standardized tests, it has been suggested that it is possible that careful and responsible use can be made of such tests by both practitioners and researchers. It is argued, that once it has been made clear that standardized tests have limitations, test users can work within those limitations. We would argue that attractive as the concept of careful, responsible use may be, its implementation is fraught with difficulties and contradictions. In spite of the best intentions, it is doubtful that existing instruments can actually be used either equitably or meaningfully to make important decisions about circumstantial bilingual individuals. We make this assertion on the basis of the empirical data reviewed up to this point and on the basis of what the major professional policy directives say about testing bilinguals.

Contemporary Policy Statements and the Testing of Circumstantial Bilinguals

In spite of the fact that the applied and research components of psychometrics continue a tradition of neglect with respect to bilingualism, some quasiregulatory committees within the psychological and educational communities have made significant acknowledgements and recommendations. Four reports are particularly germane.

In 1975, the APA's Board of Scientific Affairs commissioned a report, "Educational Uses of Tests with Disadvantaged Students" (Cleary, Humphreys, Kendrick, & Wesman, 1975). This report reasserted the validity of three historical assumptions on which tests rest. These, as already noted, are slanted and ignore the demographic, linguistic, and educational changes that are facts in contemporary America. The report also endorses prediction as the principal index for determining test bias. In its reviews of the literature up to that time, it also confirms that psychometric bias was not to be found in tests used on disadvantaged popula-

---

workplace, and the military; and (b) to recommend improvements in testing that would promote the identification and nurturing of talent, especially among racial, ethnic, and linguistic minorities.

tions. Needless to say, the report, the studies cited, and the recommendations were incomplete. Bilingualism was not considered as a possible, robust "moderator variable."

Ironically, however, the report makes one statement that virtually nullifies the rest of the report for bilingual children:

> In the elementary grades an intelligence test in English is inappropriate when the child has learned only Spanish in the home. A Spanish language test is probably a better choice in this situation than a nonlanguage performance scale. The intellectual repertoire of a bilingual child, on the other hand, can only be sampled by testing in both languages, on the basis that the repertoires in the separate languages will rarely overlap completely. Objective psychometric techniques to accomplish this have not been developed, but test administrators should assume that either language score standing alone is undoubtedly an underestimate of the bilingual child's repertoire. (p. 22)

In 1982, a Committee on Ability Testing was commissioned by the National Research Council "to conduct a broad examination of the role of testing in American life" (Wigdor & Garner, 1982, p. vii). The result was a two-volume publication on measurement, legal and societal aspects of ability, employment, and educational testing. Four pages out of the 656 focus directly on the issue of bilingualism.

In the short section on "Testing Bilingual Students" (p. 158), the Report makes several important points. First, it cautions that testing nonnative English speakers is problematic. This is an enlightened position since it sidesteps the question of L2 proficiency. Tests, as the literature has shown, are hypersensitive to the effects of a non-English language even when English is a subject's dominant language (of course, the same applies to information processing). Second, it cautions against using translations. Third, it suggests that testing bilinguals is not effectively done by just using L1 tests and L2 tests. Fourth, it labels "comparable" tests given in L1 but which use L2 norms as "nonsensical" (p. 159) (a warning that was apparently lost on the Psychological Corporation (1982) with its publication of the *Escala de Inteligencia de Wechsler en Español*). Fifth, it alerts test users to the heightened "probability of misinterpreting a bilingual pupil's test performance" when cutoff scores are used.

The second place where the report touches on bilingualism comes in the "Linguistic Bias" section. This part deals with the court cases involving Hispanic and Chinese bilingual children. It essentially comprises brief descriptions of the five cases cited.

Throughout the rest of the report, the issue of bilingualism essentially disappears. It plays no part in the voluminous citations of studies that find no ethnic or racial bias in tests (ability, educational, employment), nor in the discussions on test uses and misuses.

In 1982, the National Research Council, through a Panel on Selection and Placement of Students in Programs for the Mentally Retarded, issued a report titled *Placing Children in Special Education: A Strategy for Equity* (Heller, Holtzman, & Messick, 1982). The report essentially investigated the phenomenon of overrepresentation of minority children in classes for the mildly retarded in the United States. The report reviewed the usual legal and psychometric issues on testing ethnic children and, as usual, failed to fault tests on psychometric/predictive grounds. However, the report does attempt, and almost succeeds, in providing a balanced and broad exploration of the issues and of possible resolutions. Regrettably, with respect to bilingual issues, very little is said. Once again, however, what is said and what is relevant to bilingual pupils constitute powerful caveats to the entire report.

First, in an analysis of overrepresentation rates (1978– 79) in school districts throughout the country (previously described), Finn (1982) found that significant Hispanic overrepresentation rates occurred in small school districts with high Hispanic student populations and where there were few, if any, linguistically appropriate instructional programs (bilingual education). The assessment and diagnosis of mental retardation, in effect, was a socially constructed phenomena directly related to English-only instructional programs. Regrettably, the report never addresses the meaning of this finding in terms of psychometric, predictive validity.

Second, in three paragraphs (pp. 52, 58, 59), the report notes the following problems: Children from homes where English is not the primary language may produce test performance that is mediated not just by ability but also by familiarity with the test content ("claims about validity and meaning of test scores, then, are always population-specific"; p. 52). With limited-English-proficient children, "There appears to be no doubt that such children are at an unfair disadvantage" (p. 59) when English-language tests are used. Translating tests is a problematic procedure, particularly insofar as such tests lead to "culture specific norms" which may not be as predictive as regular norms.

Third, the report recommends that for all children, psychological assessments in schools should *follow* an assessment of the learning environment. Given Finn's finding relative to the link between bilingual instructional options and "mental retardation" rates, and given the historical experience of bilingual children in American schools, this recommendation has direct relevance to testing such children. Table 6.1 presents a modification of the report's learning environment factors that should be included in the first level of assessment, as they may relate to bilingual pupils.

TABLE 6.1
The First Level of Assessment: The Classroom

I. There should be evidence that the curriculum works with bilingual students.
Sources of Evidence: Publishers, research, school district data, standardized achievement data, results from criterion referenced tests.
II. There should be evidence that the teacher is effectively implementing the curriculum for the bilingual pupils.
Sources of Evidence: The achievement level of the class, observed quality instruction and management (e.g., adequate feedback, direction, reinforcement), amount of exposure to the curriculum by the child being considered for testing.
III. The bilingual child has not learned what was effectively and consistently presented in class.
Sources of Evidence: Tests keyed to the content presented in class.
IV. The bilingual child cannot learn even under early, individualized, intensive modifications.
Sources of Evidence: Types of modifications, the length of modifications, the results of such modifications.

In 1985, the American Educational Research Association, the American Psychological Association, and the National council on Measurement in Education published a landmark edition of the *Standards for Educational and Psychological Testing* (1985). In a quantum leap from totally ignoring bilingual issues in the 1974 edition of the *Standards*, the 1985 version devotes an entire chapter to some of the major considerations surrounding the testing of bilingual individuals. It is the strongest statement on the topic ever put forth by the testing professions. In many ways, the *Standards* in Chapter 13 virtually proscribe many of the testing practices and research procedures currently in use with bilingual populations. Unfortunately, as the studies since 1985 indicate, they are being ignored.

Chapter 13 is made up of an introductory narrative section and seven standards. The narrative, at long last, focuses attention on the ubiquitous low verbal test scores of linguistic minorities by unequivocally asserting that "every test given in English becomes, in part, a language or literacy test" (p. 73). This strong statement, however, becomes anemic when it points out that circumstantial bilinguals test scores "*may* not" [emphasis added] be valid and that test developers and test users should give "special attention to this matter." The narrative also acknowledges the unique and complex entity that is the bilingual hearer-speaker, and the possible disadvantages in processing speed associated with L2. Addressing test users and test takers again, the narrative vaguely suggests taking "language background into account" (p. 73).

On the matter of translating tests for the sake of "dual-language" testing, the criteria set forth essentially call for producing a *psychometrically* equivalent test ("content, difficulty level, reliability, and validity"; p. 73).

For example, a translation into Spanish of an English reading test "may include content equally meaningful to Spanish-speaking students" (p. 73).

On the matter of language proficiency tests *in English*, their need, use, and importance in educational programming are stressed. It is also indicated that such tests should comprehensively measure *English* language skills ("communicative competence, grammar, pronunciation, and comprehension"; p. 74). Observation of speech in "naturalistic situations" can help in determining linguistic "proficiency in *a language*" (p. 74; emphasis added). But such natural speech may not predict linguistic ability in more formal settings, such as in a classroom. For example, a child's English language ability exhibited at recess may not correctly indicate whether "instruction in English" (p. 74) will be beneficial. It is also suggested that "a broader range of tests and observations" (p. 74) of language proficiency "may be desirable" (p. 74).

Finally, the narrative section concludes by warning that test behaviors (e.g., responding to adults and length of such responses) may be mediated by cultural variables. "Resulting interpretations and prescriptions . . . may be invalid and potentially harmful" (p. 74).

Standard 13.1 and its commentary declare that with non-English linguistic backgrounds, testing should "be designed" to diminish "threats to . . . reliability and validity" (p. 74) and that this may be done by using personnel with culturally and linguistically appropriate skills ("bilingual communication"; p. 74). This proviso, in fact, is an echo of Standard 6.10, where testers are *almost* proscribed from testing individuals with linguistic backgrounds "outside the . . . [tester's] academic training or supervised experience" (p. 43).

Standard 13.2 makes a vague declaration about specificity in any language-related modifications prescribed in test manuals.

Standard 13.3 says that test makers should be explicit about whether or how their tests can be used with speakers whose L1 is not English. However, this standard recognizes that investigations on all circumstantial bilinguals are not possible.

Standard 13.4 repeats the condition for translating tests: psychometric equivalence. Interestingly, this directive is also aimed at translating tests across dialects.

Standard 13.5 is directed at all employment-related testing. The principle here is that the English language demands in the tests should be commensurate with the English language demands of the job.

Standard 13.6 is directed at tests that are available in L1 and L2 (and it seems that this applies to tests that are psychometrically sound). If they purport to be comparable, there should be proof of this.

Standard 13.7 concerns tests of English language proficiency. They should cover multiple skills.

If Chapter 13 of the *Standards for Educational and Psychological Testing* was applied or enforced, some of the criticisms of tests, testers, and testing with bilingual populations discussed in this chapter would be attenuated. However, the *Standards* themselves suffer from several flaws. These include the assumption that bilingual testing equals the sum of test scores in L1 and L2; the ambiguous directives given to test publishers; the lack of a clear and specific directive on whether testers who do not speak the test taker's language can actually test; the ignorance and silence about the widespread use of interpreters in testing limited English speakers; the lack of a clear stance on sanctions for conducting unfair, biased, harmful testing with children, particularly in the service of special education "diagnostic" testing in schools; and the manifest diminution of the importance of a non-English L1 in the narrative section and in Standards 13.5 and 13.7.

Clearly, a new set of *Standards* is needed in order to guide test users with bilingual clients. The new standards would have to operate from the recognition that unless testing technology can overcome the fact of linguistic bias ("every test given in English becomes, in part, a language or literacy test"; p. 73 of the current *Standards*) unique and heretofore unexplored directives would have to be promulgated on how to use standardized test that are inherently flawed.

Such an effort would not be a first-time enterprise. Many publications currently exist which operate precisely from such a premise (Brozovich, Oplesch, & Villegas, 1990; Hamayan & Damico, 1991; Prewitt-Diaz, 1990; Valencia & Aburto, 1991). First among these is the work of Hamayan and Damico (1991) on "*Limiting* Bias in the Assessment of Bilingual Students" [emphasis added]. Their title depicts a unique sort of tolerance in its willingness to live with bias. Hopefully, a new set of standards would go beyond Hamayan and Damico's (1991) "solution" which is to live with an unknown degree of bias for bilinguals and to "limit" bias by doing more testing in both L1 and L2.

As noted at the beginning of this chapter, the bottom line is that when a bilingual individual confronts a monolingual test, developed by monolingual individuals, and standardized and normed on a monolingual population, both the test taker and the test are asked to do something that they cannot. The bilingual test taker can't perform like a monolingual. The monolingual test can't "measure" in the other language. In this context, how can a test user give standardized tests to circumstantial bilinguals in a careful and responsible manner?

How can tests be used carefully and responsibly? We suggest that the answer to this questions depends on the purpose or the use of the test data. Resnick and Resnick (1992) provide a useful contemporary schema for examining the functions of testing. Though their analysis focuses on educational functions of tests, the schema that they use generalizes to most, if not all, standardized test functions.

Resnick and Resnick (1992), in their article "Assessing the Thinking Curriculum: New Tools for Educational Reform," carefully examine the functions of testing in order to analyze the audience concerned with each category of testing as well as the fundamental characteristics of each type of test. They identify three main classes of testing: (a) public accountability and program evaluation, (b) instructional management and monitoring, and (c) client selection and certification. According to Resnick and Resnick (1992), "each has different sets of audiences, and each places different demands on the assessment system" (p. 48).

Summarizing briefly, Resnick and Resnick argue that the focus of accountability testing is on groups and not on individuals. Test users do not depend on such tests to guide instruction, therapy, or placement; rather, tests are used by the public to obtain a broad view of how groups are performing. These tests, in essence, focus on system effects.

On the other hand, tests that are intended to guide selection and certification involve a focus on individuals themselves. Since such tests are used to make decisions about assignment or admission to particular programs, jobs, or treatments, their fundamental requirement is "that they provide information on *individuals* and that the test scores predict future performance in the institution or program for which the client is being considered."

Finally, the third category of tests involves assessment that is used in the instructional (or occupational, or therapeutic) management and monitoring of client progress. For these tests, the focus is, again, the individual; but as opposed to selection and certification tests, the audience for these tests is the instructional, occupational, or therapeutic staff. Such tests help the management of treatment. Because of their purpose and their audience, these tests must present their results quickly in order to gauge and help direct progress.

In our judgment, given the data reviewed and the policy statements promulgated since 1975, there is no justification for using standardized tests to make decisions about individual circumstantial bilinguals. We find that every extant testing practice (using the English version of a test, translating the test, using interpreters, testing in two languages, using tests developed in other countries, using tests "clinically") entails violating legal (particularly in education), professional (e.g., *Standards*), or empirical findings.

The only area wherein tests might be used carefully and responsibly is in accountability testing. When system outcomes are the focus, testing bilinguals may actually lead to the identification of error variance associated with English language proficiency and may actually be of some benefit to linguistic minorities. In academic achievement testing such a practice may actually be innovative. Many states, school districts and schools exclude bilingual pupils from their testing programs. Including them may, in fact, be not only the more honest alternative; it may also be the most useful condition insofar as taxpayers may actually get a glimpse of how effective their public school systems are in providing educational programs to all pupils.

OPTION 2: THE TEMPORARY ABOLISHMENT OF THE USE OF STANDARDIZED TESTS WITH CIRCUMSTANTIAL BILINGUALS

A second, more radical but perhaps more equitable response to the problems surrounding the testing of circumstantial bilinguals is the implementation of a policy that would temporarily suspend all testing of circumstantial bilingual persons when such tests are used to select, certify, or guide interventions for *individuals*. The basis for such a moratorium rests on the grounds that such tests provide uninterpretable information. Such a policy, although admittedly controversial, could be justified as part of a coherent national effort designed to address the procedural due-process rights of an increasingly diverse population. Such an effort might involve the following steps:

1. The declaration of a national moratorium on the testing of circumstantial bilinguals when such testing involves decision making about individuals.
2. The establishment of an information campaign explaining the moratorium and establishing guidelines for substituting direct behavioral or performance measures in all affected areas of assessment.
3. The advancement of a plan of action for research and development aimed at establishing a coherent theory of bilingual assessment.
4. The gradual phasing-in and ongoing evaluation of new assessment instrument of new alternative assessment procedures.
5. The establishment of a set of standards for testing bilingual individuals.

The abolishment of standardized testing for circumstantial bilinguals and the resulting lack of psychometric information about such students, even on a temporary basis, provokes strong reactions from practitioners and policy makers. In the current, highly charged climate surrounding assessment and measurement, arguing for the abolishment of testing for a population considered to be particularly at-risk smacks of irresponsibility. Interestingly enough, decision making informed by flawed or uninterpretable information is seen as somehow more responsible, more equitable, or perhaps more enlightened, than decision making without psychometric data. We argue that the former action is the irresponsible one.

As per our previous discussion, Resnick and Resnick's (1992) analysis of the functions of tests, a moratorium on the use of standardized testing with circumstantial bilinguals would affect two functions: selection/certification and the management of interventions.

Function: Selection/Certification

The effect of a moratorium on the testing of bilingual individuals would complicate selection and certification procedures. Because those procedures currently operate under the assumption that standardized tests can make valid comparisons among individuals, they are generally used to make decisions about college admissions, acceptance into teacher education programs, employment certification, promotion, and the like. The abolishment of such testing for circumstantial bilinguals would mean that there would be no ACT or SAT scores available for this group of individuals, no GRE or LSAT scores, no high school competency or GED scores, no NTE or CBEST scores, no MMPI profiles, and no state licensing scores for particular trades or occupations.

Without such information, it will be claimed that institutions and professions will be unable to identify and select the brightest and the best. Without comparative data for a very large group of Americans, it will be argued that rewarding merit and allocating slots will become incredibly difficult. Given the increasing hostility toward affirmative action, the ban on testing will be seen as yet another unfair ploy by minorities to obtain preferential treatment. There may be increased protests about the admission of incompetents and the exclusion of the truly talented, and members of selected professions and trades will assert that protecting the public from untrained or incompetent practitioners will be impossible.

Politically volatile as the allocation of opportunity is, it is also the case that a large number of very respected scholars have questioned the practice of using standardized test scores to identify talent (e.g., Gifford, 1989). More recently, the National Commission on Testing and Public Policy (1990) included among its recommendations the following statement about the use of testing in selection and certification:

> On its surface, using a particular score on a test to allocate opportunities appears objective and fair: all who take the test must meet the same

standard. But as we have shown, test scores used alone can result in wrong classifications about what people can or cannot do in the real worlds of school and the workplace. When such misclassifications trigger incorrect decisions, they create unfairness. Using tests as a tool for institutional accountability also seems sensible; but as we have seen, *overreliance* on tests distorts the information and diverts policy makers' attention from consideration of remedies for the underlying problems in the schools and workplace.

Thus, the Commission recommends that test scores *not* be used in isolation to make important decisions about people, groups, or institutions. Evidence that might contradict the conclusions based on a single test score must be considered. If a person who wants to dispute a speeding ticket based on a radar gun can offer evidence that the radar reading was inaccurate, or present other rebutting or mitigating evidence, test takers ought to have an analogous due process alternative.

While test scores may be useful for *informing* decisions about individuals, *past performance and experience relevant to the opportunities* should be considered in conjunction with tests scores. Traditions of fairness – as well as professional standards regarding test interpretation – demand that such decisions generally not be made on the basis of one kind of fallible evidence. Furthermore, *people and their judgments must be directly engaged* in making important decisions about other people. The Commission recognizes that human decisions about the allocation of opportunities can be biased and unfair, and that testing programs were often established to overcome such problems. Accumulated assessment evidence should be used, therefore, to evaluate the fairness and accuracy of human judgments in the allocation of opportunities. (National Commission on Testing and Public Policy, 1990, p. 30)

Clearly, in the eyes of the Commission, fairness in allocation of opportunity must involve more than a single score on a single standardized test. At the very least individuals must be given the opportunity of questioning that single score and of providing additional relevant information that might result in a more complete view of their strengths and experiences.

If this particular perspective were to be adopted for all selection and certification decisions to be made during the period of the testing moratorium, the issues of fairness and comparison could be dealt with honestly and forthrightly. We would propose that, during the period of the moratorium, other means of allocating opportunities be used. In particular, we suggest that multiple indices of competence be employed for all decisions. These indices could include: grades, personal statements, records of employment or production, recommendations, portfolios, personal interviews, written essays, observations of performance, and the like. All individuals providing a full set of acceptable indices would become part of a pool of potential candidates for a given number of slots to be chosen by lot.

A lottery system in which all individuals would have an equal chance of being chosen has the advantage of seeming just. The number of indices required by individuals in order to qualify for the lottery pool would need to be established in consultation with affected professions, minority and mainstream clients, job candidates, and policy makers. Once again, the use of these special procedures would need to be widely publicized in order to avoid the impression of deliberate unfairness or favoritism.

We contend that potentially divisive as a moratorium on testing for bilingual individuals might be, negative effects stemming from that moratorium would be minimized if it were made clear in a very public and very broad manner: (a) that research on the development of appropriate measures for the population in question would go forward at full speed; (b) that the procedures to be followed during the ban would not give unfair advantages to one group over another; and (c) that the implementation of these procedures would offer groups, individuals, and institutions concerned with selection and certification the opportunity to investigate the effects and consequences of such policies. Conceivably, society may find that multiple indices of competency benefit all and that this type of information instead of test scores may actually enhance prediction, training, and success. After all, the "best" of psychometric predictions seldom account for even 30% of the variance of various criteria (Barrett & Depinet, 1991).

Function: Management of Interventions

In this function of tests, psychometric assessment is used to manage and monitor treatment. For these tests, the focus is, again, the individual; but as opposed to selection and certification tests, the audience for these tests is the staff doing the interventions. These tests supposedly help guide treatment. In some settings, such as in classrooms, these tests "can also serve as motivators and organizers of students" study time (Resnick & Resnick, 1992, p. 50).

In abolishing the testing of circumstantial bilinguals for this management function, two points are worth noting. First, if the current tests covertly moonlight as measures of English language proficiency, how could psychiatric therapy be gauged as "effective" either in the short or the long term? How could the effects of job training be accurately ascertained or, if necessary, changed and made more effective? How can a teacher determine whether a low score on a test of academic progress reflects the impact of teaching, the amount of material learned, or the pupils limited English proficiency? Second, in the area of monitoring interventions (as in all testing functions) the suspension of testing will not lead to the suspension of judgment. An argument can be made, in fact, that in monitoring the effects of interventions, the characteristics of the interventions, of the local effort, and of the goals set by those who intervene, are far more useful for management (as multiple criteria) than a psychometric test score. In education, this argument is finding wide acceptance and is usually presented as the debate between curriculum-based testing versus psychometric testing.

A Special Case. There is one area within the educational arena where the proposed moratorium poses what may seem like a dilemma. This has to do with the assessment of language. Assessment used for instructional management involves the diagnosis of individual strengths and weaknesses for the purpose of designing appropriate instruction. In the case of circumstantial bilinguals, the issue of instructional management and monitoring becomes to some degree intertwined with that of selection. Because of the centrality of English language ability for this population, assessment used to support instruction primarily involves the measurement of language competencies. In spite of the limitations of existing language assessment instruments (reviewed here in Chapter 2) standardized language measures (e.g., BINL, LAS, BSM) are used regularly by most school districts for *both* selection *and* instructional monitoring and management. These measures are not only used in order to make decisions about appropriate program placement (e.g., whether children are eligible or not for bilingual education placement); they are also used to justify placement decisions to an audience at a distance (the community, funding agencies, state regulatory bodies) who are concerned about the education of non-English-speaking students. In order to comply, for example, with the Bilingual Education Act, school districts applying for federal funds must collect and report information on LEP (limited English-proficient) students.

Currently states vary in their requirements for the identification of students from other language backgrounds. Most require the use of a home language questionnaire in addition to language assessment test(s) in order to justify assistance program placement. In many cases, however, information obtained from teacher observations, student records, student interviews, and locally developed assessment procedures are also used. Even in those cases when the same standardized language assessment instruments are used, there is variation between states in terms of the establishment of cutoff scores. Frequently, pressure is brought upon school districts to raise or lower such scores depending on the nature of the services available.

The language assessment issue is even more complex in making decisions for program exit. The question of when a student identified as limited-English-proficient (LEP) and declared eligible for services can be classified as fluent-English-proficient (FEP) is a difficult one. In the state of California, for example, districts may use one of several methods of determining English language competence: (a) teacher observation, (b) standardized content tests, or (c) language proficiency tests. Many have argued that both teacher observation and language proficiency test results are problematic and that children should not be exited from assistance programs until their scores on standardized content tests are close to those of the mainstream school population. As we have argued earlier, however, standardized achievement tests (content tests) are in and of themselves problematic for circumstantial bilingual populations. They were never intended to be (although they may in fact be) tests of language. Their use as indicators of subject-matter knowledge is problematic enough, but their use as indicators of English fluency or even competency in academic English is even more troublesome.

A policy calling for a moratorium on standardized testing for circumstantial bilingual students would, in our opinion, prohibit the use of standardized language assessment instruments. Even though such tests focus on language itself, they are also based on a theory of assessment developed for monolingual individuals.

The result of such a policy would be that, for the period of the moratorium, other procedures for diagnosing individual children's knowledge of English would need to be used exclusively. Such procedures might involve a period of observation by the classroom teacher, complementary observations by a language specialist, a more detailed home background and language use questionnaire, student interviews, locally developed assessment procedures, and the like. In many areas of the country these procedures are already in use instead of, or in addition to, language proficiency assessment interviews.

In imposing a standardized testing moratorium in the area of student identification, a key concern would be the provision of needed instruction and services to those children needing the services. The abolishment of standardized language assessment could not be allowed to result in blanket assignments of students to either monolingual English programs or exclusively to home language programs. This would mean, then, that special monitoring procedures would need to be put in place for the period in question in order to prevent abuses.

As in the cases discussed previously, in order to diffuse angry responses from groups who would might view the moratorium as a plot against non-English-background children, much publicity would need to be given to the reasons for the moratorium, the problems present in existing language proficiency measures, and the progress of the on going research and development project.

In the case of other kinds of testing normally used by instructional staff in order to support instruction, it is not expected that a moratorium on the testing of circumstantial bilingual students would prove particularly problematic. Essentially, since the audience for such assessment is the school staff itself, the need for comparative data is more limited. Teachers would be encouraged to use a variety of indicators to identify students' strengths and weaknesses and to determine instructional support needs.

The Ongoing Research and Test Development Component

A key component of the temporary abolishment of the use of standardized tests with circumstantial bilinguals would be the funding and support of basic research on circumstantial bilingualism and the funding and support of the development of both a theory and a practice of bilingual testing. Although in our discussion of Option 3, we argue for a new conceptualization of testing and assessment, we consider that attention by the psychometric community to this effort is essential if existing assumptions about measurement remain in place.

A preliminary research agenda that might serve as a point of departure for such an effort is included in the Appendix. We maintain that in establishing a testing moratorium, elements contained in such an agenda would need to be made public. Educators, policymakers, administrators, and other concerned individuals would need to informed of the complexity of the issues and of the need to develop a means of addressing the valid assessment of circumstantial bilinguals within the existing established tradition.

The Effects of the Testing Moratorium: A Summary

In sum, the abolishment of the use of standardized tests with circumstantial bilinguals would be controversial. As we have outlined above, various different uses of testing would be affected. In many cases, the issues involved are highly charged and would lead to public controversy. In considering this second option, then, the potential problems would need to be weighed against the possibility of improvement. The choice between what would seem to be no information against what is actually flawed or uninterpretable information would need to be carefully explained.

As we have tried to make clear in our discussion of this second option, in order for it to be successfully implemented, much effort would be required.

Guidelines for dealing with accountability and program evaluation would need to be developed. Procedures for selecting and certifying individuals would need to be put in place, and finally, strategies for identifying language limitations for members of the population in question would need to be well planned. Throughout the entire period of the moratorium, the public would need to be assured of the temporary nature of the effort and of the progress of the ongoing work leading to the development of better assessment procedures for circumstantial bilinguals.

This option would also be expensive. The costs of funding the research component would be substantial. Moreover, there would be costs involved in setting up new temporary procedures and in publicizing new policies. For many, these costs will be too high. For others, the expenditure of effort and money dedicated to developing *psychometrically valid* tests for circumstantial bilinguals will seem misguided. They will argue (as will be more fully discussed later) that recent research on learning has raised profound questions about the very assumptions that undergird the psychometric tradition.

The initial reactions to such a moratorium policy are bound to be contentions. It is also quite likely that such a policy would engender a long and bitter debate. Given the likelihood that bilingual individuals would not see relief from testing errors for a long time, we recommend that, at a minimum, the following changes be considered by the testing community:

1. Studies published in scientific journals should be required to account in their designs for the possible impact of L1 on language minority samples. Designations such as "Hispanic," "American Indian," or "Asian American" are inadequate. Mercer (1979), for example, normed a large battery of psychometric tests on a representative random sample of 700, supposedly English-speaking Hispanic children. As it turned out, over 60% of them came from homes where Spanish was spoken. Virtually all the tests normed registered this fact in lowered means and altered predictive validities compromising the utility of the tests of "Hispanic" students.

2. Prestigious publications, such as the *Journal of Educational Psychology*, accept studies that use straight translations of tests normed in English. This practice should be proscribed. Data from such studies are essentially uninterpretable.

3. Textbooks on testing generally tend to provide stereotypic, irrelevant, or outdated information on linguistic minorities. The impact of bilingualism on tests is seldom treated as an important concern. The robust data on bilingualism, second language acquisition, the sociocultural factors that mediate the immigrant and language

minority experience in this country, and the issues surrounding the education of bilinguals are seldom considered. This form of intellectual alienation, often found even in reports that highlight the needs of "minorities" (e.g., Levin, 1987, 1988), has a serious longitudinal impact on test users in that it impedes their professional training, making them ill-suited to meet the needs of bilingual clients.

4. The use of interpreters in assessment and testing is a common practice that has received virtually no attention in research studies, testing standards, or the law. There is no empirically validated model for using interpreters. There are no data to substantiate the validity of this procedure. Immediate attention to this matter is urgently called for. At a minimum, the incidence and conditions under which this practice occurs should be investigated.

5. A similar set of concerns surrounds the use of tests simply translated from English to L1. Though the current standards essentially ban this procedure, practitioners still use it. A modified version of this practice can also be found in widely used tests such as the K-ABC where instructions in L1 are provided for the nonverbal parts. The validity of this practice has yet to be studied.

6. The quantity of tests available in different languages is substantial. The technical quality of most of these is suspect. Entrepreneurship more than science typify the test makers in this market. There is considerable need for critique and evaluation. A publication like the Buros volumes for the field of bilingual testing is urgently needed.

7. If a psychologist works in schools or social service settings that are heavily bilingual, are there special credentialing, certification, and licensing requirements for such a professional? Particularly, should there be a requirement that such a person should have skills in the primary language of her/his clients? The standards suggest that this might indeed be the case. There is an urgent need to clarify the policy, ethical, and legislative implications surrounding this topic.

8. New models for the study of bias and fairness when it comes to testing bilinguals should be explored. The same applies to the notion of "testing bilingually." As this text suggests, the latter may not just be the sum of scores in L1 and L2.

9. In some areas of testing, such as personality and intelligence, it may well be impossible to develop psychometric tests for large bilingual populations such as Latinos. Alternative assessment paradigms such as the Learning Assessment Potential Device may come to supplant "objective" tests for bilingual populations.

In these, professional, clinical judgment becomes paramount. The study of the validity and components of "heuristics" in bilingual assessment must be supported and encouraged in the eventuality that psychometric tests with bilingual norms may not be available.

In considering, then, the adoption of the testing moratorium option as a temporary measure designed to improve testing for circumstantial bilinguals, it will undoubtedly be necessary to examine the very nature of testing carefully. In addition to the questions and concerns raised above, both the educational and the policy communities would need to consider whether to build on a tradition that many have found to be seriously flawed or whether to engage in a meaningful rethinking of the entire question. In the next section, we will present a discussion of a third option that would need to be considered in reaching a conclusion. This third option rejects current psychometric approaches to testing.

OPTION 3: THE DEVELOPMENT OF ALTERNATIVE APPROACHES TO TESTING AND ASSESSMENT

At its core, testing technology has not changed much for nearly a century. Tests are still a variant of the Stimulus-Response model of human behavior (small questions eliciting small responses). The paradigm is essentially a reductionist one (Poplin, 1988a, 1988b) where it is assumed that the sum total of a number of small responses captures the essence of a whole, such as in the constructs of intelligence or personality. In their normative framework (and by the selection of subjects that make up the norms), tests continue to assume a relative sameness of culture, language and opportunity among those constituting the norms and, more critically, a sameness between those in the normative sample and those who take the tests. Tests continue to be seen as cost-efficient in relation to less "objective," more judgmental, and more longitudinal data collection procedures. And tests endow the test taker with a unique degree of behavioral solipsism and determinism. Context has very little if any bearing. What the score indicates from the testing session is what the individual would do in every other setting or context because supposedly the test taps something intrinsic and permanent. In this sense, tests, for many psychologists, are similar to medical procedures. An IQ is like an EEG. An MMPI is like a biopsy. An SAT is like a CAT scan. A vocational interest inventory is like a blood test.

In this book, we have attempted to demonstrate that for bilingual individuals, many of these test assumptions and characteristics simply do not apply. Reductionism in either L1 or L2 does not capture a true, miniprofile of the circumstantial bilingual. Limited English speakers are not included in norms, and the continua of bilingual skills is not controlled for in norm tables. Diversity, no matter how politically incorrect, is and will become even more of a demographic fact in America. Opportunity, perhaps more than ever, is socially stratified (Kozol, 1991). With bilingual individuals, particularly bilingual children, the societal and financial costs attached to test misdiagnosis, nonadmission, or mistreatment are far greater than the benefits attached to cost-effectiveness because of testing. Also for bilingual individuals, context, particularly linguistic and cultural contexts, determines a great deal (but not usually all) of what is operationalized. For bilingual individuals, psychometric tests function less like medical procedures and more like rules in a socially constructed game (Mehan, Herweck, & Meihls, 1986). The norms do not apply. The standardized procedures are often violated (e.g., translating, using interpreters). The interpretations and use of scores produce bias (Duran, 1983), misdiagnosis (Rueda, Figueroa, Mercado, & Carpenter, 1984) and clinical error (Guttfreund, 1991).

We would suggest, however, that the above points notwithstanding, paradigmatic and conceptual changes in the study and understanding of human behavior and human mentation are already calling into questions the uses and need for psychometric tests (Campione, Brown, & Ferrara, 1982; Gardner, 1992; Mehan, Hertweck, & Meihls, 1986; Sternberg, 1988; Taylor, 1991). Two sources of change are particularly worth nothing: (a) experimental studies of human information processing (cognitive science), and (b) the assessment of competency (McClelland, 1973; Rhodes & Dudley-Marling, 1988).

Cognitive Science. Work currently being carried out on assessment within the cognitive science perspective entails a reconceptualization of the nature of testing. This "new psychology" of intelligence and learning has much to offer to those concerned about developing assessment practices that directly support developing the potential of individuals. This conceptualization, which is derived from the cognitive science perspective is referred to here as "new" because, as O'Connor (1992) has argued, there are fundamental differences between the traditional psychometric and the more recent cognitive science perspectives on testing, differences which are profound, fundamental, and, for the most part, irreconcilable.

Summarizing briefly, according to O'Connor (1992), within the psychometric tradition, "underlying aspects of intelligent behavior or achievement are *discovered* by establishing the correlations between subjects' performance on different types of tasks" (p. *18*). Central to this perspective is the comparison of individual performance with those of a norming group and the use of a correlational approach "which locates the individual in relation to a larger group" (p. 18). Within psychometric practice, O'Connor (1992) identified three salient characteristics: (1) objects measured are precise and quantified, (2) what is measured is viewed as *static*, and (3) "the investigation of the nature of mental entities is *indirect*" (p. 19).

Additionally, Resnick and Resnick (1992) characterize traditional psychometric testing technology as being based on two key assumptions: decomposability and decontextualization. They note that both of these assumptions about the nature of human cognition and learning are now discredited. Decomposability, or the belief that thought can be described "as a collection of independent pieces of knowledge," has led, according to Resnick and Resnick, to the identification and testing of separate components or abilities, a process that has directly interfered with the effective teaching of problem solving and thinking abilities. Similarly, decontextualization or the assertion that "each component of a complex skill is fixed, and that it will take the same form no matter where it is used," has been found to be invalid. The Resnicks argue that it is now understood that "knowledge and skill cannot be detached from their contexts of practice and use" (p. 43).

Within the cognitive science perspective, on the other hand, the focus, according to O'Connor (1992), is on "understanding the processes and knowledge operating within a particular task performance, through a process of modeling what happens in a performance of that task" (p. 19). In Pellegrino's terms (1992), within the cognitive science perspective the concern is with understanding what tests test, with specifying the exact nature of the behaviors examined, and with being able, not only to count errors, but also to account for errors. The result of this view is that the emphasis is placed on the individual, on diagnosing and understanding performance at the time of assessment rather than comparing the learner with others in a larger group or with predicting future performances. Ability is not seen as static, but rather as dynamic, changeable, and context-specific. The emphasis of much of the work carried out within the cognitive science perspective is on the integration of assessment and intervention.

Currently, assessment procedures based on a cognitive science perspective are primarily in the experimental stage. These assessment procedures are designed to identify children's potential for learning. Brown et al. (1992) have identified these as including: dynamic assessment, learning potential assessment, learning tests, testing-the-limits approach, mediated assessment, evaluation of the zone of proximal or potential development, and assessment via assisted learning and transfer. According to Brown et al. (1992):

> the common feature of all these approaches is an emphasis on evaluating the psychological processes involved in learning and change. This contrasts with

standard methods of assessment that rely on product information. The argument is that individuals with comparable scores on static tests may have taken different paths to those scores and that consideration of those differences can provide information of additional diagnostic value. (p. 140)

In order to provide a more detailed view of the assumptions underlying these new assessment strategies, we will briefly describe two approaches to the assessment of children's learning potential. Before beginning such a description, it is important to note that research focusing on the assessment of children's learning potential is largely based on work carried out by Vygotsky (1978) and further developed by Feuerstein (1980). According to Brown et al. (1992), "both Vygotsky's and Feuerstein's approach was to observe students as they were actually learning to deal with novel problems and to use their performance as the basis for prediction *and remediation*" (p. 135).

Vygotsky was particularly interested in what has been termed the *zone of proximal development*. As Brown et al. (1992) explained it:

Vygotsky intended the notion of ZPD to capture the widely recognized fact that "learning should be matched in some manner with the child's developmental level" (Vygotsky 1978, 85). But he went further, arguing that one cannot understand the child's developmental level unless one considers both the actual developmental level and the potential developmental level. "The zone of proximal development is the distance between the actual developmental level as determined by independent problem solving and the level of potential development as determined through problem solving under adult guidance or in collaboration with more capable peers" (Vygotsky, 1978, 86). The actual developmental level is the result of "already completed developmental cycles." Static tests reveal "already completed development"; what is still needed is some estimate of the potential for future learning. (pp. 135–136)

Researchers working within this theoretical framework supposedly view learning as being essentially a social process. What children are first able to do with the help of others is expected to become part of what they will be able to do independently in time. In designing assessment approaches, their aim is to reveal "learning potential masked by static tests of ability" (Brown et al., 1992). In determining this learning potential, some researchers have focused on the product (how much changed has occurred), whereas other have focused on the processes involved in change. Additionally, in examining either product or process, some researchers have sought to use standardized procedures for interacting with all children, whereas others have used a more clinical approach allowing greater flexibility of interaction. Several teams of researchers have sought to evaluate "domain-general" skills and processes, whereas others have concentrated on examining skills and processes within a particular content area (e.g., reading or mathematics).

An example of a *clinical approach* developed within this perspective is the Learning Potential Assessment Device (LPAD) developed by Feuerstein. According to Brown et al. (1992), this procedure differs from traditional psychometric approaches in that: (a) "higher mental processes" are tapped that are considered to be susceptible to change; (b) during the session, the examiner interacts as an involved participant in the child's learning; (c) what is important is not the number of LPAD items the child completes, but rather how the child receives, uses, and communicates information; and (d) the test interpreter attempts to pinpoint where the child's principal problems occur. A cognitive map is created for each child, and a change is considered to have taken place when there is a decrease in the dependence on the examiner's assistance.

By comparison, an example of a research program that has used the *standardized approach* to dynamic assessment is that of the Illinois Group. This particular group has attempted to focus on the amount of aid needed by different children in order to achieve superior performance. A summary of their general approach is provided by Brown et al. (1992):

> Students of a wide range of ability (IQ 70-150) are *pretested* on their prior knowledge of the domain in question. To ensure that the tasks they are to learn are neither too hard nor too easy for them, the tasks are assigned to age groups such that most students can get easier items correct but do not perform well on harder items, the target of learning. The students then work collaboratively with a tester/teacher who provides a series of hints until the students can solve the problem. The tester estimates the level of hint required by a student, providing more or less help as needed. . . . This phase of the process continues until the student can solve an array of target problems without the teacher's help. The amount of help each student needs is taken as the estimate of her learning efficiency *within that domain* and *at that particular point in time.*

> After achieving independent learning, students are given a series of transfer problems, varying in terms of their similarity to the items learned originally. . . . This introduces the notion of "transfer distance" . . . The amount of help needed by the child to deal with each of the transfer problems is then uses ad an estimate of the student's "transfer propensity" (Campione and Brown, 1984) *in this domain at this point in time.* (p. 155)

As compared to the assessment carried out by researchers using the clinical approach, the Illinois group is able to quantify the number of hints needed by different children. Although useful in a number of ways, this ability to quantify, Brown et al. (1992) warned, is also dangerous. In particular, they fear that quantification may lead to the creation of a static "score," "thus reifying it as a cognitive entity with the same properties as traditional IQ measures" (Brown, et al., 1992, p. 186).

Regrettably, this is not the only caveat that can be leveled at some of the "alternative assessment" procedures cited by Brown et al. (1992) and noted earlier in this chapter. Many of these procedures set up artificial conditions for evaluating performance. In the case of the LPAD and Campione and Brown's work (Campione, Brown, & Ferrara, 1982), the tasks are essentially IQ-test items. Also, these "alternative assessment" procedures contradict several of the premises and assumptions which supposedly distinguish them from traditional psychometric testing. Feuerstein's dissection of cognitive deficits (Feuerstein, 1979, Chapter 2) requires that the dynamic assessor consider 27 possible cognitive deficiencies along 7 parameters from which "a mental act can be analyzed, categorized and ordered" (p. 123). This type of decomposability rivals that of one of the grandest models in the psychometric school, Guilford's Structure of Intellect (Guilford, 1956).

The assessment procedures proposed by Brown and Campione do not present a situation of learning as a social process. The tasks and the adult–child interactions are unauthentic, wholly set up by the adult, and focused on what the adult brings. This is hardly a social process. It is a testing situation. The products and the processes in these quasisocial situations may be better understood but they may not be "intelligence" or "learning ability" in any general sense. They emanate from decontextualized, contrived testing situations. They may well prove to be as predominantly situation-specific as psychometric test scores (that is, accounting for a small portion of criterion variance).

For circumstantial bilingual learners, these alternative assessment procedures are particularly problematic in that they require high degrees of psycholinguistic processing and interactions in the societal language, using decontextualized language (usually in the societal language) and without any provisions for engaging or understanding bilingual processing in artificial settings. The cognitive science school, like psychometrics, has largely ignored bilingual populations and the bilingual factor.

We have suggested throughout this book that compelling evidence exists suggesting that ability, in the bilingual learner, may well be more complex, more changeable, and more sensitive to contextual features. Alternative assessments that do not provide for these variables or that do not investigate their possible impact do not provide a better alternative.

THE ASSESSMENT OF COMPETENCY

In 1973, David McClelland wrote a provocative article in the *American Psychologist* titled "Testing for Competence Rather than for 'Intelligence'" (McClelland, 1973). He noted how pervasive testing has become in the United States and how great a role it played in the lives of those whose tests scores determined whether they were "qualified" or "less qualified" (p. 1). He also pointed to the role tests played "as a very efficient devise for screening out black, Spanish-speaking, and other minority applicants to colleges" (p. 1). For him, the validity of such tests was not "overwhelming." Further, he criticized the correlation between grades and test scores on two grounds: Grades were not very predictive of success in life and admitting only successful grade makers/ test takers into higher education seemed somewhat absurd:

> Why keep the best education for those who are already doing well at the games [tests]? . . . One would think that the purpose of education is precisely to improve the performance of those who are not doing very well. . . . To be sure, the teachers want students who will do well in their courses, but should society allow the teachers to determine who deserved to be educated, particularly when the performance of interest to teachers bears so little relation to any other type of life performance? (McClelland, 1973, p. 2)

Citing large studies on the relationship between intelligence test scores and job success, he concluded that the degree of their association may be artificially produced. Test scores allow entrance to institutions that prepare candidates (credential them with the right "habits, values, accent, interest, etc."; p. 3) in ways that are acceptable to employers and to the employers' tests. Few studies existed then which separated ability from opportunity, credentialing (often provided by admissions based on test scores) and preparation though psychologists often interpreted the very modest if not meager ($-.08, .23, .42, .45$) correlations between test scores and job success as causal links between ability and success. McClelland did not dispute the circular aspects of test validity. As he noted:

> Valid for predicting success in school? Certainly, because school success depends on taking similar types of tests. Yet, neither the tests nor school grades seem to have *much* power to predict real competence in many life outcomes, aside from the advantages that credentials convey on the individuals concerned. (McClelland, 1973, p. 6, emphasis added)

Following the general principle that tests should be validated against real-life criteria, he proposed several interesting criterion parameters. First he called for empirically and theoretically delineating performance in context, or sampling the criterion behaviors as they really happen and where they really happen. Second, he asked that the tests should account and allow for change. Tests should be dynamic and capable of measuring improvement. Third, the means for doing well in the test should be made explicit: "Faking a high score is impossible if you are performing the criterion behavior, as in tests for reading, spelling, or driving a car" (p. 9). Fourth, criteria should not be narrow but should, rather, consist of behavior and performance clusters applicable across several life outcomes. These might include "Communication skills, . . . Patience, . . . Moderate goal setting, . . . Ego development" (p 10). Fifth, tests should allow for responses that are elicited *and* those that are produced (operant) as the test taker grapples with the test stimulus. In effect, this would mean allowing for multiple types of correct answers, as in real-life situations. And sixth, the tests should define "thought codes" which govern categories of operant responses (such as, "the desire to *have impact*, to make a big splash" [p. 12], which constitutes the "thought characteristic" that drives a set of operant responses such as those in gambling, drinking, etc.).

Recently, Barret and Depinet (1991) published a strong negative response ("A Reconsideration of Testing for Competence Rather than for Intelligence") to McClelland's article. They marshall evidence purporting to show that: grades do predict to job success, intelligence and aptitude test scores are related to life outcomes, the relationship between IQ and success is not artificially created by the opportunities created by test scores, tests are not unfair to minorities, and aptitude and intelligence test scores predict better than competency scores.

Three aspects of this article are particularly noteworthy. First, Barret and Depinet's (1991) gallant defense of psychometric tests provides one of the best examples of what is wrong with testing: it is much ado about very little. Since the 1920s and 1930s, this scientific field has made great progress in statistical analyses of responses, but it has generally failed to account for much more than 30 percent of the variance of virtually everything it predicts.

Second, its treatment of ethnic minorities is simple-minded and unfair in its failure to acknowledge that the current empirical evidence has yet to seriously address the issues of bilingualism or culture. Barret and Depinet, for example, comprehensively assert that tests are not biased against minorities and that the empirical data is clear on this point. As with other similar pronouncements in the testing literature, the references used to buttress this position omit contradictory evidence (e.g., the work of Duran [1983] on test bias in college admissions for Hispanics). They even fail to acknowledge contradictory statements in some of the key references they cite. This is particularly true in the case of Wigdor and Garner (1982), as previously reviewed. Their five key pronouncements on testing bilinguals, though devoid of the available empirical evidence, make it quite clear that testing bilinguals is problematic to the point of error and bias. With respect to bilingualism their position is not what Barret and Depinet assert.

And third, they like McClelland himself, failed to see the *paradigmatic* implications for measurement in what was written in 1973 by McClelland. McClelland was really quite ahead of his time. Just like many of the researchers in the cognitive science school, his critique of psychometric testing touched on several key elements. In our judgment, these are worth reconsidering paradigmatically for developing alternative approaches to assessing bilingual persons. These key elements are: decomposability, efficiency, covariation, solipsism, and decontextualization.

Before discussing these, however, it is necessary to stress the paradigmatic aspect of such a reconsideration. McClelland, Brown, Feuerstein and others involved in the critique of psychometric testing, in our judgment, failed paradigmatically and their end products or alternatives to psychometric measures ended up looking exactly like what they criticized. A paradigmatic shift, as Heshusius (1987, pp. 1–2) noted, entails more than a theoretical shift. It means changing our "way of seeing" of "not seeing," our beliefs and "how we think about how we think about the phenomena of interest." It means a new mental picture when we say "testing" or do "assessment." The image of a subject taking a test from a test giver for the purpose of finding out what is inside the subject's brain or psyche so that she or he can be judge relative to some dimension of norm-derived competency has to be changed. For bilingual persons, this psychometric paradigm which is so analogous to how a medical doctor does tests and diagnoses, does not work. It misses too much. It cannot control for the dynamic, developmental or complex nature of bilingualism.

The sort of complexity that we speak of in the abstract (code switching, fluctuating levels of L1 and L2 proficiencies, storage-systems overlap, etc.) often does not come close to what real-life situations present in bilingual persons. Consider, for example, the case of a bilingual boy in California who underwent radical neurological surgery to remove a cancerous tumor. Postsurgery treatments (radiation) affected his hearing in such a way that he suffered from progressive hearing loss. Five years after the surgery, an assessment was requested by his high school teacher. In trying to determine what tests to give, the assessor found that his dominant language was still Spanish. The greatest amount of verbal output occured when he was talking about his home knowledge base. But he could only write in English because the school stubbornly insisted that one language would be less confusing. When he could not recall a letter or a word, retrieval was sometimes facilitated by the use of sign language (SEE). Reading comprehension was greatest in Spanish, but because of the school's language policy in this regard, he could only read at the third-grade level. He understood English, but he answered in a barely audible tone (unlike Spanish) suggesting uncertainty and lack of confidence in his English usage. And this was only a partial list of what was observed over a long period of time. It does not even begin to cover the impact of different contexts on his output. What test would work?

Where decisions, diagnoses, and treatments need to be made for bilingual individuals, the opposite of decomposability, efficiency, covariation, solipsism, and decontextualization needs to occur.

Decomposibility (Resnick & Resnick, 1992), or the assumption that human mentation can be dissected, broken down, and analyzed by small pieces, is an analogue of the reductionist approach that has worked eminently well in the physical sciences. There, the net effect has been elegant (e.g., $E = mc^2$) and powerful in explaining and predicting phenomena. In psychometrics, more than half a century of the atomistic approach has yielded very little in terms of explanations about or predictions from test-based definitions of intelligence, personality, or aptitudes. Most of the real-life variance of what these tests predict remains small and modest. It may be that test technology has not developed enough. It may also be that human behavior, mentation, and psyche are not sufficiently accessible under the assumption of decomposibility. In varying degrees, many have argued this very point (Feuerstein, 1979; Piaget & Inhelder, 1969; Poplin, 1988b; Shepard, 1991; Vygotsky, 1962). The Gestaltists were particularly insightful in maintaining that perception and thinking were more than the sum of the parts (Kohler, 1969).

Recently, Poplin (1988b) has ellaborated on this notion by underscoring how in natural situations, human mental functioning occurs "often . . . from whole to part to whole" (p. 405), where meaning is constantly being sought and negotiated, where hypotheses are tried and discarded, where authenticity is obvious, where errors are important and useful, and where the problem solver exercises some degree of control and choice. As Poplin noted, these holistic principles are antithetical to the current reductionist (drill-driven, piece-meal) models for teaching learning disabled students. They are also antithetical to the current practices in testing.

Why should there be an expectation that an unnatural, artificial and atomistic (testing) activity should produce results that account for large impacts on the real world? The fact that over the last 70 years tests correlate so highly among themselves and so poorly with real-life outcomes suggests that the current testing paradigm does well principally in its own artificial world. For the unique mental configuration that is the bilingual hearer-speaker (Grosjean, 1989), the psychometric assumption of decomposibility proves to be particularly untenable in what it fails to measure and in the degree of predictive error it engenders (Figueroa, 1991).

Tests are supposedly very efficient. Large numbers of individuals can be processed at one time and this can be done at considerable savings. The legacy of efficiency comes in great part from the role that tests are touted as playing in sorting army recruits during World Wars I and II. SAT scores, military testing programs, and employment test batteries are contemporary examples of such efficiency. This is a very attractive quality of tests that resonates particularly well in highly industrialized societies.

In gauging program and large-group treatment outcomes, efficiency is an asset. In making life decisions about individuals, however, this efficiency may not be very cost-effective. For everyone, the predictive power is too low. For bilinguals, the degree of error is too high. The societal costs associated with underrepresentation, misdiagnosis, or misplacement may also prove exorbitantly high.

Consider the example of IQ tests given to autistic children. For years, these quick, efficient tests have defined the intellectual limits of autistic persons. Their treatment and education have often been determined by their IQs. Recent work (Biklen, 1990) now suggests that the cost of such efficiency may well have been very high. It may have masked not just potential but exceptional potential; potential which if accessed through less efficient, more longitudinal procedures might actually have saved resources and also saved lives.

The same applies to the SAT's of bilingual children, the IQs of underachieving African American children, the vocational interest profiles of culturally different test takers and the TAT English-language stories of bilingual "patients." The real question boils down to what is preferable: weak but efficient measures or potentially stronger but less efficient ones (i.e., more criterion centered, more in line with how competence is manifested in real-life situations, more longitudinal, more informative about the performance behaviors in question, more predictive, more bilingual).

The link between test scores and reality, by and large, is covariation or correlation. As Cronbach (1957) noted, this is hardly a desireable condition. Not only are cause and effect linkages precluded (though they are routinely assumed in decision making based on test scores), so is definition with respect to psychological constructs and so is useful information about training or remediation. As McClelland recognized in the 1970s, the criterion behavior and the test should be inseparable. For bilingual individuals, this means that testing should be about what a person can do in natural criterion settings and in whatever linguistic code(s) is appropriate and available.

Solipsism in testing means that the test is expected to act like a scapel, cutting open and exposing the personality, the intelligence or the vocational aptitude. What tests actually expose, the validity data suggest, is a reduced and artificial version of what they try to measure. From Plato to Piaget and even to Feuerstein, another version of how individuals show what they can do and who they are suggests that the construction of meaning and the manifestation of ability may well occur best in social interaction. As Mehan et al. (1986) found, this phenomenon is so pervasive that even under the stilted strictures of IQ testing, tester and subject break standardization and negotiate meaning.

With individuals who have at their disposal two linguistic codes, the artificial conditions forced by solipsism may at best engage the lower range of what they can do. The upper range of their abilities emerges in holistic activities, in the process of operationalizing zones of proximal development, and in bilingual social interactions (Ruiz, 1988, 1989).

Psychometric testing is a world unto itself. It traps and imprisons individuals in a place where there is no context, where what will be asked cannot be known beforehand, and, often, where the ability to learn (to use what one knows, to seek out meaning, to get help from those we trust, to cogitate, and to allow enough time for insight) cannot be effectively used. Yet, test makers and test users expect optimal performance from a decontextualized testing session.

The one element of genius that truly defines the work of Feuerstein is not his test, the Learning Potential Assessment Device (LPAD). It is the process he uses to "test": in which the tester becomes an environmental architect, creating a social context rich in the negotiation of meaning and engaging the test taker in a psychopedagogical relationship. The critical flaw is LPAD. It is wholly unathentic. It is a test.

In contrast, Taylor (1991) presented an authentic model of a similar context-rich, psychopedagogical relationship. The case study that she presents could not be more germane to this discussion. The young boy, Patrick, looks and performs like an insecure, learning disabled child in a reductionist classroom and on test score profiles. When he works with Taylor, he is an avid reader and writer, a conversationalist. Context determines which Patrick emerges. For bilingual learners, the same is true (Ruiz, Figueroa, Rueda, & Beaumont, 1992). Optimal learning contexts produce optimal portraits of ability. Data collected in such contexts may well yield the best assessment information about intelligence, affect, or job-related competence.

But this is a different sort of testing psychology. Human behavior would not exist or be studied in pieces, cheaply, indirectly, ideographically, or without context. The paradigm would be different. Competency would be measured not just in real contexts, but in optimal contexts. Such "tests" would, of necessity, enhance the criterion. They would also more clearly reveal individual differences (it is a well-established axiom in educational psychology that the better the instruction the more that individual differences emerge). Further, these test contexts would directly inform about the intervention or individualized program that the individual needs.

Currently, new models in this direction are emerging. Portfolio assessment and qualitative, ethnographic-data collection procedures seem particularly promising. Some data are already appearing about bilingual children in this regard (Garcia, Rasmussen, Stobbe, & Garcia, 1990). However, this is really the topic for a future book.

As for the testers, they would have to be retrained or trained differently. Theory, heuristics, and long-term supervision would have to supplant the current one or two semester course on psychometric testing. Master's-level training would be inadequate. Bilingual proficiency would be required. Like Taylor (1991), they would have to operationalize the new paradigm. It would no longer be the MD's X-rays or CAT scans. It would be like Piaget "testing" his children or Plato "diagnosing" the slave boy in The Meno:

> What do you say of him, Meno? Were not all
> these answers given out of his own head? . . . And,
> yet, as we were just now saying, he did not
> know? . . . But still he had in him those notions of
> his—had he not? . . . then he who does not know
> may still have true notions of that which he does
> not know? . . . And at present these notions have
> just been stirred up in him, as in a dream; but if
> he were frequently asked the same questions, in
> different forms, he would know as well as anyone
> at last?

CONCLUSIONS AND RECOMMENDATIONS

In considering "solutions" to the problem of assessing circumstantial bilinguals, it is important to once again point out that, to date, the focus of even "new" approaches to testing has not been directed at this particular population. Indeed, in order to develop such a focus, researchers and practitioners would need to acquire an expertise in working with circumstantial bilingual individuals. Working with bilinguals will involve complexities not present in the case of monolingual persons. Moveover, such work must involve researches and practitioners who are themselves competent and comfortable in two languages. Adapting procedures currently in use experimentally will entail more than simply using the same procedure in non-English languages. As emphasized throughout this volume, circumstantial bilinguals, by definition, use two languages in many domains and for many purposes in their everyday lives. Their perceived strongest language may vary from moment to moment and from context to context, depending on the affect, interaction, or topic. A bilingual is not and will not ever be identical to a monolingual.

Standardized tests should not be used in any aspect of a decision-making process with bilingual populations. There is no way of minimizing the potential harm to this population resulting from seemingly "objective" and "scientific" psychometric tests. All such testing should be discontinued. This does not mean that all decisions will be made in a vacuum. It means that they have to be made under different paradigmatic, theoretical, and procedural conditions. It also means that given the national interest involved in these matters, research and development should be propelled by the federal government. Such research should include the participation of specialists in the area of bilingualism from a number of different backgrounds (sociolinguistics, psycholinguistics, linguistics, educational anthropologists).

As we indicated in this chapter, given the little that test contribute to the reduction of error, the results may prove to be exceedingly beneficial to the entire society.

APPENDIX

Toward The Development of a Research Agenda on Bilingualism and Testing

EXPLAINING BILINGUALS' PERFORMANCE ON STANDARDIZED TESTS

As was made clear in this volume, circumstantial bilingual individuals have not done well on standardized tests. In attempting to account for these differences, a number of explanations have been offered. Among them are the following:

- standardized tests are culturally biased,
- standardized tests are linguistically biased, and
- students who come from homes where a non-English language is spoken may perform poorly on tests because their English is limited.

Although this list of explanations is not exhaustive, in essence, most researchers who have investigated the performance of bilingual minority children on standardized tests have taken what we consider to be a limited view. Specifically, these researchers have focused on three principal areas: (a) the characteristics of standardized tests themselves, (b) the inherent talent and/or the academic achievement of non-White individuals, and (c) the degree to which bilingual minority students have mastered the English language. Even though each of these three areas is important to the understanding of why bilingual students "test" poorly, it is our purpose here to suggest that in order to account fully for the difference in performance on standardized tests between bilingual minority individuals and mainstream, monolingual individuals, attention must be focused on what we have termed here "the unique mental processing characteristics of bilingual minds."

Given the traditions that have been followed in the study of bilingualism, and the assumptions generally made by the field of educational measurement, the development of a coherent research agenda that seeks to address these issues must include the following ordered steps:

Step 1: The examination and study of the problems surrounding the measurement of bilingualism.

Step 2: The study of the nature of minority or circumstantial bilingualism in comparison to the nature of middle-class elective bilingualism.

Step 3: The review and examination of existing research which has focused on the relationship between bilingualism and cognitive difference

Step 4: The development of a list of key questions which will guide research in psychometrics and measurement.

In essence, a research agenda designed to produce a body of knowledge that can explain how and why bilingual individuals perform as they do on standardized tests cannot continue to replicate the existing limitations of current and past research on bilinguals and bilingualism. That it is to say, it cannot ignore the complexity of bilingualism itself and the difficulties involved in its measurement. It cannot pretend that research conducted on "ideal" or balanced bilinguals can answer questions about the children of working-class immigrants. Finally, such research must be based on an understanding of the implications *and* limitations of our existing knowledge about bilingualism and cognition.

In the section that follows, we will discuss each of the steps which would need to be supported in the development of a research agenda. Our intent is to present an outline of the types of questions that might be examined at each step and to provide only a brief discussion of the reasoning behind their inclusion.

STEPS IN THE DEVELOPMENT OF A RESEARCH AGENDA ON BILINGUALISM AND TESTING

Step 1: The Examination and Study of the Problems Surrounding the Measurement of Bilingualism

In spite of the complexity and the difficulty of measuring bilingual abilities, research on bilingual individuals which hopes to examine the nature of bilingual processing or bilingual cognition in order to understand how and whether standardized tests include or exclude mental content must begin by carefully examining the bilingualism of different types of individuals. What this means is that if research is conducted on test taking by bilinguals, on problem solving, or on information processing, it is imperative that individual differences in terms of relative language proficiency be accounted for carefully.

A careful investigation of the measurement of bilingualism by researchers interested in conducting research on the nature of bilingualism and its relationship to testing would begin with questions such as the following:

1. What is bilingualism? How can bilingualism be defined? What are the advantages and disadvantages of using a narrow versus a broad definition? What kinds of individuals are included and excluded by different definitions?

2. How has bilingualism been measured? What are the strengths and limitations of each of these methods? How well can each method distinguish between bilinguals of different types? How can each method of assessment be improved? What additional information is obtained about different bilingual individuals by using a combination of strategies and methods of assessment? Which combination of strategies appear to yield the most meaningful information about bilingual individuals?

3. Which combination of strategies result in information that makes possible the categorization of individuals into different kinds or types of bilinguals? What are these categories? What kinds of factors are they based on? Do these factors reflect the actual functional use of language by bilinguals? Is this important? What are the characteristics of the different types of bilinguals? What are the limitations of the proposed categorization?

4. What is the difference between measuring language proficiency and measuring language dominance? What is language dominance as opposed to language proficiency? What constitutes proficiency? dominance? What kinds of behaviors are indicative of language dominance? of language proficiency?

5. What constitutes bilingual "balance?" Is the notion of balance a useful construct? What are its problems? What are its limitations? How many bilinguals perform equivalently on measures of their two languages? What accounts for this equivalent performance in middle-class elective bilinguals? in minority circumstantial bilinguals?

Clearly, this list of questions is not complete. Our purpose in including it has been to suggest the range of concerns that must inform the work of researchers at this stage of the research process. Without involving themselves deeply in the measurement of bilingualism, without a first-hand understanding of the range of language abilities represented by even a group of individuals who appear to have similar life histories, researchers may fail to comprehend the limits of previous work on bilingual assessment and may fail to account and control for the ubiquitous source of error in all forms of measurement: the bilingual factor.

Step 2: The Study of the Nature of Minority or Circumstantial Bilingualism in Comparison to the Nature of Middle-Class Elective Bilingualism

In the United States, concern about the relationship between bilingualism and testing stems from the fact that large numbers of minority children of non-English-speaking backgrounds have been penalized in school or in the working world as a result of their poor performance on standardized tests. In developing a research agenda and in establishing points of departure for such an endeavor, it is important to emphasize that the while a great deal of work has been carried out on bilingualism and school-age children in other countries, we view this agenda-setting endeavor as one which must focus on American bilingual minorities and on the specific characteristics of their bilingualism.

For example, even though American educators and researchers might share a fundamental interest in the nature of elective or additive bilingualism as it has been examined by Canadian researchers, this country's concern cannot be focused primarily (as theirs has been) on instructed or schooled bilingualism for majority children and on the positive or negative aspect of this elective condition.

On the contrary, a research agenda designed to guide future work in this country must be concerned with *how* and *whether* tests can be constructed which can fairly and accurately assess the abilities of bilingual minority children. In other words, the question in the United States is not whether children should become bilingual or not. As opposed to the Canadian researchers who have focused primarily on immersion education[1] and on

---

[1]Immersion education in Canada involves the enrollment of Anglophone children in programs in which the medium of instruction is French. Teachers are bilingual in French and English. Children are allowed to respond in either language in the early years although all instruction is carried out in French. No native French-speaking children are enrolled in such programs. There is no competition with peers who are already fluent speakers of the language, but there is also no opportunity for using French with same-age native speakers of the language. Research on the effectiveness of such programs indicate that French is acquired with some limitations and that English academic skills are developed at the same rate as those of students enrolled in all-English-language medium schools.

children who can at any point opt out of becoming bilingual, the concern of researchers working in the United States must be with children whose life's circumstances have dictated that they should acquire this country's majority language, that is, with children who do not themselves have a choice about becoming bilingual.

From the research perspective, what this means is that, valuable as the Canadian research has been, it is limited in its application to American bilingual minority children in that most of it has been carried out with children very unlike our Mexican, Hmong, Chinese, Filipino, and Puerto Rican minorities. Moreover, the principal intent of Canadian research (especially that of recent work focusing on the cognitive advantage of bilingualism) has been to compare monolinguals and bilinguals and to discover how "balanced" or true bilinguals perform in comparison to monolinguals.[2]

From our perspective, research on bilingualism and testing conducted in the United States must focus on the study of minority individuals whose life circumstances have resulted in their becoming bilingual. Research conducted in other countries should be used only as a point of reference and only after careful attention has been given to the purposes of the research and the types of bilingual individuals studied. Specifically, American research directed at understanding the performance of bilingual minority children on standardized tests should explore the following questions.

1. In the American context, how and why do immigrant minority children learn English?

    What are the contexts in which this learning takes place? How many minority children learn English primarily at school? How many are enrolled in special programs (e.g., bilingual education, ESL instruction)? In what other contexts does language learning take place? How does learning progress over time? How and with whom is English used? How and with whom is the ethnic language used? To what degree do members of minority

---

[2]For a criticism of this research and of its limitations, the reader is directed to McNab (1979). Summarizing McNab's critique briefly, it can be said that he found fault with the fact that this research tends to select only "balanced" bilinguals who: (a) generate words in response to stimulus words, (b) can find words in embedded letters, (c) comprehend words given in English, and (d) have high self-ratings of understanding, speaking, reading, and writing English. By focusing on such bilingual individuals, the researchers in question excluded immigrant children, that is, children who would have been most like American circumstantial bilingual children. For example, of a population of 364 children, Peal and Lambert (1962) found only 89 children to be "balanced" bilinguals. The type or kind of bilingualism demonstrated by the other children was of no interest.

communities feel that their children have a choice about learning or not learning English? To what degree is the English language learning of minority children an elective process, and to what extent is it circumstantial? What is the impact of the various types of English language learning on psychometric tests?

2. Are there differences between bilingual minority children and majority group children who study a foreign language? between bilingual minority children and upper middle-class and middle-class foreign students who decide to study in the United States? How can these differences be described? To what degree is the study of a foreign language in this country an elective process? Is there a difference between foreign students who study in the United States and recently arrived permanent residents who have immigrated here from the same country? What are the differences between the circumstantial nature of some types of elective bilingualism and the circumstances of the immigrant minority experience? Are these differences linguistic? attitudinal? social? Are there similarities between these two different groups? How do psychometric tests register these differences?

3. Is there a point at which circumstantial bilinguals can no longer be considered to be "learners" of their second language? Is there a point at which their second language becomes "stronger" than their first? Are there circumstantial bilinguals for whom a "weaker" language cannot be identified consistently? What is the relationship between perceived limitations and strengths and actual functional abilities? How can this relationship be studied in tests, testing practices, and test users?

4. Can circumstantial bilinguals be classified into different types? How many different types of circumstantial bilinguals can be identified? Are there background factors (e.g., age of acquisition, exposure to dominant community, frequency of use of ethnic language) which are related to differences in language abilities? To what degree are classifications based on language abilities expected to be stable? How do circumstantial bilinguals change over time? Do these factors operate as independent sources of test variance?

5. Are there circumstantial bilinguals that *do* perform well on standardized tests? What kinds of tests do they perform well on? Is this typical or exceptional for their ethnic group? Has the performance of the entire group changed over time? What is the language history, educational history, and familial history of bilingual individuals who *do* perform well on standardized tests? Does the ethnic

group include individuals who are middle class? Are there differences between working-class circumstantial bilinguals and middle-class circumstantial bilinguals in their performance on tests? Are there language ability differences between these two groups of circumstantial bilinguals? What is the nature of these differences?

In this step, what is important is that researchers have an opportunity to compare and contrast circumstantial with elective bilinguals *and* circumstantial bilinguals with each other. This step, together with Step 1 has as its purpose involving test developers and test users—whose interest in bilingualism per se is limited—in the study of American bilingual minorities and their preformance on tests.

Step 3: The Review and Examination of Existing Research That Has Focused on the Relationship Between Bilingualism and Cognitive Difference

As was made clear in our discussion of bilingualism in the first part of this volume, bilingual individuals share with each other the fact that they have *more than one language competence*; that is to say, they are able to function (i.e., speak, understand, read, or write) even to a very limited degree in *more than one* language. As this definition of bilingualism makes obvious, there are many different kinds and types of bilingual individuals. At one end of the continuum, there are bilinguals who may indeed be accepted as native speakers of each of their two languages by other native speakers; and, at the other end of the continuum, there are bilinguals whose only ability in L2 maybe be limited to reading with the aid of a bilingual dictionary.

The question is, are these bilingual individuals, these circumstantial bilinguals of various backgrounds and origins different from monolinguals in "important" ways; that is, in ways which might directly affect their performance on standardized tests? How might these differences be discovered? How might these differences be manifested?

To date, a number of different areas of research on bilingualism and bilingual individuals suggest that bilinguals may indeed be different from monolinguals. As was discussed in the first part of this volume, research on what may be the unique processing characteristics of bilingual minds (e.g., the psychological verbal storage systems of bilinguals and their possible neurological representations, the nature of bilingual information processing, and the nature of the greater cognitive flexibility of bilinguals) implies that bilingual persons are cognitively more complex than monolinguals.

What is not known is what this cognitive difference consists of. Is cognitive difference a simple by-product of becoming bilingual? To date, a number of different areas of research on bilingualism and bilingual individuals suggest that bilinguals may indeed be different from monolinguals. These areas are: (a) the investigation of cognitive development in bilinguals, (b) the neuropsychological work on hemispheric involvement in the learning and processing of first and second languages, and (c) current work on language and information processing in bilinguals. The development of a coherent research agenda that focuses on the study of bilingualism and testing must look carefully into the work carried out in these three areas.

Step 3, then, has been designed to involve would-be researchers on bilingualism and testing in a careful reading of the research literature on each of the three areas identified above. Such reading and examination is expected to identify a number of research questions and research directions which will be further refined in Step 4. Examples of these questions are:

1. What is unique about the processing characteristics of bilingual minds?
2. In what ways are bilinguals cognitively different from monolinguals?
3. How does this complexity manifest itself in tests?
4. Do these differences result in there being a "bilingual factor" (e.g., a complex of variables that interact with other variables) which directly impacts on test performance?
5. Is there evidence that tests fail to measure mental processes and abilities that are the product of bilingualism? and
6. Is there evidence that tests may exclude mental content that is available to bilinguals in their other language?

Step 4: The Development of a List of Key Questions That Will Guide Future Research on Bilingualism and Testing

The development of a list of key questions and areas of study that would guide future research on bilingualism and testing must be based on two different but complementary set of directions: (a) directions for research on the cognitive complexity of bilinguals suggested by the literature, and (b) directions for research suggested by the nature of standardized testing. In this section, each of these two directions will be discussed briefly.

Directions for Research on the Cognitive Complexity of Bilinguals Suggested by the Literature. As the discussion of Step 3 in the process of developing a coherent research agenda undoubtedly made clear, the identification of key questions and fundamental research directions must be based on a review and analysis of the existing research. This analysis must be sensitive to a number of concerns, among which is the need to understand *why* bilingual minority students perform poorly on standardized tests.

It is expected – given our own preliminary analysis of that research – that questions such as the following would be included in a final listing of research directions:

1. Are all bilinguals significantly different from monolinguals?
2. Are certain kinds of bilinguals different from monolinguals?
3. What kinds of bilinguals are different from monolinguals? How can bilinguals belonging to this class be identified? How are they like and unlike other bilinguals?
4. How can the differences between bilinguals and monolinguals be described?
5. Does evidence that there is a difference support the conclusion that bilinguals are more cognitively complex than monolinguals?
6. In what ways are bilinguals more cognitively complex than monolinguals?
7. How does this complexity manifest itself?
8. How might this complexity affect the normal everyday functioning of bilinguals?
9. How might this complexity affect bilinguals' performance in school?
10. How might this complexity affect bilinguals' processing of information on tasks involving very high information load or task stress?
11. How might this complexity affect bilinguals' performance on standardized tests?

Directions for Research Suggested by the Nature of Standardized Testing. In conjunction with the above questions, a number of related research directions are suggested by the nature of standardized testing itself. These directions include:

Direction 1. What do standardized tests test in the case of middle-class monolingual individuals? What do standardized tests test in the case of circumstantial bilingual minority persons?

This question is clearly fundamental, and it has already been asked by others. Work carried out by researchers such as Mulholland, Pellegrino, and Glaser (1980), for example, specifically addresses the issue. In the researchers' own words:

Until recently, questions about the nature of individual differences in cognition have been addressed primarily by the psychometric branch of psychology. This field has been successful in developing test instruments having reasonable predictive validity. The tests tap significant aspects of human behavior that are related to the processing of verbal and nonverbal information and that are useful in discriminating among individuals who are more or less likely to succeed in academic and related endeavors. What is lacking in the field is a clear idea of the nature of the processes that underlie performance on the tests, how individuals differ in terms of these processes, and the task characteristics that influence these performance differences.

These same individuals have suggested (Pellegrino & Glaser, 1979) that questions of the form "What do intelligence tests test" must be sought through rational and empirical analyses of the information processing demands of the specific tasks that comprise these tests.

In identifying key questions which would logically form the basis of research investigating the relationship between bilingualism and testing, it is important to echo Cronbach's (1957) concern about the fact that psychometricians have measured differences between individuals without much concern for the process by which subjects attack tests, and experimental psychologists have studied processes in general without regard for the differences between individuals. We would argue that in the case of bilingual individuals, psychologists' interest in bilingual storage systems, bilingual information processing, hemispheric involvement, and the like, has not extended to an exploration of how these same bilinguals function during tests of different types. Psychometricians, on the other hand, have pretended that there were few differences between bilinguals and monolinguals.

If, however, we wish to understand what it is that tests test, that is, if we want to understand the nature of the demands that such instruments make on individuals both monolingual and bilingual, research must focus on questions such as the following:

1. What kinds of demands do tests normally make on monolinguals? What is known about the difficulties experienced by mainstream middle-class monolinguals on standardized tests?
2. Are there differences between mainstream middle-class monolinguals who test well and those who do not?
3. How can these differences be described?
4. Are there differences in the way successful and unsuccessful examinees function during test-taking conditions?
5. What are these differences?
6. How do bilinguals of different types function during test-taking conditions?

7. How are they like and unlike mainstream monolinguals who ordinarily perform well on standardized tests?
8. How are they like or unlike mainstream monolinguals who ordinarily perform poorly on standardized tests?

Direction 2. What types of demands do standardized tests make on
bilingual individuals? Are these demands information processing demands
or language processing demands? Are these demands different than those
made on monolingual individuals? How are they the same? How are they
different?

Direction 3. Are difficulties experienced by bilinguals on standardized
tests caused by task stress or by language limitations? To what degree can
poor performance on tests be attributed to limitations of knowledge? to
limitations of potential? to differences in ways in which information is
processed? to language limitations? or to an interaction between all or
some of these elements?

Direction 4. Does there appear to be a "bilingual factor" operating (e.g.,
a complex of variables that interacts with other variables) which directly
impacts on test performance?

Direction 5. What is the relationship between language proficiency
and performance on standardized tests? What evidence is there that there
is a certain "threshold" level which must be reached by bilinguals in their
first language (L1) before they are able to perform well on standardized
tests in their second language (L2)?

This question is a central one in the area of bilingualism and education
because it has been hypothesized by Cummins (1979, 1981) that there is a
certain threshold of first language development that must be reached by
children before they will be in a position to benefit from the cognitive
advantages currently attributed to bilingualism. According to Cummins,
unless children are able to develop language abilities in their first language
which allow them to process decontextualized cognitively demanding
materials, they will not be able to develop the ability to do so in their
second language. For Cummins, academic tasks are cognitively demanding and decontextualized in ways in which everyday communication
and interaction is not. He therefore argues that immigrant children should
not be placed in classrooms where instruction is conducted solely in the
majority language and expected to succeed academically only because
they appear to speak this language well enough to interact normally in
informal interactions. Such placement, he argued, will lead to the unfor-

tunate condition of "semilingualism," a state in which neither the first nor the second language are "fully" developed.

Interesting as Cummins's hypotheses are, and supportive as they are of bilingual education, they are based on research conducted on bilingual children's performance on standardized tests. In Cummins's research, in particular, academic success has been operationalized as scores on a variety of standardized measures. From his perspective, children who have not received instruction in their first language perform poorly on such measures in their second language *because* of their lack of development in their *first* language. For Cummins, "cognitive" development in or by means of L1 is not only directly available for cognitively demanding activities in L2, but is also the primary basis for development of such abilities in the second language.

Specifically, for Cummins, immigrant children (circumstantial bilingual children) perform poorly academically (i.e., on standardized tests in English), not because of limitations in this second language, but because they have not developed cognitive academic proficiency in their first language.

What this suggests for researchers interested in the relationship between bilingualism and testing is that tests may make demands on bilinguals that have less to do with language proficiency in the language of the test than they do with other factors as yet undefined and undescribed. Cummins's critics, particularly those who denounce the concept of semilingualism (e.g., Edelsky et al., 1983; Martin-Jones & Romaine, 1987) suggest that these factors may involve what has been termed "testwiseness" more than they involve either cognitive academic language proficiency or basic interpersonal communication skills.

Given the fact that this research has been based on a multitude of studies which have also used standardized tests as measures of ability or performance, a further investigation of questions such as the following would contribute much to our understanding of the role of second language proficiency in standardized testing:

1. How much English do children need to know (speak and understand, read and write) in order to perform well on standardized tests? How can this knowledge be measured *without* the use of standardized tests?
2. Is it possible for children who have been schooled in their first language and/or who have had experience with the process of test taking to outscore children who speak more English than they do on English-language standardized tests?
3. How much English must such children know? How can it be measured?

4. What kinds of activities or functions must they be able to carry out in their first language? in everyday interaction? in school settings? on experimental tasks in their first language before this "better" performance can take place?
5. How do proficiencies in English and in the first language of "academically successful" children compare with those of unsuccessful children?
6. What does the process of test taking involve for both groups of children?
7. Is there evidence to suggest that standardized tests require a special kind of language proficiency?

Direction 6.   What evidence is there that tests in one language exclude mental content that is available to bilinguals in their other language? How can such exclusion be documented? What means can be used to measure the excluded content in the light of what is known about the nature of circumstantial bilingualism?

As will be noted, each of these research directions is related, either directly or indirectly, to other questions which in turn have been suggested either by the literature on the nature of bilingualism, or by problems currently facing young circumstantial bilinguals in American schools. Although a final listing of research directions for a fully developed agenda might well differ from those suggested earlier, it is expected that issues, such as those discussed here, would form the core of such a research agenda. It would be hoped that the questions raised in the course of developing a complete agenda would be brought to the attention of both practitioners and researchers as well as policy makers who are in the position to make monies available to support this research endeavor.

References

Aiken, L. R. (1987). *Assessment of intellectual functioning.* Boston: Allyn & Bacon.

Albanese, J. (1985). Language lateralization in English-French bilinguals. *Brain and Language, 24,* 284–296.

Albert, M., & Obler, L. (1978). *The bilingual brain.* New York: Academic Press.

Alderman, D. L. (1982). Language proficiency as a moderator variable in testing academic aptitude. *Journal of Educational Psychology, 74,* 580–587.

Amastae, J. (1981). The writing needs of Hispanic students. In B. Cronnell (Ed.), *The writing needs of linguistically different students* (pp. 99–128). Los Alamitos, CA: SWRL Educational and Research Development.

Amastae, J. (1984). Pan-American project. In J. Ornstein-Galacia (Ed.), *Form and function in Chicano English* (pp. 135–142). Rowley, MA: Newbury House.

Ambert, A. N. (1986). Identifying language disorders in Spanish speakers. *Journal of Reading, writing, & Learning Disabilities International, 2,* 21–41.

American Educational Research Association, American Psychological Association, National Council on Measurement in Education. (1985). *Standards for educational and psychological testing.* Washington, DC: American Psychological Association. (Also published 1974, 1969)

Ammon, P. (1985). Helping children learn to write in English as a second language: Some observations and hypotheses. In S. Freedman (Ed.), *The acquisition of written language: Revision and response* (pp. 65–84). Norwood, NJ: Ablex.

Anderson, A., Estrada, E., & Teale, W. (1980). Low income children's preschool literacy experiences: Some naturalistic observations. *Quarterly Newsletter of the Laboratory of Comparative Human Cognition, 2(3),* 59–65.

Angelis, P. J. (1977). Language testing and intelligence testing: Friends or foes? In J. E. Reddon (Ed.), *Proceedings of the First International Conference on Frontiers in Language Proficiency and Dominance Testing* (Occasional Papers on Linguistics, No. 1). Carbondale, IL: Southern Illinois University.

Angoff, W. H., & Sharon, A. T. (1971). A comparison of scores earned on the test of English as a foreign language by native American college students and foreign applicants to U.S. colleges. *TESOL Quarterly, 5,* 129–136.

Appel, R., & Muysken, P. (1987). *Language contact and bilingualism*. London: Edward Arnold.

Argulewicz, E. N., & Abel, R. R. (1984). Internal evidence of bias in the PPVT-R for Anglo-American and Mexican-American children. *Journal of School Psychology, 22,* 299–303.

Argulewicz, E. N., Bingenheimer, L. T., & Anderson, C. C. (1983). Concurrent validity of the PPVT-R for Anglo-American and Mexican-American students. *Journal of Psychoeducational Assessment, 1*(2), 163–167.

Argulewicz, E. N., Anderson, C. C., & Bingenheimer, L. T. (1983). Alternate form reliability of the PPVT-R for Anglo American and Mexican American school children. *Educational and Psychological Research, 3*(1), 19–24.

Argulewicz, E. N., & Kush, J. C. (1983). Equivalence of Forms L and M of the PPVT-R for use with Anglo-American and Mexican-American learning disabled students. *Psychological Reports, 52,* 827–830.

Arias, B. (Ed.). (1986). The education of Hispanic Americans: A challenge for the future. *American Journal of Education, 95.*

Arlitt, A. H. (1921). On the need for caution in establishing race norms. *Journal of Applied Psychology, 5,* 179–183.

Armour-Thomas, E. (1992). Intellectual assessment of children from culturally diverse backgrounds. *School Psychology Review, 21,* 552–565.

Arnedt, C., & Gentile, J. R. (1986). A test of dual coding theory for bilingual memory. *Canadian Journal of Psychology, 40*(3), 290–299.

Arnold, R. D. (1969). Reliability of test scores for the young bilingual disadvantaged. *Reading Teacher, 22,* 341–345.

Arreola v. Santa Ana Board of Education (Orange County, California). No. 160–577. (1968).

Asian American Task Force on University Admissions. (1985). *Task Force Report* (1–19). Davis, CA: University of California.

Bachman, L. F. (1990). *Fundamental considerations in language testing*. Oxford: Oxford University Press.

Baetens-Beardsmore, H. (1982). *Bilingualism basic principles*. Clevedon, Avon: Tieto.

Bain, B. (1974). Bilingualism and cognition: Toward a general theory. In S. T. Carey (Ed.), *Bilingualism, biculturalism, and education: Proceedings from the conference at College Universitaire Saint Jean*. Edmonton: The University of Alberta.

Bain, B., & Yu, A. (1984). The development of the body percept among working- and middle-class unilinguals and bilinguals. In M. Paradis & Y. Lebrun (Ed.), *Early bilingualism and child development*. Lisse: Swets & Zeitlinger BV.

Baker, C. (1988). Normative testing and bilingual populations. *Journal of Multilingual and Multicultural Development, 9,* 399–409.

Baker, K. (1986). Selecting students for bilingual education under the Keyes Agreement. *La Raza Law Journal, 1*(3), 330–341.

Baker, K., & de Kanter, A. A. (1981). *Effectiveness of bilingual education: A review of the literature* (Final draft report). Washington, DC: Office of Technical and Analytic Systems, Office of Planning and Budget, U.S. Department of Education.

Balkan, L. (1970). *Les effets du bilinguism Français-Anglais sur les aptitudes intellectuelles*. Bruxelles: Aimav.

Ballmer, T. T. (1981). A typology of native speakers. In F. Coulmas (Ed.), *A festschrift for native speaker* (pp. 51–67). The Hague: Mouton.

Baratz-Snowden, J., Pollack, J., & Rock, D. (1988). *Quality of responses of selected items on NAEP special study student survey*. Princeton, NJ: National Assessment of Educational Progress.

Baratz-Snowden, J., Rock, D., Pollack, J., & Wilder, G. (1988). *The educational progress of language minority children: Findings from the 1985–86 special study.* Princeton, NJ: Educational Testing Service.

Barke, E. M., & Perry-Williams, D. E. (1938). A further study of the comparative intelligence of children in certain bilingual and monoglot schools in South Wales. *British Journal of Educational Psychology, 8,* 63–77.

Barnett, D. W., & Zucker, K. B. (1990). *The personal and social assessment of children.* Boston: Allyn & Bacon.

Barona, A. (1989). Differential effects of WISC-R factors on special education eligibility for three ethnic groups. *Journal of Psychoeducational Assessment, 7,* 31–38.

Beebe, L. M. (1988). *Issues in second language acquisition.* New York: Newbury House.

Bell, R. (1935). *Public school education of second-generation Japanese in California.* Stanford, CA: Stanford University Press.

Ben-Zeev, S. (1976). The effects of bilingualism in children from Spanish-English low economic neighborhoods on cognitive development and cognitive strategy. *Working Papers on Bilingualism, 9,* 83–122.

Ben-Zeev, S. (1977a). The influence of bilingualism on cognitive strategy and cognitive development. *Child Development, 48,* 1009–1018.

Ben-Zeev, S. (1977b). Mechanisms by which childhood bilingualism affects understanding of language and cognitive structures. In P. A. Hornby (Ed.), *Bilingualism: Psychological, social, and educational implications* (pp. 29–55). New York: Academic Press.

Berk, R. A., Bridges, W. P., & Shih, A. (1981). Does IQ really matter? A study of the use of IQ scores for the tracking of the mentally retarded. *American Sociological Review, 46,* 58–71.

Bialystok, E., & Sharwood-Smith, M. (1985). Interlanguage is not a state of mind: An evaluation of the construct for second language acquisition. *Applied Linguistics, 6,* 101–117.

Blair, D., & Harris, R. (1981). A test of interlingual interaction in comprehension by bilinguals. *Journal of Psycholinguistic Research, 10,* 457–467.

Blanc, M. (1987). Preface/Foreword. In M. Blanc & J. F. Hamers (Eds.), *Theoretical and methodological issues in the study of languages/dialects in contact at the macro- and micro-logical levels of analysis* (pp. 3–8). Quebec: International Center for Research on Bilingualism.

Bloomfield, L. (1933). *Language.* New York: Henry Holt.

Bond, M. H., & Yang, K. S. (1982). Ethnic affirmation versus cross-cultural accommodation: The variable impact of questionnaire language on Chinese bilinguals in Hong Kong. *Journal of Cross-Cultural Psychology, 13,* 169–185.

Bourdieu, P. (1977). *Outline of a theory of practice.* London: Cambridge University Press.

Bourdieu, P., & Passeron, J.-C. (1977). *Reproduction in education, society and culture.* Beverly Hills, CA: Sage.

Braff, E. (1981). *Hispanics in special education in California: OCR data.* San Francisco, CA: California Rural Legal Assistance (CRLA).

Bracken, B. A., Barona, A., Bauermeister, J. J., Howell, K. K., Paggioli, L., & Puente, A. (1990). Multinational validation of the Spanish Bracken Basic Concept Scale for cross-cultural assessments. *Journal of School Psychology, 28,* 325–341.

Bredemeir, M. (1991). IQ test ban for Blacks called unconstitutional. *CASP TODAY, XLI,* 22–23.

Breland, H. M., & Duran, R. P. (1985). Assessing English composition skills in Spanish-speaking populations. *Educational and Psychological Development, 45*(2), 309–18.

Brent-Palmer, C. (1979). A sociolinguistic assessment of the notion of 'immigrant semilingualism' from a social conflict perspective. *Working Papers on Bilingualism, 17,* 135–180.

Brigance, A. H. (1983). *Assessment of basic skills: Spanish edition.* North Billerica, MA: Curriculum Associates.

Brigham, C. C. (1923). *A study of American intelligence.* Princeton, NJ: Princeton University Press.

Brill, M. (1936). Studies of Jewish and non-Jewish intelligence. *Journal of Educational Psychology, 27*(5), 331–352.

Brimner, L. D. (1982). The effects of praise and blame on writing. *English Journal, 71*(1), 58–60.

Brislin, R. W. (1983). Cross-cultural psychology. *Annual Review of Psychology, 34*, 363–400.

Brislin, R. W. (1986). The wording and translation of research instruments. In W. J. Lonner & J. W. Berry (Eds.), *Field methods in cross-cultural research* (pp. 137–164). Beverly Hills, CA: Sage.

Brislin, R. W., Lonner, W. J., & Thorndike, R. M. (Eds.). (1973). *Cross-cultural research methods.* New York: Wiley.

Brizuela, C. S. (1975). Semantic differential responses of bilinguals in Argentina. *Dissertation Abstracts International, 36*(12-B), 6439. (University Microfilms No. 76-13, 514)

Brown, A. L., Campione, J. C., Webber, L. S., & McGilly, K. (1992). Interactive learning environments: A new look at assessment and instruction. In B. R. Gifford & M. C. O'Connor (Ed.), *Changing assessments: Alternative views of aptitude, achievement, and instruction* (pp. 121–211). Boston: Kluwer.

Brown, G. L. (1992). Intelligence as related to nationality. *Journal of Educational Research, 5*(4), 324–327.

Brown, F. G. (1984). *Principles of educational and psychological testing.* New York: Holt, Rinehart & Winston.

Brown v. Board of Education. 347 U.S. 483 (1954).

Buriel, R. (1975). Cognitive style among three generations of Mexican-American children. *Journal of Cross-Cultural Psychology, 6,* 417–429.

Buros, O. K. (1978). *The eighth mental measurements yearbook* (Vols. I & II). Highland Park, NJ: Gryphon.

Campos, L. P. (1989). Adverse impact, unfairness, and bias in the psychological screening of Hispanic peace officers. *Hispanic Journal of Behavioral Sciences, 11*(2), 122–135.

Canale, M., & Swain, M. (1980). Theoretical bases of communicative approaches to second language teaching and testing. *Applied Linguistics, 1,* 1–47.

Cancino, H., & Hakuta, K. (1981). *The acquisition of English by working class adult speakers of Spanish* (Final Report). Washington, DC: National Institute of Education.

Candell, G. L., & Hulin, C. L. (1987). Cross-language and cross-cultural comparisons in scale translations: Independent sources of information about item nonequivalence. *Journal of cross-cultural Psychology, 17,* 417–440.

Canner, J. (1989). *Preliminary report New York City norms for the EIWN-R.* New York: New York City Board of Education.

Cantwell, Z. (1986). Assessment of developed general intellectual ability with nonverbal measures. *Journal of Psychology, 120*(5), 473–478.

Carroll, F. (1978). Cerebral dominance for language: A dichotic listening study of Navajo-English bilinguals. In H. Key, S. McCullogh, & J. Sawyer (Eds.), *The bilingual in a pluralistic society* (pp. 11–17). Long Beach: California State University at Long Beach.

Carroll, F. W. (1980). Neurolinguistic processing of a second language: Experimental evidence. In R. Scarcella & S. Krashen (Eds.), *Research in second language acquisition.* Rowley, MA: Newbury House.

Carroll, J. B. (1971). Development of native language skills beyond the early years. In C. E. Reed (Ed.), *The learning of language* (pp. 97–156). New York: Appleton-Century Crofts.

Carrow, S. M. A. (1957). Linguistic functioning of bilingual and monolingual children. *Journal of Speech and Hearing Disorders, 22,* 371–380.

CASP. (1991). *The Use of Individually Administered Tests of Cognitive Ability, Intelligence.* Millbrae, CA: California Association of School Psychologists.

CASP. (1992). *The Use of Intelligence Tests with African American Students.* Millbrae, CA: California Association of School Psychologists.

CASP. (1992, September/October). *CASP TODAY, XLII.*

Chandler, J., & Plakos, J. (1969). *Spanish speaking pupils classified as EMR.* Sacramento: California State Department of Education.

Chavez, E. L. (1982). Analysis of a Spanish translation of the Peabody Picture Vocabulary Test. *Perceptual and Motor Skills, 54,* 1335–1338.

Chelala, S. I. (1981). *Composing process of two Spanish speakers and the coherence of their text: A case study.* Unpublished dissertation, New York University, NY

Chenowith, A. N. (1987). The need to teach rewriting. *ELT Journal, 41*(1), 25–29.

Chernigovskaya, T., Balonov, L., & Deglin, V. (1983). Bilingualism and brain functional asymmetry. *Brain and Language, 20,* 195–216.

Chomsky, N. (1980). *Rules and explanations.* New York: Columbia University Press.

Chomsky, N. (1981). *Lectures on government and binding.* Dordrecht: Forris.

Church, A. T. (1987). Personality research in a non-western culture: The Philippines. *Psychological Bulletin, 102*(2), 272–292.

Clark, J. L. D. (1977). *The performance of native speakers of English on the Test of English as a Foreign Language* (TOEFL Research Rep. No. 1). Princeton, NJ: Educational Testing Service.

Clark, L. A. (1987). Mutual relevance of mainstream and cross-cultural psychology. *Journal of Consulting and Clinical Psychology, 55,* 461–470.

Cleary, T. A., & Hilton, T. L. (1968). An investigation of item bias. *Educational and Psychological Measurement, 28,* 61–75.

Cleary, T. A., Humphreys, L. G., Kendrick, S. A., & Wesman, A. (1975). Educational uses of tests with disadvantaged students. *American Psychologist, 15,* 15–40.

Collado-Herrell, L. I. (1976). An exploration of affective and cognitive components of bilingualism. *Dissertation Abstracts International, 37*(6-B), 3044–3045. (University Microfilms No. 76-27, 391)

Conroy, AA. (1982), The testing of minority language students. *The Journal of Educational Issues and Language Minority Students, 11,* 175–186.

Corballis, M. C. (1980). Laterality and Myth. *American Psychologist, 35,* 284–295.

Corman, L., & Budoff, M. (1974). Factor structures of Spanish-speaking and non-Spanish-speaking children on Raven's Progressive Matrices. *Educational and Psychological Measurement, 34,* 977–981.

Costantino, G., Malgaby, R. G., Casullo, M. M., & Castillo, A. (1991). Cross-cultural standardization of TEMAS in three Hispanic subcultures. *Hispanic Journal of Behavioral Sciences, 13,* 48–62.

Cotter, D. E., & Berk, R. A. (1981, April). *Item bias in the WISC-R using Black, White, and Hispanic learning disabled children.* Paper presented at the Annual Meeting of the American Educational Research Association, Los Angeles, CA.

Coulmas, F. (1981). *A festschrift for native speaker.* The Hague: Mouton.

Covarrubias v. San Diego Unified School District. No. 70-394-T, San Diego, CA. (1972).

Crawford, J. (1989). *Bilingual education: History, politics, theory and practice.* Trenton, NJ: Crane.

Crawford v. Honig, No. C-89-0014 (N.D. Cal).RFP.

Crawford v. Honig, Memorandum and Order, No. C-89-0014 RFP, No. C-71-2270, RFP. (1992, August 31).

Cronbach, L. J. (1975). The two disciplines of scientific psychology. *American Psychologist, 12,* 671–684.

222   REFERENCES

Cronbach, L. J. (1975). Five decades of public controversy over mental testing. *American Psychologist, 30*, 1–14.

Cronbach, L. J. (1984). *Essentials of psychological testing* (4th ed.). NY: Harper & Row.

Cummins, J. (1973). A theoretical perspective on the relationship between bilingualism and thought. *Working Papers on Bilingualism, 1*, 1–9.

Cummins, J. (1976). The influence of bilingualism on cognitive growth: A synthesis of research findings and explanatory hypotheses. *Working Papers on Bilingualism, 9*, 1–43.

Cummins, J. (1977a). Cognitive factors associated with the attainment of intermediate levels of bilingual skill. *Modern Language Journal, 61*, 3–12.

Cummins, J. (1977b). *Metalinguistic development of children in bilingual education programs: Data from Irish and Canadian Ukrainian-English programs.* Columbia, SC: Hornbeam Press.

Cummins, J. (1978). Bilingualism and the development of metalinguistic awareness. *Journal of Cross-Cultural Psychology, 9*, 139–149.

Cummins, J. (1979). Linguistic interdependence and the educational development of bilingual children. *Review of Educational Research, 49*, 222–251.

Cummins, J. (1981). The role of primary language development in promoting educational success for language minority students. In C. S. D. O. E. Office of Bilingual Bicultural Education (Ed.), *Schooling and language minority students: A theoretical framework.* Los Angeles: California State University, Evaluation, Dissemination and Assessment Center.

Cummins, J. (1984a). *Bilingualism and special education: Issues in assessment and pedagogy.* San Diego, CA: College Hill Press.

Cummins, J. (1984b). Wanted: A theoretical framework for relating language proficiency to academic achievement among bilingual students. In C. Rivera (Ed.), *Language proficiency and academic achievement* (p. 10). Clevedon, Avon: Multilingual Matters.

Cunningham, G. K. (1986). *Educational and psychological measurement.* New York: Macmillan.

Curtis, M. E. (1987). Cognitive analyses of verbal aptitude tests. In R. A. Freedle & R. P. Duran (Eds.), *Cognitive and linguistic analyses of test performance* (pp. 151–161). Norwood, NJ: Ablex.

Dandonoli, P. (1987). ACTFL's current research in proficiency testing. In H. Byrnes & M. Canale (Eds.), *Defining and developing proficiency: Guidelines, implementations and concepts* (pp. 75–96). Lincolnwood, IL: National Textbook Company.

Darcy, N. T. (1946). The effect of bilingualism upon the measurement of the intelligence of children of preschool age. *Journal of Educational Psychology, 38*(1), 21–44.

Darcy, N. T. (1953). A review of the literature on the effects of bilingualism upon the measurement of intelligence. *Journal of Genetic Psychology, 82*, 21–57.

Darsie, M. L. (1926). The mental capacity of American-born Japanese children. *Comparative Psychology Monographs, 3*, 1–89.

Davenport, E. L. (1932). The intelligence quotients of Mexican and non-Mexican siblings. *School and Society, 36*(923), 304–306.

Davies, A. (1982). Language testing. In V. Kinsella (Ed.), *Surveys: Eight state-of-the-art articles on key areas in language teaching.* Cambridge: Cambridge University Press.

Dean, R. S. (1977). Analysis of the PIAT with Anglo and Mexican American children. *Journal of School Psychology, 15*, 329–333.

Dean, R. S. (1979). Predictive validity of the WISC-R with Mexican-American children. *Journal of School Psychology, 17*, 55–58.

De Avila, E. A., & Duncan, S. (1985). The language-minority child: A psychological, linguistic, and social analysis. In S. F. Chipman, J. W. Segal, & R. Glaser (Eds.), *Thinking and learning skills: Volume 2: Research and open questions* (pp. 245–274). Hillsdale, NJ: Erlbaum.

Del Castillo, J. C. (1970). The influence of language upon symptomatology in foreign-born patients. *American Journal of Psychiatry, 127,* 242–244.

De Jesus, S. (1982). *The relationship between Spanish and English writing proficiency.* Unpublished dissertation, New York University, New York.

Diana v. California State Board of Education. No. C-70-37, United States District Court of Northern California. (1970).

Diaz, R. M. (1983). The impact of bilingualism on cognitive development. *Review of Research in Education,* (Vol. 10). Washington DC: American Educational Research Association.

Diaz-Guerrero, R. (1988). *Psicologia del Mexicano* [Psychology of the Mexican] (4th ed.). Mexico: Editorial Trillas.

Dil, A. S. (Ed.). (1972). *Language, psychology and culture: Essays by Wallace E. Lambert.* Stanford, CA: Stanford University Press.

Diller, K. (1970). "Compound" and "coordinate" bilingualism: A conceptual strategy. *Word, 26,* 254–261.

Dodson, C. J. (1985). Second language acquisition and bilingual development: A theoretical framework. *Journal of Multilingual and Multicultural Development, 5*(6), 325–346.

Domingo, R. (1980). *The development of a language arts program designed to improve reading and writing skills in Spanish of bilingual secondary level students using interest and motivation.* Unpublished dissertation, New York University, New York.

Dornic, S. (1977). *Information processing and bilingualism.* Department of Psychology, University of Stockholm.

Dornic, S. (1978a). *Nosie and language dominance.* Department of Psychology, University of Stockholm.

Dornic, S. (1978b). The bilingual's performance: Language dominance, stress, and individual differences. In D. Gerver & H. Sinaiko (Eds.), *Language Interpretation and Communication.* New York: Plenum Press.

Dornic, S. (1979). Information processing in bilinguals: Some selected issues. *Psychological Research, 40,* 329–348.

Doyle, A., Champagne, M., & Segalowitz, N. (1977). Some issues on the assessment of linguistic consequences of early bilingualism. *Working Papers on Bilingualism, 14,* 21–30.

Duncan, S. E., & DeAvila, E. (1979). Bilingualism and cognition: Some recent findings. *NABE Journal, 4,* 15–50.

Dunn, L. (1987). *Bilingual Hispanic children in the U.S. mainland: A review of research on their cognitive, linguistic, and scholastic development.* Circle Pines, MN: American Guidance Service.

Dunn, L., Padilla, E., Lugo, D., & Dunn, L. (1986). *Test de vocabulario en Imágenes Peabody* [The Peabody Picture Vocabulary Test]. Circle Pines, MN: American Guidance Service.

Duran, R. A., Knight, M. A., & Rock, D. A. (1985). *Language factors and Hispanic freshmen's student profile* (College Board Report NO.85-3 ETS RR No.85-44). New York: College Entrance Examination Board.

Duran, R. P. (1983). *Hispanics' education and background: Predictors of college achievement.* New York: College Entrance Examination Board.

Duran, R. P. (1985). Influences of language skills on bilinguals' problem solving. In S. F. Chipman, J. W. Siegal, & R. Glaser (Ed.), *Thinking and learning skills* (pp. 187–207). Hillsdale, NJ: L Erlbaum.

Durgunoglu, A. Y., & Roediger, H. L. (1987). Test differences in accessing bilingual memory. *Journal of Memory and Language, 26,* 377–391.

Ebel, R. L., & Frisbie, D. A. (1986). *Essentials of educational measurement* (4th ed.). Englewood Cliffs, NJ:Prentice-Hall.

Edelsky, C. (1982). Writing in a bilingual program: The relation of L1 and L2 tests. *TESOL Quarterly, 16*(2), 211–228.

Edelsky, C. (1983). Segmentation and punctuation: Developmental data from young writers in a bilingual program. *Research in the Teaching of English, 17*(2), 135–156.

Edelsky, C. (1986). *Habia una vez: Writing in a bilingual program.* Norwood, NJ: Ablex.

Edelsky, C., Flores, B., Barkin, F., Altwerger, B., & Jilbert, K. (1983). Seimilinugalism and language deficit. *Applied Linguistics, 4*(1), 1–22.

Edgerton, R. B., & Karno, M. (1971). Mexican-American bilingualism and the perception of mental illness. *Archives of General Psychiatry, 24*, 286–290.

Eels, W. C. (1933). Mental ability of the native races of Alaska. *Journal of Applied Psychology, 17*, 417–438.

Elliot, S. N., Argulewicz, E. N., & Turco, T. L. (1986). Predictive validity of the scales for rating the behavioral characteristics of superior students for gifted children from three sociocultural groups. *Journal of Experimental Education, 55*(1), 27–32.

Elliot, S. N., & Boeve, K. (1987). Stability of WISC-R IQs: An investigation of ethnic differences over time. *Educational and Psychological Measurement, 47*, 461–465.

Elliot, S. N., Piersel, W. C., Witt, J. C., Argulewicz, E. N., Gutkin, T. B., & Galvin, G. A. (1985). Three-year stability of WISC-R IQs for handicapped children from three racial/ ethnic groups. *Journal of Psychoeducational Assessment, 3*, 233–244.

Emerling, F. (1990). An investigation of test bias in two nonverbal cognitive measures for two ethnic groups. *Journal of Psychoeducational Assessment, 8*, 34–41.

Ervin, S. (1961). Learning and recall in bilinguals. *The American Journal of Psychology, 74*(3), 446–451.

Ervin, S. (1964a). Language and TAT content in bilinguals. *Journal of Abnormal and Social Psychology, 68*, 500–507.

Ervin, S. (1964b). An analysis of the interaction of language, topic and listener. *American Anthropologist, 66*(2), No. 6.

Faniband, D. K. (1976). Effects of coordinate bilingualism on TAT responses. *Dissertation Abstracts International, 37*(3-B), 1430. (University Microfilms No. 76-19, 649)

Fantini, A. E. (1985). *Language acquisition of a bilingual child: A sociolinguistic perspective.* Clevedon: Multilingual Matters.

Fass, P. (1989). *Outside in: Minorities and the transformation of American education.* Oxford: Oxford University Press.

Feingold, G. A. (1924). Intelligence of the first generation of immigrant groups. *Journal of Educational Psychology, 15*, 65–82.

Feldman, C., &. Shen, M. (1971). Some language-related cognitive advantages of bilingual five-year-olds. *Journal of Genetic Psychology, 118*, 235–244.

Ferris, M. R., & Politzer R. L. (1981). Effects of early and delayed second language acquisition: English composition skills of Spanish-speaking junior high school students. *TESOL Quarterly, 15*(3), 263–74.

Feuerstein, R. (1980). *Instrument enrichment: An intervention program for cognitive modifiability.* Baltimore: University Park Press.

Figueroa, R. A. (1983). Test bias and Hispanic children. *Journal of Special Education, 17*, 431–440.

Figueroa, R. A. (1987). *Special education assessment of Hispanic pupils in California: Looking ahead to the 1990s,* Sacramento: California State Department of Education, Office of Special Education.

Figueroa, R. A. (1989) Psychological testing of linguistic-minority students: Knowledge gaps and regulations. *Exceptional Children, 56*, 145–153.

Figueroa, R. A. (1990). Assessment of linguistic minority group children. In C. R. Reynolds & R. W. Kamphaus (Eds.), *Handbook of psychological and educational assessment of children: Vol. 1. Intelligence and achievement.* New York: Guilford.

Figueroa, R. A., Delgado, G. L., & Ruiz, N. T. (1984). Assessment of Hispanic children:

Implications for Hispanic hearing-impaired children. In G. L. Delgado (Ed.), *The Hispanic deaf: Issues and challenges for bilingual special education* (pp. 124-153). Washington, DC: Gallaudet College Press.

Figueroa, R. A., & Sassenrath, J. M. (1984). *The validation study of the system of multicultural pluralistic assessment* (Final Report). Davis, CA: University of California, Department of Education.

Figueroa, R. A., & Sassenrath, J. M. (1989). A longitudinal study of the predictive validity of the System of Multicultural Pluralistic Assessment (SOMPA). *Psychology in the Schools, 26,* 5-19.

Fillmore, L. W. (1982). Language minority students and school participation: What kind of English is needed? *Journal of Education, 164-165*(2), 143-156.

Finn, J. D. (1982). Patterns in special education placement as revealed by OCR surveys. In K. A. Keller, W. H. Holtzman, & S. Messick (Eds.), *Placing children in special education: A strategy for equity* (pp. 322-381). Washington, DC: National Academy Press.

First, J., & Carrera, J. (1988). *New voices: Immigrant students in U.S. public schools.* Boston, MA: National Coalition of Advocates for Students.

Fishman, J. A. (1964). Language maintenance and language shift as a field of inquiry. *Linguistics, 9,* 32-70.

Fishman, J. A. (1965). Who speaks what language to whom and when? *La Linguistique, 2,* 67-68.

Fishman, J. A. (1967). Bilingualism with and without diglossia; Diglossia with and without bilingualism. *Journal of Social Issues, 32,* 29-38.

Fishman, J. A. (1968). Sociolinguistic perspective on the study of bilingualism. *Linguistics, 39,* 21-49.

Fishman, J. A. (1977). A review of "Bilingualism and Primary Education" by J. Nacnamara. *Irish Journal of Education, 1,* 79-83.

Fishman, J. A. (1980). Bilingualism and biculturalism as individual and societal phenomena. *Journal of Multilingual and Multicultural Development, 1,* 1-13.

Fishman, J. A., Cooper, R., & Ma, R. (1971). *Bilingualism in the barrio.* Bloomington, IN: Indiana University Press.

Fletcher, T. (1989). A comparison of the Mexican version of the Wechster Intelligence Scale for Children-Revised and the Woodcock Psycho-educational Battery in Spanish. *Journal of Psychoeducational Assessment, 7,* 56-65.

Flynn, S., & O'Neil, W. (1988). *Linguistic theory in second language acquisition.* Dordrecht: Kluwer Academic Publishers.

Fouad, N., & Bracken, B. (1986). Cross-cultural translation and validation of two U.S. psychoeducational assessment instruments. *School Psychology International, 7*(3), 167-172.

Fouad, N., Cudeck, R., & Hansen, J. (1984). Convergent validity of the Spanish and English forms of the Strong-Campbell Interest Inventory for bilingual Hispanic high school students. *Journal of Counseling Psychology, 31*(7), 339-348.

Fouad, N., & Hansen, J. (1987, April). Cross-cultural predictive accuracy of the Strong-Campbell Interest Inventory. *Measurement and Evaluation in Counseling and Development,* pp. 3-10.

Fourqurean, J. M. (1987). A K-ABC and WISC-R comparison for Latino learning-disabled children of limited English proficiency. *Journal of School Psychology, 25,* 15-21.

Fuchs, D., Fuchs, L. S. (1989). Effects of examiner familiarity on Black, Caucasian, and Hispanic Children: A meta-analysis. *Exceptional Children, 4,* 303-308.

Fukuda, T. (1923). Some data on the intelligence of Japanese children. *American Journal of Psychology, 34*(4), 599-602.

Galloway, L. (1978). Language impairment and recovery in polyglot aphasia: A case study of a hepta-lingual. In M. Paradis (Ed.), *Aspects of bilingualism* (pp. 139–148). Columbia, SC: Hornbeam Press.

Galloway, L. (1981). The convolutions of second language: A theoretical article with a critical review and some new hypotheses towards a neuropsychological model of bilingualism and second language performance. *Language Learning, 31*(2), 439–464.

Galloway, L. (1982). Bilingualism: Neuropsychological considerations. *Journal of Research and Development in Education, 15*(3), 12–28.

Galloway, L., & Scarcella, R. (1982). Cerebral organization in adult second language acquisition. *Brain and Language, 16*(1), 56–60.

Galvan, M. (1985). *The writing processes of Spanish-speaking bilingual/bicultural graduate students: An ethnographic perspective.* Unpublished dissertation, Hofstra University, Hempstead, NY.

Gandara, P., Keogh, B. K., & Yoshioka-Maxwell, B. (1980). Predicting academic performance of Anglo and Mexican American Kindergarten children. *Psychology in the Schools, 17,* 174–177.

Garcia, S. B. (1985, Fall). Characteristics of limited English proficient Hispanic students served in programs for the learning disabled: Implications for policy, practice and research (Part 1). *Bilingual Special Education Newsletter,* pp. 1–5.

Garretson, O. K. (1928). A study of causes of retardation among Mexican children in a small public school system in Arizona. *Journal of Educational Psychology, 19,* 31–40.

Garth, T. R. (1920). Racial differences in mental fatigue. *Journal of Applied Psychology, 4,* 235–244.

Garth, T. R. (1923). A comparison of the intelligence of Mexican and mixed and full blood Indian children. *Psychological Review, 30,* 388–401.

Garth, T. R. (1925). The intelligence of full blood Indians. *Journal of Applied Psychology, 9,* 382–389.

Garth, T. R. (1926). Mental fatigue of Indians of nomadic and sedentary tribes. *Journal of Applied Psychology, 10,* 437–452.

Geary, O. C., & Whitworth, R. H. (1988). Is the factor structure of the WISC-R different for Anglo- and Mexican- American children? *Journal of Psychoeducational Assessment, 6,* 253–260.

Genesee, F. (1988). Neuropsychology and second language acquisition. In L. M. Beebe (Ed.), *Issues in second language acquisition: Multiple perspectives* (pp. 81–111). Rowley, MA: Newbury House.

Genesee, F., Hamers, J., Lambert, W., Mononen, L., Seitz, M., & Stark, R. (1978). Language processing in bilinguals. *Brain and Language, 5,* 1–12.

Gifford, B. R. (1989). The allocation of opportunities and the politics of testing: A policy analytic perspective. In B. R. Gifford (Ed.), *Test policy and the politics of opportunity allocation: The workplace and the law.* Boston: Kluwer Academic Publishers.

Glanzer, M., & Duarte, A. (1971). Repetition between and within languages in free recall. *Journal of Verbal Learning and Verbal Behavior, 10,* 625–630.

Glutting, J. J. (1986). Potthoff bias analyses of K-ABC MPC and nonverbal scale IQs among Anglo, Black, and Puerto Rican kindergarten children. *Professional School Psychology, 1*(4), 225–234.

Goldman, R. D., & Hartig, L. K. (1976). The WISC may not be a valid predictor of school performance for primary-grade minority children. *American Journal of Mental Deficiency, 80,* 583–587.

Goldman, R. D., & Hewitt, B. N. (1975). An investigation of test bias for Mexican American college students. *Journal of Educational Measurement, 12,* 187–196.

Gomez-Palacio, M. M., Padilla, E. R., & Roll, S. (1983). *Escala de Inteligencia para Nivel Escolar Wechsler* [Wechsler Intelligence Scale for Children-Revised]. Mexico City: El Manual Moderna, S. A. de C. V.

Gomez-Palacio, M., Rangel-Hinojosa, E., & Padilla, E. (1985). *Kaufman Bateria de Evaluacion Intelectual: Manual de aplicación y calificación* [Kaufman Assessment Battery: Manual of application and scoring]. Mexico: Direccion General de Educacion Especial.

Gonzalez, J. R. (1978). Language factors affecting treatment of bilingual schizophrenics. *Psychiatric Annals, 8,* 68–70.

Gonzalez, A., & Bautista, L. S. (1986). *Language surveys in the Philippines (1966–1984).* Manila, Philippines: De La Salle University.

Gonzalez, R. D. (1982). Teaching Mexican-American students to write: Capitalizing on the culture. *The English Journal, 71*(7), 20–24.

Gonzalez-Reigoza, F. (1976). The anxiety-arousing effect of taboo words in bilinguals. In C. D. Spielberger & R. Diaz-Guerrero (Eds.), *Cross-cultural anxiety* (pp. 89–105). Washington, DC: Hemisphere.

Goodenough, F. L. (1926). Racial differences in the intelligence of school children. *Journal of Experimental Psychology, 9,* 388–397.

Gordon, R. A. (1977). Examining labelling theory: The case of mental retardation. In W. R. Gove (Ed.), *The labeling of deviance: Evaluating a perspective* (pp. 83–146). New York: Halsted Press.

Gordon, R. A. (1980). Labelling theory, mental retardation, and public policy: Larry P. and other developments since 1974. In W. R. Gove (Ed.), *The labelling of deviance* (2nd ed.). Beverly Hills, CA: Sage.

Gottfredson, L. S. (1986). Special groups and the beneficial use of vocational interest inventories. In W. B. Walsh & S. H. Osipow (Eds.), *Advances in vocational psychology: Vol. 1. The assessment of interests* (pp. 127–194). Hillsdale, NJ: Erlbaum.

Grabo, R. P. (1931). *A study of comparative vocabularies of junior high school pupils from English and Italian speaking homes* (Bulletin No. 13). Washington, DC: U.S. Office of Education.

Grand, S., Marcos, L., Freedman, N., & Barroso, F. (1977). Relation of psychopathology and bilingualism to kinesic aspects of interview behavior in schizophrenia. *Journal of Abnormal Psychology, 86*(5), 492–500.

Grainger, J., & Beauvillain, C. (1987). Language blocking and lexical access in bilinguals. *Quarterly Journal of Experimental Psychology, 39A,* 295–319.

Grosjean, F. (1982). *Life with two languages.* Cambridge, MA: Harvard University Press.

Grosjean, F. (1985a). The bilingual as a competent but specific speaker-hearer. *The Journal of Multilingual and Multicultural Development, 6,* 467–477.

Grosjean, F. (1985b). Polyglot aphasics and language mixing: A comment on Perecman. *Brain and Language, 26,* 349–355.

Grosjean, F. (1989). Neurolinguists, beware! The bilingual is not two monolinguals in one person. *Brain and Language, 36,* 3–15.

Guadalupe Organization v. Tempe Elementary School District. 587 F.2d 1022, U.S. Dist. Court of Arizona. (1978).

Gutkin, T. B., & Reynolds, C. R. (1980). Factorial similarity of the WISC-R for Anglos and Chicanos referred for psychological services. *Journal of School Psychology, 18,* 34–39.

Hakuta, K. (1986). *Mirror of language: The debate on bilingualism.* NY: Basic Books.

Hakuta, K. & Diaz, R. (1985). The relationship between bilingualism and cognitive ability: A critical discussion and some new longitudinal data. In K. E. Nelson (Ed.), *Children's language* (Vol. 5). Hillsdale, NJ: Erlbaum.

Hakuta, K., Ferdman, B. M., & Diaz, R. M. (1986). *Bilingualism and cognitive development: Three perspectives and methodological implications.* Los Angeles: University of California, Los Angeles. Center for Language Education and Research.

Hakuta, K., Ferdman, B. M., & Diaz, R. M. (1986).Bilingualism and cognitive development: Three perspectives. In S. E. Rosenberg (Ed.), *Advances in applied Psycholinguistics* (Vol. 2). New York: Cambridge University Press.

Hakuta, K., & Garcia, E. E. (1989). Bilingualism and education. *American Psychologist, 44,* 374–379.

Hamers, J. F., & Blanc, M. H. A. (1989). *Bilinguality and bilingualism.* Cambridge: Cambridge University Press.

Hamers, J. F. & Lambert., W. (1977). Visual field and cerebral hemisphere preferences in bilinguals. In S. Segalowitz & F. Gruber (Eds.), *Language development and neurological theory* (pp. 59–63). New York: Academic Press.

Hansen, J. (1987, January). Cross-cultural research on vocational interests. *Measurement and Evaluation in Counseling and Development* (pp. 163–176). Harley, (1986).

Harley, B. (1986). *Age in second language acquisition.* San Diego: College Hill Press.

Harnisch, D. L., & Linn, R. L. (1982). *Identification of aberrant response patterns* (Final Report, National Institute of Education Grant No. G-80-0003). Champaign, IL: University of Illinois.

Harris, C. W. (1948). An exploration of language skill patterns. *Journal of Educational Psychology, 32,* 351–364.

Haugen, E., & (1956). *Bilingualism in the Americas: A bibliography and research guide.* University, AL: University of Alabama Press.

Haugen, E. (1953). *The Norwegian language in America: A study in bilingual behavior.* Philadelphia: University of Pennsylvania Press.

Haugen, E. (1972). The stigmata of bilingualism. In A. S. Dil (Ed.), *The ecology of language* (pp. 307–324). Stanford: Stanford University Press.

Haugen, E. (1973). Bilingualism, language contact and immigrant languages in the United States: A research report. In T. A. Sebeok (Ed.), *Current Trends in Linguistics* (pp. 505–591). The Hague: Mouton.

Haught, B. F. (1934). Mental growth of the Southwestern Indian. *Journal of Applied Psychology, 18,* 137–142.

Haven, S. E. (1931). The relative effort of children of native vs. foreign born parents. *Journal of Educational Psychology, 22*(6), 523–535.

Haviland, M., & Hansen, J. (1987, January). Criterion validity of the Strong-Campbell Interest Inventory for American Indian college students. *Measurement and Evaluation in Counseling and Development,* (pp. 196–201).

Hays, J. R., & Smith, A. L. (1980). Comparison of WISC-R and Culture Fair Intelligence Test scores for three ethnic groups of juvenile delinquents. *Psychological Reports, 46,* 931–934.

Heber, R. (1961). A manual on terminology and classification in mental retardation. *American Journal on Mental Deficiency* [Monograph Suppl.].

Heller, K. A., Holtzman, W. H., & Messick, S. (1982). *Placing children in special education: A strategy for equity.* Washington, DC: National Academy Press.

Henderson, R. W., & Rankin, R. J. (1973). WPPSI reliability and predictive validity with disadvantaged Mexican-American children. *Journal of School Psychology, 11,* 16–20.

Herrick, E. M. (1984). Interference of Spanish phonology in written English. In J. Ornstein-Galacia (Ed.), *Form and function in Chicano English* (pp. 60–70). Rowley, MA: Newbury House.

Hiltonsmith, R. W., Hayman, P. M., & Kleinman, P. (1984). Predicting WAIS-R scores from the Revised Beta for low functioning minority group offenders. *Journal of Clinical Psychology, 40*(4), 1063–1066.

Hiltonsmith, R. W., Hayman, P. M., & Ursprung, A. W. (1982). Beta-WAIS comparisons with low functioning minority group offenders: A cautionary note. *Journal of Clinical Psychology, 38*(4), 864–866.

Hobson v. Hansen. (1967). 269 F. Supp. 401 (D.D.C.).

Hoffman, M. N. (1934). *The measurement of bilingual background.* New York: Teachers College, Columbia University.

Holtzman, W. H., Diaz-Guerrero, R., & Swartz, J. D. (1975). *Personality development in two cultures: A cross-cultural longitudinal study of school children in Mexico and the United States*. Austin: University of Texas Press.

Homel, P., Palij, M., & Aaronson, D. (1987). *Childhood bilingualism: Aspects of linguistic, cognitive and social development*. Hillsdale NJ: Earlbaum,

Honig, B. (1992). *Declaration of Superintendent Honig in Support of Stipulated Request to Extend Data Reporting Requirements*. *Larry P. v. Riles*, No. C-71-2270. (1992, June 9).

Hoosian, R., & Salili, F. (1987). Language differences in pronunciation speed for numbers, digit span, and mathematical ability. *Psychologia, 30*, 34–38.

Hung Hsiao, H. (1929). The mentality of the Chinese and Japanese. *Journal of Applied Psychology, 13*, 9–31.

Hurt, M., & Mishra, S. P. (1970). Reliability and validity of the metropolitan achievement tests for Mexican-American children. *Educational and Psychological Measurement, 30*, 989–992.

Hyltenstam, K., & Obler, L. K. (1989). *Bilingualism across the lifespan: Aspects of acquisition, maturity, and loss*. Cambridge: Cambridge University Press.

Hymes, D. (1972). On communicative competence. In J. B. Pride & J. Holmes (Ed.), *Sociolinguistics*. Harmondsworth: Penguin Books.

Hymes, D. (1985). Toward linguistic competence. *Revuew de l'AILA: AILA Review, 2*, 9–23.

Ianco-Worrall, A. D. (1972). Bilingualism and cognitive development. *Child Development, 43*, 1390–1400.

Institute of Education. (1983). *Linguistic minorities in England: A report from the linguistics minorities project*. London: University of London.

Intelligence and its measurement [Special Issue]. (1921). *Journal of Educational Psychology, 12*.

Jensen, A. R. (1969). How much can we boost IQ and scholastic achievement? *Harvard Educational Review, 39*, 1–123.

Jensen, A. R. (1973). *Educability and group differences*. New York: Harper & Row.

Jensen, A. R. (1974). How biased are culture-loaded tests? *Genetic Psychology Monographs, 90*, 185–244.

Jensen, A. R. (1976). Construct validity and test bias. *Phi Delta Kappan, 58*, 340–346.

Jensen, A. R. (1977, September 14). *The nature of intelligence and its relation to learning*. Theodore A. Fink Memorial Lecture delivered at the University of Melbourne, Australia.

Jensen, A. R. (1980). *Bias in mental testing*. New York: Free Press.

Jensen, A. R. (1982). Reaction time and psychometric g. In H. J. Eysenck (Ed.), *A model for intelligence* (pp. 93–132). New York: Springer.

Jensen, A. R. (1984). Test bias: Concepts and criticisms. In C. R. Reynolds & R. T. Brown (Eds.), *Perspectives on bias in mental testing* (pp. 507–586). New York: Plenum.

Jensen, A. R., & Inouye, A. R. (1980). Level I and Level II abilities in Asian, White, and Black children. *Intelligence, 4*, 41–49.

Johnson, L. W. (1938). A comparison of the vocabularies of Anglo-American and Spanish-American high school pupils. *Journal of Educational Psychology, 29*, 135–144.

Johnson, E. (1986). The role of bilingualism in color naming. *Psychologia, 29*, 156–164.

Johnson, D. L., & McGowan, R. J. (1984). Comparison of three intelligence tests as predictors of academic achievement and classroom behaviors of Mexican-American children. *Journal of Psychoeducational Assessment, 2*, 345–352.

Jones, E. E., & Thorne, A. (1987). Rediscovery of the subject: Intercultural approaches to clinical assessment. *Journal of Consulting and Clinical Psychology, 55*, 488–495.

Jones, M. A. (1980). *An investigation to determine the rate of syntactic growth as a result of sentence combining practice in freshman English*. Unpublished dissertation, Auburn University, Auburn, Alabama.

Jose P. v. Ambach, No. C–270 (E.D.N.Y. 1979)

Jungué, C., Vendrell, P., Vendrell-Brucet, J., & Tobeña, A. (1989). Differential recovery in naming in bilingual aphasics. *Brain and Language, 36*, 16–22.

Kagan, S. &. Buriel, R. (1977). Field dependence-independence and Mexican-American culture and education. In J. L. Martinez (Ed.), *Chicano psychology* (pp. 279–328). New York: Academic Press.

Kamphaus, R., & Reynolds, C. (1987). *Clinical and research applications of the K-ABC*. Circle Pines, MN: American Guidance Service.

Karabinus, R. A., & Hurt, M., Jr. (1969). The Van Alstyne Picture Vocabulary Test used with six-year-old Mexican-American children. *Educational and Psychological Measurement, 29*, 935–939.

Kardash, C., Amlund, J., Kulhavy, R., & Ellison, G. (1988). Bilingual referents in cognitive processing. *Contemporary Educational Psychology, 13*, 45–57.

Kaufman, A. S. (1979). *Intelligent testing with the WISC-R*. New York: Wiley Interscience.

Kaufman, A. S., & Kaufman, N. L. (1983). *K-ABC: Kaufman Assessment Battery for Children*. Circle Pines, MN: American Guidance Service.

Kaufman, A. S., & Wang, J-J. (1992). Gender, race and education differences on the K-BIT at ages 4 to 90 years. *Journal of Psychoeducational Assessment, 10*, 219–229.

Kazemek, F. E. (1984). "I wanted to become a tencra to help Penp to I . . .": Writing for adult beginning learners. *Journal of Reading, 27*(7), 614–619.

Kelin, W., & Dittmar, N. (1979). *Developing grammars: The acquisition of German syntax by foreign workers*. New York: Springer-Verlag.

Kelly, L. G. (1969). *Description and measurement of bilingualism: An international seminar*. Toronto: University of Toronto Press.

Kestenbaum, C. J., & Williams, D. T. (1988). *Handbook of clinical assessment of children and adolescents* (Vol. 1, Vol. II). New York: New York University Press.

Kirp, D. L., Kuriloff, P. J., & Buss, W. G. (1975). Legal mandates and organizational change. In N. Hobbs (Ed.), *Issues in the classification of children* (pp. 319–382). San Francisco: Jossey-Bass.

Klein, W. (1986). *Second language acquisition*. Cambridge: Cambridge University Press.

Knoff, H. M. (1983). Effect of diagnostic information on special education placement decisions. *Exceptional Children, 49*, 440–444.

Knoff, H. M. (Ed.). (1986). *The assessment of child and adolescent personality*. New York: Guilford Press.

Knudson, R. E. (1993). Effects of ethnicity in attitudes toward writing. *Psychological Reports, 72*, 39–45.

Koch, H. L., & Simmons, R. (1926). A study of the test performance of American, Mexican and Negro children. *Psychology Monographs, 35*, 1–116.

Kolers, P. A. (1963). Interlingual word associations. *Journal of Verbal Learning and Verbal Behavior, 2*, 291–300.

Kolers, P. A. (1965). Bilingualism and bicodalism. *Language and Speech, 8*, 122–126.

Kolers, P. A. (1966a). Interlingual facilitation of short-term memory. *Journal of Verbal Learning and Verbal Behavior, 5*, 314–319.

Kolers, P. A. (1966b). Reading and talking bilingually. *American Journal of Psychology, 79*, 357–376.

Kolers, P. A., & Brison, S. J. (1984). Commentary: On pictures, words, and their mental representations. *Journal of Verbal Learning and Verbal Behavior, 23*, 105–113.

Kolers, P. A., & Gonzales, E. (1980). Memory for words, synonyms, and translations. *Journal of Experimental Psychology: Human Learning and Memory, 6*, 53–65.

Kozol, J. (1991). *Savage inequalities: Children in America's schools*. New York: Crown.

Lamb, E. O. (1930). Racial differences in bi-manual dexterity of Latin and American children. *Child Development, 1*, 204–231.

Lambert, W. E. (1955). Measurement of the linguistic dominance in bilinguals. *Journal of Abnormal and Social Psychology, 50,* 197–200.

Lambert, W. E. (1969). Psychological studies of interdependencies of the bilingual's two languages. In J. Puhvel (Ed.), *Substance and structure of language.* Los Angeles: University of California Press.

Lambert, W. (1972). The influence of language-acquisition contexts on bilingualism. In A. S. Dil (Ed.), *Language, psychology and culture* (pp. 50–62). Stanford, CA: Stanford University Press.

Lambert, W. E. (1974). Culture and language as factors in learning and education. In F. E. Aboud & R. D. Meaade (Ed.), *Cultural factors in learning.* Bellingham, WA: Western Washington State College.

Lambert, W. E. (1977). Effects of bilingualism on the individual. In P. A. Hornby (Ed.), *Bilingualism: Psychological, social and educational implications* (pp. 15–27). New York: Academic Press.

Lambert, W. E., Havelka, J., & Crosby, C. (1958). The influence of language acquisition contexts on bilingualism. *Journal of Abnormal and Social Psychology, 56,* 239–244.

Lambert, W. E., Havelka, J., & Gardner, R. C. (1959). Linguistic manifestations of bilingualism. *American Journal of Psychology, 72,* 77–82.

Lambert, W. E., &. Moore, N. (1966). Word-association responses: Comparison of American and French monolinguals with Canadian monolinguals and bilinguals. *Journal of Personality and Social Psychology, 3,* 313–320.

Landry, R. G. (1974). A comparison of second language learners and monolinguals on divergent thinking tasks at the elementary school level. *Modern Language Journal, 58,* 10–15.

Langdon, H. W. (1986). *The interpreter/translator in a school setting.* Sacramento, CA: California State Department of Education, Office of Special Education.

Laosa, L. M., Swartz, J. O., & Diaz-Guerrero, R. (1974). Perceptual-cognitive and personality development of Mexican and Anglo-American children as measured by Human Figure Drawings. *Developmental Psychology, 10,* 131–139.

Larry P. v. Riles. 343 F. Supp. 1306 (N. D. Cal. 1972) *aff'r* 502 F.2d 963 (9th Cir. 1974); 495 F. Supp. 926 (N. D. Cal. 1979); appeal docketed, No. 80–4027 (9th Cir., Jan. 17, 1980).

Larry P. v. Riles, Order Modifying Judgment, No. C-71-2270, RFP. (1986, September 25).

Lau v. Nichols. 414 U.S. 563 (1974).

Lauver, P. J., & Jones, B. M. (1991). Factors associated with perceived career options in American Indian, White, and Hispanic rural high school students. *Journal of Counseling Psychology, 18,* 159–166.

Lavandera, B. A. (1978a). The variable component in bilingual performance. In J. E. Alatis (Ed.), *Georgetown University roundtable on languages and linguistics 1978* (pp. 391–409). Washington, DC: Georgetown University Press.

Levin, H. M. (1987, August). *Accelerating elementary education for disadvantaged students.* Paper presented at the Summer Institute of the Council of Chief State School Officers (CCSSO), Whitefish, MT.

Levin, H. M. (1988, April). *Structuring schools for greater effectiveness with educationally disadvantaged or at-risk students.* Paper presented at the meeting of the American Educational Research Association, New Orleans, LA.

Levin, H. M. (1991). Review of J. H. Hartigan and A. K. Wigdor, Eds., Fairness in employment testing: Validity generalization, minority issues, and the General Aptitude Test Battery. *Journal of Educational Measurement, 28,* 358–363.

Liedtke, W. W., & Nelson, L. D. (1968). Concept formation and bilingualism. *Alberta Journal of Educational Research, 14,* 225–232.

Lindholm, J. J., & Padilla, A. M. (1978). Language mixing in bilingual children. *Journal of Child Language, 5,* 327–335.

Livesay, T. M. (1936). Racial comparisons in performance on the American Council Psychological Examination. *Journal of Educational Psychology, 28,* 631–634.

Lopez, R. P., Braden, J. B., & Sneed, T. G. (1991). *Support Paper on CASP's IQ Stand: Tools Worth Keeping.* El Camino, CA: California Association of School Psychologists.

Lopez, M., Hicks, R. E., & Young, R. R. (1974). Retroactive inhibition in a bilingual A-B, A'-B' paradigm. *Journal of Experimental Psychology, 103,* 85–90.

Lopez, M., & Young, R. R. (1974). The linguistic interdependence of bilinguals. *Journal of Experimental Psychology, 6,* 981–983.

Lora v. Board of Education of the City of New York, 587 F. Supp. 1592 (E.D.N.Y. 1984).

Louttit, C. M. (1931). Test performance of a selected group of part-Hawaiians. *Journal of Applied Psychology, 15,* 43–52.

Lubin, B., Larsen, R. M., & Matarazzu, J. D. (1984). Patterns of psychological test usage in the United States: 1935–1982. *American Psychologist, 39,* 451–454.

Lucero, R. O. (1985, March). *ATP racial/ethnic data report: Comparative data 1981-1982-1983-1984.* Princeton, NJ: College Board.

Luh, C. W., & Wy, T. M. (1931). A comparative study of the intelligence of Chinese children on the Pintner performance and the Binet tests. *Journal of Social Psychology, 2,* 402–408.

Lynn, R., Hampson, S., & Bingham, R. (1987). Japanese, British and American adolescents compared for Spearman's G and for the verbal, numerical and visuospatial abilities. *Psychologia, 30,* 137–144.

Mack, M. (1986). A study of semantic and syntactic processing in monolinguals and fluent early bilinguals. *Journal of Psycholinguistic Research, 15*(6), 463–488.

Mackey, W. F. (1962). The description of bilingualism. *Canadian Journal of Linguistics, 7,* 51–85.

Mackey, W. F. (1967). *Bilingualism as a world problem/ Le bilinguisme: phenomene mondial.* Montreal: Harvest House.

Mackey, W. F. (1970). A typology of bilingual education. In T. Anderson & M. Boyer (Eds.), *Bilingual schooling in the United States.* Austin, TX: National Educational Laboratory.

Macnamara, J. (1967). The linguistic independence of bilinguals. *Journal of Verbal Learning and Verbal Behavior, 6,* 729–736.

MacNamara, J. (1969). How can one measure the extent of a person's bilingual dominance? In L. G. Kelly (Ed.), *Description and measurement of bilingualism* Toronto: University of Toronto Press.

Macnamara, J. (1969). Comment mesurer le bilinguisme d'une personne? In L. G. Kelly (Ed.), *Description and measurement of bilingualism.* Toronto: Toronto University Press.

Macnamara, J. & Kushnir, S. (1971). Linguistic interdependence of bilinguals: The input switch. *Journal of Verbal Learning and Verbal Behavior, 10,* 480–487.

Magiste, E. (1979). The competing language systems of the multilingual: A developmental study of decoding and encoding processes. *Journal of Verbal Learning and Verbal Behavior, 18,* 79–89.

Magiste, E. (1980). Memory for numbers in monolinguals and bilinguals. *Acta Psychologica, 46,* 63–68.

Magiste, E. (1985a). Automaticity and interference in bilinguals. *Psychological Research, 44,* 29–43.

Magiste, E. (1985b). Development of intra- and interlingual interference in bilinguals. *Journal of Psycholinguistic Research, 14,* 137–154.

Malgady, R., Constantino, G., & Rogler, L. (1984). Development of a thematic apperception test (TEMAS) for urban Hispanic children. *Journal of Consulting and Clinical Psychology, 52*(6), 986–996.

Malmberg, B. (1977). Finns halvsprakighet? *Sydvenska Dagbladet, 21*(11).

Manuel, H. T. (1932). The intelligence and drawing ability of young Mexican children.

Journal of Applied Psychology, 16, 382–387.

Manuel, H. T. (1935). Spanish and English editions of the Stanford-Binet in relation to the abilities of Mexican children. *University of Texas Bulletin* (No. 3532). Austin: University of Texas.

Marcos, L., & Alpert, M. (1976). Strategies and risks in psychotherapy with bilingual patients: The phenomenon of language independence. *American Journal of Psychiatry, 133*(11), 1275–1278.

Marcos, L., Alpert, M., Urcuyo, L., & Kesselman, M. (1973). The effect of interview language on the evaluation of psychopathology in Spanish-American schizophrenic patients. *American Journal of Psychiatry, 130,* 549–553.

Marcos, L., Urcuyo, L., Kesselman, M., & Alpert, M. (1973). The language barrier in evaluating Spanish-American patients. *Archives of General Psychiatry, 29,* 655–659.

Martinez, M. A. (1985). Toward a bilingual school psychology model. *Educational Psychologist, 20,* 143–152.

Martin-Jones, M., & Romaine, S. (1987). Semilingualism: A half-baked theory of communicative competence. *Applied Linguistics, 7*(1), 26–38.

Maspons, M. M., & Liabre, M. M. (1985). The influence of training Hispanics in test taking on the psychometric properties of a test. *Journal for Research in Mathematics Education, 16,* 177–183.

McArthur, D. L. (Ed.). (1987). *Alternative approaches to the assessment of achievement.* Boston MA: Kluwer.

McElwee, E. W. (1935). Differences in reading attainment of Italian and Jewish children. *Journal of Applied Psychology, 19,* 730–732.

McGowan, R. J., Johnson, D. L., & Maxwell, S. E. (1981). Relations between infant behavior ratings and concurrent and subsequent mental test scores. *Developmental Psychology, 17*(5), 542–553.

McLaughlin, J. A., & Lewis, R. B. (1990). *Assessing special students.* New York: McMillan.

McNab, G. (1979). Cognition and bilingualism: A reanalysis of studies. *Linguistics, 17,* 231–255.

Mehan, H., Hertweck, H., & Meihls, J. L. (1986). *Handicapping the handicapped.* Palo Alto, CA: Stanford University Press.

Mehrens, W. A., & Lehmann, I. J. (1987). *Using standardized tests in education* (4th ed.). NY: Longman.

Mercer, J. R. (1971). The meaning of mental retardation. In R. Koch & J. C. Dobson (Eds.), *The mentally retarded child and his family: A multidisciplinary handbook* (pp. 23–46). NY: Brunner & Mazel.

Mercer, J. R. (1972, September). IQ: The lethal label. *Psychology Today,* pp. 44–47, 95–97.

Mercer, J. R. (1973). *Labeling the mentally retarded.* Berkeley: University of California Press.

Mercer, J. R. (1977). *Implications of current assessment procedures for Mexican-American children* (Vol. 1, No. 1). California State University, Los Angeles, National Dissemination and Assessment Center.

Mercer, J. R. (1979). *The system of multicultural pluralistic assessment: Technical manual.* New York: Psychological Corporation.

Mercer, J. R., & Lewis, J. F. (1977). *SOMPA parent interview manual.* New York: Psychological Corporation.

Miele, F. (1979). Cultural bias in the WISC. *Intelligence, 3,* 149–164.

Miller, H. (1916). *The school and the immigrant.* Cleveland: Survey Committee of the Cleveland Foundation.

Miller-Jones, D. (1989). Culture and testing. *American Psychologist, 44,* 360–366.

Mishra, S. P. (1981a). Factor analysis of the McCarthy Scales for groups of white and Mexican-American children. *Journal of School Psychology, 19,* 178–182.

Mishra, S. P. (1981b). Reliability and validity of the WRAT with Mexican-American children. *Psychology in the Schools, 18,* 154–158.

Mishra, S. P. (1982). The WISC-R and evidence of item bias for Native-American Navajos. *Psychology in the Schools, 19,* 458–464.

Mishra, S. P. (1983). Validity of WISC-R IQ's and factor scores in predicting achievement for Mexican American children. *Psychology in the Schools, 20,* 442–444.

Mishra, S. P., & Hurt, M. J. (1970). The use of Metropolitan Readiness Tests with Mexican-American children. *California Journal of Educational Research, 21,* 182–187.

Montgomery, G. T., & Orozco, S. (1985). Mexican American's performance on the MMPI as a function of level of acculturation. *Journal of Clinical Psychology, 41,* 203–212.

Mullholland, T. M., Pellegrino, J. W., & Glaser, R. (1980). Components of geometric analogy solution. *Cognitive Psychology, 12,* 254–284.

Myers, B., & Goldstein, D. (1979). Cognitive development in bilingual and monolingual lower-class children. *Psychology in the Schools, 16*(1), 137–142.

National Commission on Testing and Public Policy. (1990). *From gatekeeper to gateway: transforming testing in America.* Chestnut Hill, MA: Boston College.

Naveh-Benjamin, M., & Ayres, T. (1986). Digit span, reading rate, and linguistic relativity. *Quarterly Journal of Experimental Psychology, 38A,* 739–751.

Nielsen, R., & Fernandez, R. M. (1981). *Hispanic students in American high schools: Background characteristics and achievements.* Washington, DC: National Center for Educational Statistics.

Nuttal, D. L. (Ed.). (1986). *Assessing educational achievement.* Philadelphia: Falmer.

Oakland, T. (1980). Nonbiased assessment of minority group children. *Exceptional Education Quarterly, 1,* 31–46.

Oakland, T. (1983). Concurrent and predictive validity estimates for the WISC-R IQs and ELPs by racial-ethnic and SES groups. *School Psychology Review, 12*(1), 57–61.

Oakes, J. (1985). *Keeping track.* New Haven, CT: Yale University Press.

Obler, L., Albert, M., & Gordon, H. (1975). *Assymetry of cerebral dominance in Hebrew-English bilinguals.* Presented at the 13th Academy of Aphasia.

O'Brian, B. (1982). *Comparative response forms for selected Hispanic and non-Hispanic subjects in a syntax test.* Unpublished dissertation, Marquette University, Milwaukee, WI.

O'Connor, M. C. (1989). Aspects of differential performance by minorities on standardized tests: Linguistic and sociocultural factors. In B. R. Gifford (Ed.), *Test policy and test performance: Education, language and culture* (pp. 129–173). Boston: Kluwer.

O'Connor, M. C. (1992). Rethinking aptitude, achievement and instruction: Cognitive science research and the framing of assessment policy. In B. R. Gifford, & M. C. O'Connor (Ed.), *Changing Assessments: Alternative Views of Aptitude, Achievement, and Instruction* (pp. 9–35). Boston: Kluwer.

Office of the General Counsel (1992). *Analysis of Judge Peckham's August 31, 1992 Decision in Larry P. v. Riles and Crawford v. Honig.* Sacramento, CA: California Department of Education.

Oller, J. W. (1979). *Language tests at school.* London: Longman.

Oplesch, M., & Genshaft, J. (1981). Comparison of bilingual children on the WISC-R and the Escala de Inteligencia Wechsler para niños. *Psychology in the Schools, 18,* 159–163.

Ortiz, A. A. (1986, Spring). Characteristics of limited English proficient Hispanic students served in programs for the learning disabled: Implications for policy and practice (Part II). *Bilingual Special Education Newsletter,* pp. 1–5.

Ortiz, A. A., & Maldonado-Colon, E. (1986). Recognizing learning disabilities in bilingual children: How to lessen inappropriate referral of language minority students to special education. *Journal of Reading, Writing, and Learning Disabilities International, 43*(1), 47–56.

Ortiz, A. A., & Polyzoi, E. (1986). *Characteristics of limited English-proficient Hispanic students served in programs for the learning disabled: Implications for policy and practice.* Austin: University of Texas. (ERIC Document Reproduction Service No. ED 267 597)

Ortiz, A. A., & Polyzoi, E. (1987). *Language assessment of Hispanic learning disabled and speech and language handicapped students: Research in progress.* Austin: University of Texas, Department of Special Education, Handicapped Minority Research Institute on Language Proficiency.

Ortiz, A. A., & Yates, J. R. (1987). *Characteristics of learning disabled, mentally retarded, and speech-language handicapped Hispanic students at initial evaluation and re-evaluation.* Unpublished manuscript, University of Texas at Austin.

Ortiz-Franco, L. (1990). Interrelationships of seven mathematical abilities across languages. *Hispanic Journal of Behavioral Sciences, 12,* 299–312.

Paivio, A., Clark, J., & Lambert, W. (1988). Bilingual dual-coding theory and semantic repetition effects on recall. *Journal of Experimental Psychology, 14*(1), 163–172.

Palomares, U. H., & Johnson, L. C. (1966). Evaluation of Mexican-American pupils for EMR classes. *California Education, 3,* 27–29.

Paradis, M. (1977). Bilingualism and aphasia. In H. Whitaker & H. Whitaker (Eds.), *Studies in neurolinguistics* (pp. 65–121). New York: Academic Press.

Paradis, M. (1978). *Aspects of bilingualism.* Columbia, SC: Hornbeam Press.

Parents in Action on Special Education (PASE) v. Hannon. No. 74 C 3586 (N.D. III. 1980).

Paschal, F. C., & Sullivan, L. R. (1925). Racial influences in the mental and physical development of Mexican children. *Comparative Psychology Monographs, 3,* 1–76.

Paulston, C. B. (1975). Ethnic relations and bilingual education: Accounting for contradictory data. *Working Papers on Bilingualism, 6,* 1–44.

Paulston, C. B. (1977). Theoretical perspectives on bilingual education. *Working Papers on Bilingualism, 13,* 130–177.

Peal, E., & Lambert, W. E. (1962). The relation of bilingualism to intelligence. *Psychological Monographs: General and Applied, 76,* 1–23.

Pearson, C. A. (1988). Cognitive differences between bilingual and monolingual children on the Kaufman Assessment Battery for Children. *Journal of Psychoeducational Assessment, 6,* 271–279.

Pellegrino, J. W. (1992). Understanding what we measure and measuring what we understand. In B. R. Gifford, & M. C. O'Connor (Ed.), *Changing assessments: Alternative views of aptitude, achievement, and instruction* (pp. 275–300). Boston: Kluwer.

Pellegrino, J. W., & Glaser, R. (1979). Cognitive correlates and components in the analysis of individual differences. *Intelligence, 3,* 187–214.

Peña, A., & Bernal, E. M. (1978). Malpractices in language assessment for Hispanic children. In J. E. Redden (Ed.), *Proceedings of the Second International Conference on Frontiers in Language Proficiency and Dominance Testing. Occasional Papers on Linguistics Number 3* (pp. 102–108). Carbondale, ILL: Southern Illinois University.

Penfield, J. (1984). Vernacular base of literacy development in Chicano English. In J. Ornstien-Galacia (Ed.), *Form and function in Chicano English* (pp. 71–84). Rowley, MA: Newbury House.

Pennock-Roman, M. (1986). New directions for research on Spanish-language tests and test-item bias. In M. A. Olivas (Ed.), *Latino college students* (pp. 193–220). New York: Teachers College Press.

Piersel, W. C., & Reynolds, C. R. (1981). Factorial validity of item classification on the Boehm Test of Basic Concepts (BTBC), Forms A and B. *Educational and Psychological Measurement, 41*(2), 579–583.

Pilkington, C., Piersel, W., & Ponterotto, J. (1988). Home language as a predictor of first grade achievement for Anglo- and Mexican-American children. *Contemporary Educational Psychology*, *13*(1), 1-14.

Pintner, R., & Arsenian, S. (1937). The relation of bilingualism to verbal intelligence and school adjustment. *Journal of Educational Research*, *31*(4), 255-263.

Pintner, R., & Keller, R. (1922). Intelligence tests of foreign children. *Journal of Educational Psychology*, *13*, 214-222.

P. L. *94-142, Education for All Handicapped Children Act of 1975*. Washington, DC: 94th Congress.

Plata, M. (1985). The use of criterion referenced assessment with bilingual handicapped students. *Journal of Instructional Psychology*, *12*, 200.

Pletcher, B. P., Locks, N. A., Reynolds, D. F., & Sisson, B. G. (1978). *A guide to assessment instruments for limited English-speaking students*. New York: Santillana.

Portenier, L. G. (1947). Abilities and interests of Japanese-American high school seniors. *Journal of Social Psychology*, *25*, 53-61.

Powers, S., Barkan, J. H., & Jones, P. B. (1986). Reliability of the Standard Progress Matrices Test for Hispanic and Anglo-American children. *Perceptual and Motor skills*, *62*, 348-350.

Powers, S., Escamilla, K., & Houssler, M. (1986). The California Achievement Test as a predictor of reading ability across race and sex. *Educational and Psychological Measurement*, *46*, 1067-1070.

Powers, S., & Jones, P. (1984). Factorial invariance of the California Achievement Tests across race and sex. *Educational and Psychological Measurement*, *44*, 967-970.

Powers, S., Rossman, M., & Douglas, P. (1986). Reliability of the Boehm Test of Basic Concepts for Hispanic and non-Hispanic kindergarten pupils. *Psychology in the Schools*, *23*, 34-36.

Pratt, H. G. (1929). Some conclusions from a comparison of school achievement of certain racial groups. *Journal of Educational Psychology*, *20*, 661-668.

Prewitt Diaz, J. O. (1990). *The process and procedures for identifying exceptional language minority children*. University Park, PA: Pennsylvania State University.

Prewitt Diaz, J. O., Rodriguez, M. D., & Ruiz, D. R. (1986). The predictive validity of the Spanish translation of the WISC-R (EIWN-R) with Puerto Rican students in Puerto Rico and the United States. *Educational and Psychological Measurement*, *46*, 401-407.

Price, C. S., & Cuellar, I. (1981). Effects of language and related variables on the expression of psychopathology in Mexican American psychiatric patients. *Hispanic Journal of Behavioral Sciences*, *3*(2), 145-160.

Project, L. M. (1983). *Linguistic minorities in England*. London: Tinga Tinga (Heinemann Educational Books).

Psychological Corporation (Trans.). (1982). *Manual para la Escala de Inteligencia Wechsler para Niños-Revisada* [Manual for the Wechsler Intelligence Scale for Children-Revised]. New York: Psychological Corporation.

Rappaport, N. B., & McAnulty, D. P. (1985). The effect of accented speech on the scoring of ambiguous WISC-R responses by prejudiced and nonprejudiced raters. *Journal of Psychoeducational Assessment*, *3*, 275-283.

Rapport, R. L., Tan, C. T., & Whitaker, H. A., (1983). *Language Function and Dysfunction Among Chinese- and English-speaking Polyglots: Cortical Stimulation, Wada Testing, and Clinical Studies*, *18*, 342-366.

Ramirez, M. (1973). Cognitive styles and cultural democracy in education. *Social Science Quarterly*, *53*, 895-904.

Ramirez, M. & Castaneda, A. (1974). *Cultural democracy, bicognitive development, and education*. New York: Academic Press.

Ramirez, M., Castaneda, A, & Herold, P. L. (1974). The relationship of acculturation to cognitive style among Mexican-Americans. *Journal of Cross-Cultural Psychology, 5,* 425–433.

Ramirez, M. & Price-Williams, D. (1974). Cognitive styles in children: Two Mexican communities. *International Journal of Psychology, 8,* 93–100.

Ramirez, J. D., Wolfson, R., Talmadge, G. K., & Merino, B. (1986). *First year report: Longitudinal study of immersion programs for language minority children* (Submitted to U.S. Department of Education, Washington, DC). Mountain View, CA: SRA Associates.

Rastogi, K. G., & Singh, L. C. (1976). Influence of language and script on effective meaning. *Indian Educational Review, 11,* 61–69.

Reschly, D. J. (1978). WISC-R factor structures among Anglos, Blacks, Chicanos, and Native American Papagos. *Journal of Consulting and Clinical Psychology, 46,* 417–422.

Reschly, D. J. (1982). Assessing mild mental retardation: The influence of adaptive behavior, sociocultural status, and prospects for nonbiased assessment. In C. R. Reynolds & T. B. Gutkin (Eds.), *The handbook of school psychology* (pp. 209–242). New York: Wiley.

Reschly, D. J., & Reschly, J. E. (1979). Validity of WISC-R factor scores in predicting achievement and attention for four sociocultural groups. *Journal of School Psychology, 17,* 355–361.

Reschly, D. J., & Saber, D. L. (1979). Analysis of test bias in four groups, with the regression definition. *Journal of Educational Measurement, 16,* 1–9.

Resnick, L. B., & Resnick, D., P. (1992a). Assessing the thinking curriculum: new tools for educational reform. In B. R. Gifford, & M. C. O'Connor (Ed.), *Changing Assessments: Alternative views of aptitude, achievement and instruction* (pp. 37–75). Boston: Kluwer.

Resnick, L., & Resnick, D. (1992b). *The new standards project, 1992–1995, A proposal.* Pittsburgh: Learning Research and Development Center, University of Pittsburgh

Reynolds, A. (1933, reprinted 1973). *The education of Spanish-speaking children in five southwestern states* (1933, Bulletin No. 11). Washington, DC: U.S. Department of the Interior.

Reynolds, A. G. (1991). *Bilingualism, multiculturalism and second language learning: The McGill Conference in honor of Wallace E. Lambert.* Hillsdale NJ: Erlbaum.

Reynolds, C. R. (1982). The problem of bias in psychological assessment. In C. R. Reynolds & T. B. Gutkin (Eds.), *The handbook of school psychology* (pp. 178–208). New York: Wiley.

Reynolds, C. R., & Gutkin, T. B. (1980). A regression analysis of test bias on the WISC-R for Anglos and Chicanos referred to psychological services. *Journal of Abnormal Child Psychology, 8,* 237–243.

Reynolds, C. R., & Gutkin, T. B. (Eds.). (1982). *The handbook of school psychology.* New York: Wiley.

Reynolds, C. R., & Kaiser, S. M. (1990). Test bias in psychological assessment. In T. B. Gutking & C. R. Reynolds (Eds.), *The Handbook of School Psychology* (2nd ed.) (pp. 487–525). New York: Wiley.

Rivera, C. (1986). *The national assessment of educational progress: Issues and concerns for the assessment of Hispanic students.* Chicago: Spencer Foundation.

Rivera, C., & Pennock-Roman, M. (1987). *Issues in race/ethnicity identification procedures in the national assessment of educational progress, Part I: A comparison of observer reports and self-identification.* Princeton, NJ: Educational Testing Service.

Rosado, J. W. (1986). Toward an interfacing of Hispanic cultural variables with school psychology service delivery systems. *Professional Psychology: Research and Practice, 17,* 191–199.

Rose, R. G. (1980). Second language performance and language of thought. *The Journal of General Psychology, 103,* 245–250.

Rubin, A. (1973). *Affidavit dated September 19, 1973 in response to plaintiffs' motion for a Civil Contempt Order. (Diana file).* Sacramento: California State Department of Education, Legal Office Library.

Rueda, R., Cardoza, D., Mercer, J. R., & Carpenter, L. (1984). *An examination of special education decision-making with Hispanic first-time referrals in large urban school districts.* Los Alamitos, CA: Southwest Regional Laboratory.

Rueda, R., Figueroa, R., Mercado, P., & Cardoza, D. (1984). *Performance of Hispanic educable mentally retarded, learning disabled and nonclassified students on the WISC-RM, SOMPA and S-KABC.* Los Alamitos, CA: Southwest Regional Laboratory.

Ruiz, E. J. (1975). Influence of bilingualism on communication in groups. *International Journal of Group Psychotherapy, 25,* 391–395.

Ruiz, N. T. (1988). *The nature of bilingualism: Implications for special education.* Sacramento: California State Department of Education, Resources in Special Education.

Ruiz, N. T. (1989). An optimal learning environment for Rosemary. *Exceptional Children, 56,* 29–41.

Ruiz v. State Board of Education. C. A. No. 218394 (Super. Ct. Cal., Sacramento County, 1971).

Rupp, J. (1980). *Cerebral language dominance in Vietnamese-English bilingual children.* Doctoral dissertation, University of New Mexico.

Saer, D. J. (1923). The effect of bilingualism on intelligence. *British Journal of Psychology, 14,* 25–38.

Salvia, J., & Ysseldyke, J. (1988). *Assessment in special and remedial education* (4th ed.). Boston: Houghton Mifflin.

Samway, K. (1987). Formal evaluation of children's writing: An incompete story. *Language Arts, 64*(3), 289–298.

Sanchez, G. I. (1934). Bilingualism and mental measures: A word of caution. *Journal of Applied Psychology, 18,* 756–772.

Sanders, M., Scholz, J. P., & Kagan, S. (1976). Three social motives and field independence-dependence in Anglo American and Mexican American children. *Journal of Cross-Cultural Psychology, 7,* 451–462.

Sandiford, P., & Kerr, R. (1926). Intelligence of Chinese and Japanese children. *Journal of Educational Psychology, 17*(6), 361–367.

Sandoval, J. (1979). The WISC-R and internal evidence of test bias with minority groups. *Journal of Consulting and Clinical Psychology, 47,* 919–927.

Sandoval, J., Zimmerman, I. L., & Woo, J. M. (1980, September). *Cultural differences on WISC-R verbal items.* Paper presented at the annual convention of the American Psychological Association, Montreal, Canada.

Sato, T., Takeya, M., Kurata, M., Marimoto, Y., & Chimura, H. (1981). An instructional data analysis machine with a microprocessor–SPEEDY. *NEC Research and Development, 61,* 55–63.

Sattler, J. (1982). *Assessment of children's intelligence and special abilities* (2nd ed.). Boston: Allyn & Bacon.

Sattler, J. (1988, 1992). *Assessment of children* (3rd ed.). San Diego, CA: Sattler.

Sattler, J. M., & Altes, L. M. (1984). Performance of bilingual and monolingual Hispanic children on the Peabody Picture Vocabulary Test-Revised and the McCarthy Perceptual Performance Scale. *Psychology in the Schools, 21,* 313–316.

Sattler, J., Avila, V., Houston, W., & Toney, D. (1980). Performance of bilingual Mexican-American children on Spanish and English versions of the Peabody Picture Vocabulary Test. *Journal of Consulting and Clinical Psychology, 48*(6), 782–784.

Savignon, S. J. (1985). Evaluation of communicative competence: The ACTFL proficiency guidlines. *Modern Language Journal, 70,* 129–34.

Scheuneman, J. (1975, March-April). *A new method of assessing bias in test items.* Paper presented at the annual meeting of the American Educational Research Association, Washington, DC.

Scheuneman, J. (1978, March). *Ethnic group bias in intelligence test items.* Paper presented at the annual meeting of the American Educational Research Association, Toronto.

Schmitt, A. P. (1988). Language and cultural characteristics that explain differential item functioning for Hispanic examinees on the Scholastic Aptitude Test. *Journal of Educational Measurement, 25,* 1–13.

Schneiderman, E. I. (1986). Learning to the right: Some thoughts on hemisphere involvement in language acquisition. In J. Vaid (Ed.), *Language processing in bilinguals: Psycholinguistic and neuropsychological perspectives.* Hillsdale, NJ: Erlbaum.

Schneidermann, E., &. Wesche., M. (1980). *Right hemisphere participation in second language acquisition.* The Third Los Angeles Second Language Research Forum, Los Angeles, CA.

Schroeder, G. B., & Bemis, K. A. (1969). *The use of the Goodenough Draw-a-Man Test as a predictor of academic achievement.* Albuquerque, NM: Southwestern Cooperative Educational Laboratory.

Schulkind, L. (1992). *Letter to Betty Henry, President of CASP, November 23, 1992.* San Francisco, CA: Public Advocates.

Segalowitz, N. (1986). Skilled reading in the second language. In J. Vaid (Ed.), *Language processing in bilinguals* (pp. 3–19). Hillsdale, NJ: Erlbaum.

Seliger, H. W., & Vago, R. M. (1991). *First language attrition.* Cambridge, MA: Cambridge University Press,

Selinker, L. (1972). Interlanguage. *International Review of Applied Linguistics, 10,* 209–231.

Shuman, A. (1983). Collaborative literacy in an urban multiethnic neighborhood. *International Journal of Sociology of Language, 42,* 69–81.

Shuy, R. W. (1978). Problems in assessing language ability in bilingual education programs. In H. Lafontaine, B. Persky, & L. H. Golubchick (Eds.), *Bilingual education* (pp. 376–380). Wayne, NJ: Avery.

Skrtic, R. (1991a). *Behind special education.* Denver, CO: Love.

Skrtic, R. (1991b). The special education paradox: Equity as the way to excellence. *Harvard Educational Review, 61,* 148–186.

Skutnabb-Kangas, T. (1981). *Bilingualism or not: The education of minorities.* Clevedon, England: Multilingual Matters.

Slaughter, H. B. (1988). A sociolinguistic paradigm for bilingual language proficiency assessment. In J. Fine (Ed.), *Second language discourse: A textbook of current research* (pp. 89–143). Norwood, NJ: Ablex.

Smith, M. E. (1942). The effect of bilingual background on college aptitude scores and grade point ratios earned by students at the University of Hawaii. *Journal of Educational Psychology, 33,* 356–364.

Soares, C., &. Grosjean, F. (1980). Left hemisphere language lateralization in bilinguals and monolinguals. *Perception and Psychophysics, 29*(6), 599–604.

Soares, C., & Grosjean, F. (1984). Bilinguals in a monolingual and a bilingual speech mode: The effect on lexical access. *Memory & Cognition, 12*(4), 380–386.

Solin, D. (1989). The systematic misrepresentation of bilingual-crossed aphasia data and its consequences. *Brain and Language, 36,* 92–116.

Spielberger, C. D., & Butcher, J. N. (1985, 1987, 1988). *Advances in personality assessment* (Vols. 5, 6, & 7). Hillsdale, NJ: Erlbaum.

Spolsky, B. (1975). Language testing: Art or science? *Proceedings of the Fourth International Congress of Applied Linguistics* (pp. 9–28). Stuttgart, Germany: Sonderdruck.

Staff. (n.d.). Hispanics underrepresented in special education. *Bilingual Special Education News, 1*(1), 1–2. (Available from University of Texas at Austin, College of Education, Department of Special Education.)

Sternberg, R. J., Conway, B. E., Ketron, J. L., & Bernstein, M. (1981). People's conceptions of intelligence. *Journal of Personality and Social Psychology, 41,* 37–55.

Stone, B. J. (1992). Prediction of achievement by Asian-American and White children. *Journal of School Psychology, 30,* 91–99.

Suarez-Orozco, M. (1990). Speaking the unspeakable: Toward a psychological understanding of responses to terror. *Ethos, 18,* 353–383.

Sussman, H., Franklin, P., & Simon, T. (1982). Bilingual speech: Bilateral control? *Brain and Language, 15,* 125–142.

Swedo, J. (1987). Effective teaching strategies for handicapped limited English-proficient students. *Bilingual Special Education Newsletter,* pp. 1–5.

Tarone, E. (1988). *Variation in interlanguage.* London: Edward Arnold.

Taylor, R. L., & Richards, S. B. (1991). Patterns of intellectual differences of Black, Hispanic, and white children. *Psychology in the Schools, 28,* 5–8.

Taylor, R. L., & Ziegler, E. W. (1987). Comparison of the first principal factor in the WISC-R across ethnic groups. *Educational and Psychological Measurement, 47,* 691–694.

Teale, W. H. (1986). Home background and young children's literacy development. In W. H. Teale & E. Sulzby (Eds.), *Emergent literacy.* Norwood, NJ: Ablex.

Temple, C. (1979, November 29-December 1). *Learning to spell in Spanish.* (ERIC #189 891). Paper presented at The 29th Annual Meeting of The National Reading Conference, San Antonio, TX.

Teuber, J., & Furlong, M. (1985). The concurrent validity of the Expressive One-Word Picture Vocabulary Test for Mexican-American children. *Psychology in the Schools, 22,* 269–273.

Tharp, R. (1989). Psychocultural variables and constants. *American Psychologist, 44,* 349–359.

Thorndike, R. (1973). *Reading comprehension education in fifteen countries.* New York: Wiley.

Torrance, E. P., Wu, J. J., Gowan, J. C., & Aliotti, N. C. (1970). Creative functioning of monolingual and bilingual children in Singapore. *Journal of Educational Psychology, 61,* 72–75.

Toukomaa, P., & Skutnabb-Kangas, T. (1977). *The intensive teaching of the mother tongue to the migrant children of preschool age and children in the lower level of comprehensive school.* Helsinki: Finnish National Commission for UNESCO.

Trueba, H. T. (1987). Organizing classroom instruction in specific sociocultural contexts: Teaching Mexican youth to write in English. In S. R. Goldman & H. T. Trueba (Eds.), *Becoming literate in English as a second language* (pp. 235–252). Norwood, NJ: Ablex.

Tucker, J. A. (1980). Ethnic proportions in classes for the learning disabled: Issues in nonbiased assessment. *Journal of Special Education, 14,* 93–105.

Twomey, S. C., Gallegos, C., Anderson, L., Williamson, B., & Williamson, J. (1980). *A study of the effectiveness of various nondiscriminatory and linguistically and culturally appropriate assessment criteria for placement of minority students in special education programs.* Merced, CA: Planning Associates.

Ulibarri, D. M. (1985). *Standardized achievement testing of non-native English-speaking students in elementary and secondary schools.* Rosslyn, VA: National Clearinghouse for Bilingual Education.

Ulibarri, D. M., Spencer, M. L., & Rivas, G. A. (1981). Language proficiency and academic achievement: A study of language proficiency tests and their relationship to school ratings as predictors of academic achievement. *NABE Journal, 5*(3), 47–80.

U.S. Commission on Civil Rights. (1973). *Teachers and students: Differences in teacher interaction with Mexican-American and Anglo students* (Report V: Mexican American Educational Study). Washington, DC: U.S. Government Printing Office.

U.S. Commission on Civil Rights. (1974). *Toward quality education for Mexican-Americans*

(Report VI: Mexican-American Educational Study). Washington, DC: U.S. Government Printing Office.

U.S. Controller General. (1981). *Report to the Chairman, Subcommittee on Select Education, Committee on Education and Labor, House of Representatives.* Gaithersburg, MD: U.S. General Accounting Office.

U.S. Department of Health, Education, & Welfare/Office for Civil Rights. (1978). *Directory of Elementary and Secondary School Districts, and Schools in Selected School Districts: School Year 1976-1977.* Washington, DC: U.S. Government Printing Office.

U.S. Department of Education/Office for Civil Rights. (1980). *Directory of Elementary and Secondary School Districts, and Schools in Selected School Districts: School Year 1978-1979.* Washington, DC: U.S. Government Printing Office.

U.S. Office for Civil Rights. (1978). *State and National Summaries of Data Collected by the 1976 Elementary-Secondary Schools Civil Rights Survey.* Washington, DC: Department of Health, Education & Welfare.

Vaid, J. (1981a). Bilingualism and brain lateralization. In S. Segalowitz (Ed.), *Language functions and brain organization.* New York: Academic Press.

Vaid, J. (1981b). *Cerebral lateralization of Hindi and Urdu: A pilot tachistoscopic Stroop study.* Unpublished manuscript, McGill University.

Vaid, J. (1984). Visual, phonetic, and semantic processing in early and late bilinguals. In M. Paradis (Ed.), *Leburn, Y* (pp. 175-191). USSE: Swets & Zeitlinger.

Vaid, J. (1986). *Language processing in bilinguals: Psycholinguistic and neuropsychological perspectives.* Hillsdale, NJ: Erlbaum.,

Vaid, J. (1988). Bilingual memory representation: A further test of dual coding theory. *Canadian Journal of Psychology, 42*(1), 84-90.

Vaid, J. &. Grosjean, F. (1980). Neuropsychological approaches to bilingualism. *Canadian Journal of Psychology, 34,* 417-445.

Vaid, J., & Lambert, W. (1979). Differential cerebral involvement in the cognitive functioning of bilinguals. *Brain and Language, 8,* 92-110.

Valdés, G. (1980). Is code-switching interference, in tegration or neither? In E. Blansitt (Ed.), *Fetschrift for Jacob Ornstein* (pp. 314-325). Rowley, MA: Newbury House.

Valdes, G. (1989a). Teaching Spanish to Hispanic bilinguals: A look at oral proficiency testing and the proficiency movement. *Hispania, 72,* 392-401.

Valdes, G. (1989b). Testing bilingual proficiency for specialized occupations: Issues and implications. In B. R. Gifford (Ed.), *Test policy and test performance: Education, language, and culture* (pp. 207-229). Boston: Kluwer.

Valdés, G. (1992). The role of the foreign language teaching profession in maintaining non-English languages in the United States. In H. Byrnes (Ed.), *Language for a multicultural world in transition* (pp. 29-71). Lincolnwood, Ill: National Textbook Company.

Valdez, R. S., & Valdez, C. (1983). Detecting predictive bias: The WISC-R vs. achievement scores of Mexican-American and non-minority students. *Learning Disability Quarterly, 6*(4), 440-447.

Valencia, R. R. (1979). Comparison of intellectual performance of Chicano and Anglo third-grade boys on the Raven's Coloured Progressive Matrices. *Psychology in the Schools, 16,* 448-453.

Valencia, R. R. (1982). Predicting academic achievement of Mexican-American children: Preliminary analysis of the McCarthy Scales. *Educational and Psychological Measurement, 42,* 1269-1278.

Valencia, R. R. (1983). Stability of the McCarthy Scales of Children's Abilities over a one-year period for Mexican-American children. *Psychology in the Schools, 20,* 29-34.

Valencia, R. R. (1984). Reliability of the Raven Coloured Progressive Matrices for Anglo and for Mexican American children. *Psychology in the Schools, 21,* 49-52.

Valencia, R. R. (1985a). Predicting academic achievement in Mexican-American children using the Kaufman Assessment Battery for Children. *Educational and Psychological Research, 5*, 11–17.

Valencia, R. R. (1985b). Stability of the Kaufman Assessment Battery for Children for a sample of Mexican-American children. *Journal of School Psychology, 23*, 189–193.

Valencia, R. R. (1988). The McCarthy Scales and Hispanic children: A review of psychometric research. *Hispanic Journal of Behavioral Sciences, 16*, 81–104.

Valencia, R. R., Henderson, R. W., & Rankin, R. J. (1981). Relationship of family constellation and schooling to intellectual performance of Mexican American children. *Journal of Educational Psychology, 73*(4), 524–532.

Valencia, R. R., & Rankin, R. J. (1983). Concurrent validity and reliability of the Kaufman version of the McCarthy Scales Short Form for a sample of Mexican-American children. *Educational and Psychological Measurement, 43*, 915–925.

Valencia, R. R., & Rankin, R. J. (1985). Evidence of content bias on the McCarthy Scales with Mexican-American children: Implications for test translation and nonbiased assessment. *Journal of Educational Psychology, 77*(2), 197–207.

Valencia, R. R., & Rankin, R. J. (1986). Factor analysis of the K-ABC for groups of Anglo and Mexican-American children. *Journal of Educational Measurement, 23*(3), 209–219.

Valencia, R. R., & Rankin, R. J. (1988). Evidence of bias in predictive validity on the Kaufman Assessment Battery for Children in samples of Anglo and Mexican-American children. *Psychology in the Schools, 25*(3), 257–263.

Valencia, R. R., & Rothwell, J. G. (1984). Concurrent validity and the APPSI with Mexican-American preschool children. *Educational and Psychological Measurements, 44*, 955–961.

Vernon, P. E. (1982). *The abilities and achievements of Orientals in North America.* New York: Academic Press.

Vukovich, D., & Figueroa, R. A. (1982) *The validation of the system of multicultural pluralistic assessment: 1980-1982.* Unpublished manuscript, University of California at Davis, Department of Education.

Vygotsky, L. S. (1962). *Thought and language.* Boston: MIT Press.

Vygotsky, L. S. (1975). *Mulitilingualism in children* (M. Gulutsan & I. Arki, Trans.). Edmonton: The University of Alberta. (Original work published 1935).

Vygotsky, L. S. (1978). *Mind in society: The development of higher psychological processes.* In M. Cole, V. John-Steiner, S. Scribner, & E. Souberman (Eds.), Cambridge, MA: Harvard University Press.

Wald, B. (1987). The development of writing skills among Hispanic high school students. In S. E. Goldman & H. T. Trueba (Eds.), *Becoming literate in English as a second language* (pp. 155–185). Norwood, NJ: Ablex.

Walters, J., & Zatorre, R. (1978). Laterality differences for word identification in bilinguals. *Brain and Language, 2*, 158–167.

Watson, D. L., Grouell, S., Heller, B., & Omark, D. (1980). *Nondiscriminatory assessment: Test matrix, V2.* San Diego, CA: Superintendent of Schools, Department of Education, San Diego County.

Weinreich, U. (1974). *Languages in contact.* The Hague: Mouton.

Weisner, T. S., Gallimore, R., & Jordan, C. (1988). Unpackaging cultural effects on classroom learning: Native Hawaiian peer assistance and child-generated activity. *Anthropology & Education Quarterly, 19*, 327–353.

Wells, G. L. (1975). For Blacks, Chicanos, Puerto Ricans, and other minorities: The language experience approach to learning. *Adolescence, 10*(39), 409–18.

Westermeyer, J. (1987). Cultural factors in clinical assessment. *Journal of Consulting and Clinical Psychology, 55*, 471–478.

Wheeler, L. R. (1932). The mental growth of dull Italian children. *Journal of Applied*

Psychology, 16, 650–667.
Whitaker, H. A. (1989). Bilingualism and neurolinguistics: A note on the issues. *Brain and Language, 36,* 1–2.
Whitworth, R. H., & Barrientos, G. A. (1990). Comparison of Hispanic and Anglo Graduate Record Examination scores and academic performance. *Journal of Psycho educational Assessment, 8,* 128–132.
Whitworth, R. H., & Chrisman, S. M. (1987). Validation of the Kaufman Assessment Battery for Children comparing Anglo and Mexican-American preschoolers. *Educational and Psychological Measurement, 47*(3), 695–702.
Wigdor, A., & Garner, W. R. (Eds.). (1982). *Ability testing: Uses, consequences, and controversies.* Washington, DC: National Academy Press.
Wilen, D. K., & Sweeting, C. M. (1986). Assessment of limited English proficient Hispanic students. *School Psychology Review, 15,* 59–75.
Wilkinson, C. Y., & Holtzman, Jr., W. H. (n.d.). *Relationships among language proficiency, language of test administration and special education eligibility for bilingual Hispanic students with suspected learning disabilities.* Austin: University of Texas, Department of Special Education, Handicapped Minority Research Institute.
Wilkinson, C. Y., & Ortiz, A. A. (1986). *Characteristics of limited English-proficient and English-proficient learning disabled Hispanic students at initial assessment and at reevaluation.* Austin: University of Texas, Handicapped Minority Research Institute on Language Proficiency.
William, U. (1971). The construction of standardized tests for Welsh-speaking students. *Educational Research, 14*(1), 29–34.
Williams, R. L. (1970). Black pride, academic relevance and individual achievement. *Counseling Psychologist, 2*(1), 18–22.
Williams, R. L. (1971). Abuses and misuses in testing black children. *Counseling Psychology, 2*(3), 62–73.
Willig, A. C. (1985). A meta-analysis of selected studies on the effectiveness of bilingual education. *Review of Educational Research, 55,* 269–317.
Willig, A. C., & Swedo, J. J. (1987, April). *Improving teaching strategies for exceptional Hispanic limited-English proficient students: An exploratory study of task engagement and teaching strategies.* Paper presented at the annual meeting of the American Educational Research Association, Washington, DC.
Witkin, H. A., & Goodenough, D. R. (1977). *Field dependence revisited* (Research Bulletin 77-16). Princeton, NJ: Educational Testing Service.
Wood, M. M. (1929). Mental test findings with Armenian, Turkish, Greek and Bulgarian subjects. *Journal of Applied Psychology, 13,* 266–273.
Woodcock, R. W. (1982). *Bateria Woodcock Psico-Educativa en Español* [Woodcock Psycho-Educational Battery in Spanish]. Hingham, MA: Teaching Resources Corporation.
Woody, R. H. (1980). *Encyclopedia of clinical assessment.* San Francisco: Jossey-Bass.
Worthington, G. B., & Benning, M. E. (1988). Use of the Kaufman Assessment Battery for Children in predicting achievement among students referred for special education services. *Journal of Learning Disabilities, 21*(6), 370–374.
Wulfeck, B. B., Juarez, L., Bates, E. A., & Kilborn, K. (1986). Sentence interpretation strategies in healthy and aphasic bilingual adults. In J. Vaid (Ed.), *Language processing in bilinguals: Psycholinguistic and neuropsychological perspectives* (pp. 199–219). Hillsdale, NJ: Erlbaum.
Yang, K. S., & Bond, M. H. (1980). Ethnic affirmation by Chinese bilinguals. *Journal of Cross-Cultural Psychology, 11*(4), 411–425.
Yeung, K. T. (1921). The intelligence of Chinese children in San Francisco and vicinity. *Journal of Applied Psychology, 5,* 267–274.

Yoder, D. (1928). Present status of the question of racial differences. *Journal of Educational Psychology, 19*, 463–470.

Zatorre, R. J. (1989). On the representation of multiple languages in the brain: Old problems and new directions. *Brain and Language, 36*, 127–147.

Zatorre, R. &. Piazza, D. (1979). *Right ear advantage for dichotic listening in bilingual children.* Unpublished manuscript, Brown University, Providence, RI

Author Index

Subject Index

Achievement testing, 109–118
  bilingual achievement testing,
    114–115
  historical literature, 110–111
  National Assessment of Educational
    Progress, 115–118
  professional literature, 111–112
  psychometric properties and bias,
    112–114
Acquisition of L1 and L2, hemispheric
  involvement, 73–75
Alternatives to testing and
  assessment, 190–195
  cognitive science, 191–195
    Learning Potential Assessment
    Device, 194–195
    Zone of Proximal Development,
    193
Assessment of competency, 195–202

Bias and achievement tests, 112–115
Bias in intelligence tests, 90–109
  cultural bias, 95–99
  linguistic bias, 99–104
    concurrence, 103–104
    factor structures, 102
    item analyses, 101
    prediction, 102–103

  reliability, 101
  test translation, 104–107
Bilingual achievement testing,
  114–115
Bilingual individuals
  circumstantial bilinguals, 11–15
  cognitive development of, 69–73
  elective bilinguals, 11–15
  immigrant bilinguals, 15–18
  language and information
    processing, 75–77
  types of bilinguals, 8–9, 10–11
Bilingualism
  definitions, 7–10
  typologies, 10–11
Bilingualism and testing, research
  agenda, 204–216
  bilingualism and cognitive
    differences, 204–216
  defining bilingualism, 205–210
  key questions, 211–216

Cognition and bilingualism, 68–86,
  210–211
Courts and special education testing,
  129–152
  Brown v. Board of Education,
    130–131